GERMAN WAR BIRDS
FROM WORLD WAR 1
TO NATO ALLY

GERMAN WAR BIRDS FROM WORLD WAR 1 TO NATO ALLY

Kenneth Munson
AMRAeS   ARHistS

Art Editor
John W. Wood

NEW ORCHARD EDITIONS
Poole · New York · Sydney

First published in the UK 1986 by New Orchard
Editions, Robert Rogers House, New Orchard, Poole,
Dorset BH15 1LU

Distributed in the United States by Sterling Publishing
Company Inc, Two Park Avenue, New York 10016

Distributed in Australia by Capricorn Link (Australia) Pty Ltd,
P.O. Box 665, Lane Cove, NSW 2066

ISBN 185079 044 2

Typeset by Poole Typesetting (Wessex) Ltd, England

Printed in Italy by
New Interlitho SpA, Milan

CONTENTS

PREFACE AND ACKNOWLEDGEMENTS

This book brings together the best German military material from the fourteen volume *Pocket Encyclopaedia of World Aircraft in Color* published by Blandford Press between 1966 and 1977. This series enjoyed immense popularity and success — well over 1,000,000 copies were sold in nine languages. The selection in this book starts with the primitive and ends with the sophisticated, missile armed, radar guided, nuclear weapon carrying aircraft of today.

Any selection for a volume of this size must necessarily be an arbitrary one. It is hoped however that this book will provide a 'ready reckoner' for the aviation enthusiast, and that the marking and camouflage schemes, many infrequently illustrated in color, will provide inspiration for the aircraft modeller. Several aircraft are presented in periods of service or in the markings of services which may appear unfamiliar, but it is hoped that this will lend depth to the perspective.

The **color plates** are arranged in approximate chronological order of the aircraft's first entry into service. The 'split' plan view depicts the markings appearing above and below either the port side or the starboard side of the aircraft, according to the aspect shown in the side elevation. It should not be assumed however that the unseen portion of the plan view is neccesarily a 'mirror image' of the half portrayed. Neither should it be assumed that all color plates necessarily show either a standard color scheme or a pristine, ex-works finish; indeed the intention has been to illustrate a wide variety of finishes, from ex-works to much-weathered aircraft.

The **specifications** relate to the specific machine illustrated, and may not necessarily apply in all details to the type or sub-type in general.

Preparation of the color plates owes a tremendous amount to Ian Huntley, whose comprehensive knowledge of aircraft colors and markings, based upon extensive researches, and whose general advice, formed the foundation upon which the plates were based. The plates were executed under art editor and director John W. Wood, by Michael Baber, Norman Dinnage, Frank Friend, Brian Hiley, Bill Hobson, Alan ('Doc') Holiday, James Jessop, Tony Mitchell, Jack Pelling and Allen Randall.

The Publishers

Rumpler (Etrich) Taube

Taube (probably Rumpler-built) of the Imperial German Military Aviation Service, October 1914

Engine: One 100hp Argus water-cooled in-line
Span: 45ft 11¼in (14·00m)
Length: 33ft 9½in (10·30m)
Wing area: 344·4sq ft (32·00sq m)
Take-off weight: 1,190lb (540kg)
Maximum speed: 59mph (95km/hr) at sea level
Service ceiling: 9,840ft (3,000m)
Endurance: 4hr 0min

The Austrian engineer Igo Etrich designed and flew his first tractor monoplane on 20 July 1909, and the first *Taube* prototype in July 1910. In late 1910 Etrich negotiated a manufacturing licence with Lohner in Austria and Rumpler in Germany, and the latter company produced most of the *Tauben* built from then until the outbreak of World War 1. Those built from 1911 onward reflected a host of dimensional and other variations, but the 2-seat military version produced by Rumpler in 1912 was the most widespread and may be taken as typical. At the outbreak of war in Europe on 4 August 1914 *Tauben* were already in service with the air forces of Italy, Germany and Austro-Hungary as observation and training aircraft, and many later-famous German pilots learned to fly on aircraft of this type. Privately owned *Tauben* were impressed for military service, and a large-scale production programme was put in hand. By this time Dr. Etrich had relinquished his copyright in the design, following a dispute with Rumpler, and this left the way clear for *Tauben* for various types to be built in Germany by the Albatros, DFW, Gotha, Halberstadt, Jeannin, Kondor, Krieger, LVG, Lübeck-Travemünde and Rumpler factories. Etrich, meanwhile, joined forces with industrialist Gottfried Krüger in early 1914 to form the Brandenburgische (later Hansa-und-Branden-burgische) Flugzeugwerke GmbH. About five hundred *Tauben* were built in Germany, those by DFW and Jeannin being known as *Stahltauben* because of their steel-framed fuselages. A wide variety of engines, with output ranging from 70 to 120hp, were fitted to German-built machines, the most popular being the Mercedes or Argus inlines of 100 or 120hp. The two versions in Austro-Hungarian service were the Lohner-built A.1 (with 85hp Austro-Daimler and overhead radiators) and the A.11 (120hp Austro-Daimler with frontal radiator), built by Lohner and (as the Series 71 and 72) by the K.u.K. Flieger Arsenal at Fischamend. In August 1914 the *Taube* quickly proved its worth as a reconnaissance aircraft when it gave the Germans warning of a Russian advance during the Battle of Tannenburg. Later that month it was used for bombing when Lt. von Hiddesen dropped a small load of tiny bombs on Paris. The *Taube* was a stable aircraft with pleasant flying characteristics, and considering that it was already four years old when war broke out, its performance for 1914-15 was not at all bad. However, it was not highly manoeuvrable, and since it carried no armament (other than crew members' revolvers or rifles), it was of little front-line value by the spring of 1915. It remained in use for a year or more thereafter as a very useful training type.

Albatros biplanes

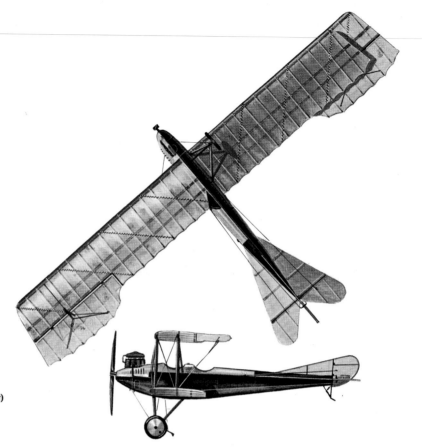

Albatros 2-seat biplane of 1913-1914

Engine: One 75hp Mercedes 4-cylinder
    water-cooled in-line
Span: 47ft 6⅛in (14·50m)
Length: 26ft 3in (8·00m)
Height: approx 10ft 9in (3·28m)
Wing area: 480.0sq ft (44·60sq m)
Take-off weight: approx 2,756lb (1,250kg)
Speed: 65mph (105km/hr)

In its early years, the Albatros-Werke GmbH of Johannisthal bei Berlin acquired its initial experience in the realm of aviation by building foreign designs under licence. It chose these well, for the two most important types undertaken were the excellent Antoinette and Etrich *Taube* monoplanes. The *Taube* in particular exercised a strong influence upon Albatros' own early designs, although the latter were mostly biplane types. At the Berlin Air Exhibitions of 1912 and 1913 the Albatros company displayed two enclosed-cabin *Taube*-type monoplanes, and a biplane whose wing and tail contours were also strikingly similar to those of the Austrian design. A feature of early Albatros biplanes was the unusual configuration of the radiator, installed under the nose and shaped to follow the curved contour of the lower engine cowling. One such machine, exhibited at Berlin in 1913, had a four-wheel, twin-skid main landing gear and mounted a searchlight between the mainplanes on the starboard side for use when making night flights. Another version, powered by a fully-cowled Daimler engine with a frontal radiator, had raised decking round the two cockpits, non-overhanging ailerons,

the lower wings set below the fuselage and a wheels-only main undercarriage instead of the more usual wheels and centre skid arrangement of early Albatroses. These various designs were the forerunners of the unarmed military B types and the subsequent wartime C types built by Albatros, and were themselves responsible for several impressive pre-war performances. Josef Sablatnig, a well-known competition flier in Germany and later the constructor of a series of successful wartime seaplanes, piloted an Albatros carrying three passengers to an altitude of 9,282ft (2,830m) at Johannisthal on 28 September 1913. Like the *Taube* – which, flown solo, could remain in the air for more than five hours – the Albatroses were also noted for their powers of endurance. On 27–28 June 1914 one of the military biplanes, flown by Landmann, stayed aloft over Johannisthal for a record 21hr 50min, during which he covered more than 1,200 miles (1,931km) through the air. His record was short-lived, for on 10–11 July Reinhold Böhm, in the same machine and carrying a 132 Imp gal (600 litre) fuel load, remained airborne for 24hr 12min to complete the first 24-hour nonstop flight over a closed circuit in aviation history.

Albatros B types

Albatros B.II of the Imperial German Military
Aviation Service, *ca* April 1916

Engine: One 100hp Mercedes D.I water-
   cooled in-line
Span: 42ft 0in (12·80m)
Length: 25ft 0¾in (7·63m)
Wing area: 431·8sq ft (40·12sq m)
Take-off weight: 2,361lb (1,071kg)
Maximum speed: 65·2mph (105km/hr) at
   sea level
Service ceiling: 9,845ft (3,000m)
Endurance: 4hr 0min

The unarmed 2-seat Albatros biplanes that served Germany in one capacity or another throughout World War 1 were probably the best reconnaissance machines in German service at the outbreak of war. Their design had been undertaken by Ernst Heinkel early in 1914, and the original version had entered production in a small way before the war started. They were impressed for war service, given the military designation B.I and allocated to Feld Flieger Abteilung (Field Reconnaissance) units in August 1914. Production was not especially standardised, and the B.I appeared in 1-, 2- and 3-bay forms with either a 100hp Mercedes D.I or 120hp D.II engine, the radiator for which was mounted above the cylinder block. As was the fashion at the time, the pilot sat in the rear cockpit while the observer occupied the front seat under the cabane trestle. No fixed defensive armament was carried, but during the early months of the war the observer usually armed himself with a rifle or carbine. Two batches of Albatros B.Is (Series 23 and 24) were built in Austro-Hungary by Phönix. A second Albatros 2-seater had also flown during 1914, and in the summer it set an altitude record of 4,500m (14,764ft). A 2-bay biplane with a shorter span than the B.I, the B.II, as this version became known, was powered at first by a 100hp Mercedes D.I. The Albatros B.II was one of the most widely used reconnaissance and observation types during the first year of the war, and was the subject of an extensive production programme. To improve the downward view for both pilot and observer, small cut-outs were made in the lower-wing roots. A small batch of B.Is and B.IIs (Series 21) was supplied to Austro-Hungary, and it is thought that some or all of these may have been fitted with a rudimentary mounting for a machine-gun in the front cockpit. Later production B.IIs were of the B.IIa model, with a strengthened and aerodynamically improved airframe, dual controls and a 120hp engine – either the Mercedes D.II or the Argus As.II. The final Albatros B type was the B.III, which was built in small numbers in 1915 for reconnaissance work with both the German Army and Navy. This retained more or less the same fuselage as the B.II, but had shorter-span wings and a new, high-aspect-ratio vertical tail and curved tailplane similar to those later employed on the C.III. With the introduction of the C category of armed 2-seaters in summer 1915, the B types became obsolete as observation aircraft. However, the Albatros machines' excellent flying qualities made them ideally suited to a training role, and they were extensively employed in this capacity throughout the remainder of the war. Production of the Albatros B series was undertaken by the BFW, LFG, Linke-Hofmann, Merkur, Kondor and Refla companies in Germany, in addition to those built by the Ostdeutsche Albatros Werke. Some Albatros B types were in military service in Sweden in 1918–19.

Lloyd-built C.II of the Austro-Hungarian Air Service, 1915

Engine: One 145hp Hiero water-cooled in-line
Span: 45ft 11½in (14·00m)
Length: 29ft 6½in (9·00m)
Wing area: approx 374·0sq ft (34·75sq m)
Take-off weight: approx 2,976lb (1,350kg)
Maximum speed: approx 79·5mph (128km/hr) at sea level
Service ceiling: 9,845ft (3,000m)
Endurance: approx 2hr 30min

The C type 2-seat reconnaissance aircraft built by the Ungarische Lloyd Flugzeug und Motorenfabrik are among the lesser-known aircraft of World War 1, despite the fact that between four and five hundred aircraft of this type were built and used quite extensively by both Austro-Hungarian air services during the first half of the war. They originated before the outbreak of war with the C.I (Series 41), one example of which was flown to an altitude of 6,170m (20,243ft) at Vienna in the summer of 1914. Aircraft of this type were already in military service when the war commenced. They were followed early in 1915 by the Lloyd C.II (Series 42), whose general appearance was typical of the Lloyd machines up to the time of the C.V. One hundred C.IIs were completed, fifty by Lloyd and fifty by WKF. They were powered by 145hp Hiero engines and had a communal cockpit for the 2-man crew; the wing span was slightly larger than that of the C.I. The C.IIs were at first unarmed, but later aircraft in service were fitted with a Schwarzlose machine-gun for the observer. In 1916 the C.III appeared, being basically similar to the C.II

except for its more powerful 160hp Austro-Daimler engine in a somewhat deeper cowling. WKF built fifty C.IIIs (Series 43.51), and they were employed on the Italian and Romanian Fronts in 1916–17. Some were fitted with a second machine-gun mounted on top of the wings. Little is known about the C.IV: it is thought to have been a single-bay version of the C.III, built by Lloyd and WKF as Series 44 and 44.51, but its operational employment has not been confirmed. The final Lloyd C type was the C.V (Series 46), with smaller dimensions, an aerodynamically refined airframe including a spinnered propeller and a taller fin with a rounded rudder. Powered by 185hp Austro-Daimlers in the first fifty aircraft and 220hp locally built Benz Bz.IVs in the second fifty, the C.V was some 32km/hr (20mph) faster than the C.III. It was also built in Series 82 form by WKF with 200hp Bz.IV engines, but by the time the C.V appeared, later and more efficient reconnaissance aircraft were in service, and the Lloyd C types were transferred to training duties.

Lohner B and C types

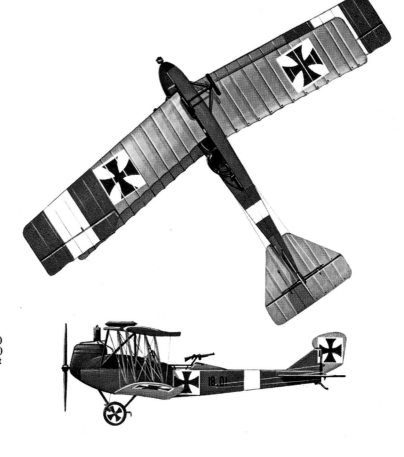

Lohner-built C.I of the Austro-Hungarian Air Service, 1916

Engine: One 160hp Austro-Daimler water-cooled in-line
Span: 44ft 1½in (13·45m)
Length: 29ft 3in (9·22m)
Wing area: approx 413·3sq ft (38·40sq m)
Take-off weight: approx 2,998lb (1,360kg)
Maximum speed: 85·1mph (137km/hr) at sea level
Service ceiling: 11,485ft (3,500m)
Endurance: approx 3hr 0min

The Jakob Lohner Werke of Vienna is best known for the range of marine aircraft that it produced during 1914–18, but, like its lesser-known compatriot, Lloyd, it also produced a range of 2-seat reconnaissance biplanes during the early part of the war. The first of these, the Lohner Type B, was in fact a 1913 design, several of which had been built before the outbreak of war with 100hp Austro-Daimler engines. Some of them were given individual names, all beginning with the letter B. After the outbreak of war, production was increased, and the type was designated B.I. It was built by Lohner (as Series 11) and by the government factory at Fischamend (as Series 73), some aircraft having 120hp engines. Although unarmed, the B.Is were used in some numbers during the early months of hostilities for observation and communications work. The Lohner Type C, or B.II, differed chiefly in having a longer fuselage, balanced rudder and an 85hp Hiero engine. This type was built by Lohner, Fischamend and Ufag with Series numbers 12, 74 and 12.41 respectively. The third B type to enter service was the B.IV (Lohner Type E), which equipped several Fliegerkompagnien in 1915. It was powered by a 100hp Mercedes D.I engine, had a further-extended fuselage and a neater undercarriage. It was the first B type to

be properly armed, having a Schwarzlose machine-gun in the rear for use by the observer. Built by Lohner (Series 15) and Ufag (Series 15.51), the B.IV was of limited value to the Austro-Hungarian air service since it could only maintain its performance effectively at altitudes below 2,000m (6,560ft). Later, in 1915, the B.IV was followed by the B.VII (Lohner Type I), which had a much more powerful engine and a far better performance. This version was built by Lohner as Series 17 with the 150hp Austro-Daimler, and by Ufag as Series 17.51 with the 160hp Austro-Daimler. The rear-mounted Schwarzlose machine-gun was retained as standard equipment. Although numerically earlier, the Lohner B.VI (Type H) did not enter service until 1916, after the appearance of the B.VII. Powered by a 145hp Rapp engine, the B.VI had a shorter fuselage than its predecessors and lower wings of extended span. The sweepback of both upper and lower planes was reduced, and the interplane bracing simplified. The B.VI was built by Lohner as Series 16.10. The same basic airframe, with a 160hp Austro-Daimler engine, was used in the construction of the Lohner C.I, or Type K. This entered service early in 1916 and remained in use throughout that year, being built by Lohner only as Series 18.

13

Aviatik B types

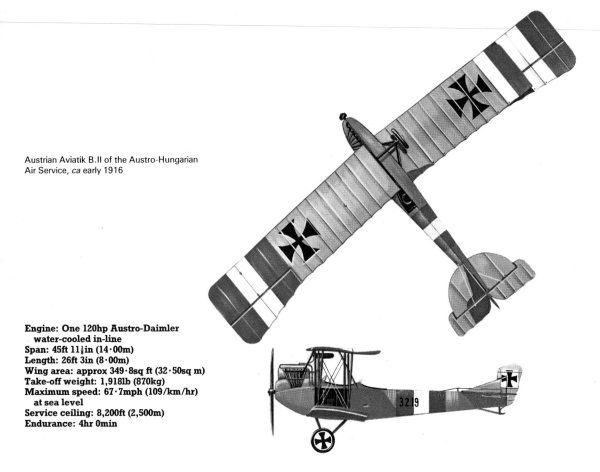

Austrian Aviatik B.II of the Austro-Hungarian
Air Service, *ca* early 1916

Engine: One 120hp Austro-Daimler
  water-cooled in-line
Span: 45ft 11½in (14·00m)
Length: 26ft 3in (8·00m)
Wing area: approx 349·8sq ft (32·50sq m)
Take-off weight: 1,918lb (870kg)
Maximum speed: 67·7mph (109/km/hr)
  at sea level
Service ceiling: 8,200ft (2,500m)
Endurance: 4hr 0min

In 1914–15 the German Automobil und Aviatik AG of Leipzig built a small, 2-seat reconnaissance aircraft designated B.I, powered by a 100hp Mercedes D.I engine, which was employed in small numbers on the Western Front for observation during the early months of World War 1. The company's Austrian subsidiary, the Oesterreichische-Ungarische Flugzeugfabrik Aviatik of Vienna, in 1915 built a variation of this design with similar-pattern fuselage and wings, a characteristic of which were the strut-braced outer sections. Chief points of distinction between the German and Austrian Aviatiks were the horn-balanced, overhung elevators and rudder of the latter. The Austrian B.II was built in a small series (Series 32) in 1915, powered by a 120hp Austro-Daimler engine. It carried no defensive armament other than the observer's rifle or revolver, but was able to carry a pair of 10kg bombs for 'nuisance' raids. It was followed by the B.III (Series 33), which was ostensibly an improved version. This was powered by a 160hp Austro-Daimler, with a box radiator mounted over the engine instead of the B.II's side radiators. The wings were of increased span, with raked-back tips; the fin was strut-braced; and instead of the B.II's separate cockpits, the B.III featured a long, communal cockpit in which the

pilot now sat in the front seat and the observer at the rear had a Schwarzlose machine-gun on a flexible mounting. Like the B.II, the B.III had an excellent range, and was used in some numbers for long-distance reconnaissance on the Russian Front. It could carry three 10kg bombs. Unfortunately, the B.III's flying qualities were nowhere near as good as those of its predecessor: it did not respond very quickly to its flight controls, and this caused it to swing about when flying in windy conditions, earning it such nicknames as 'gondola' and 'rocking-chair'. Because of its unsatisfactory flying tendencies, a second series of B.II aircraft were built – the Series 34. These retained the former basic B.II airframe, but incorporated the 160hp Austro-Daimler engine with its box radiator and the machine-gun installation of the B.III. Bomb load was increased to three 20kg bombs. In its Series 34 form the B.II was considerably more stable in flight, faster than the B.III and could climb to twice the altitude of the original B.II. Though they were not outstanding machines, the Austrian Aviatiks performed useful service in theatres where their long range was an asset, but by early 1916 they had been withdrawn from the front line and relegated to training duties.

DFW B and C types

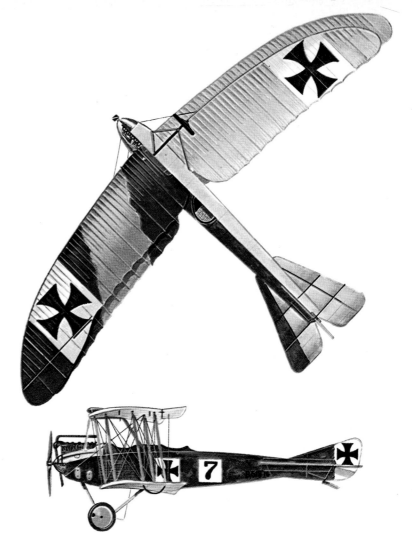

DFW B.I of the Imperial German Military
Aviation Service, 1915

Engine: One 100hp Mercedes D.I water-
     cooled in-line
Span: 45ft 11½in (14·00m)
Length: 27ft 6⅔in (8·40m)
Wing area: approx 369·2sq ft (34·30sq m)
Take-off weight: 2,238lb (1,015kg)
Maximum speed: 74·6mph (120km/hr) at
     sea level
Service ceiling: approx 9,845ft (3,000m)
Endurance: approx 4hr 0min

In the years preceding World War 1 one of the types built by
the Deutsche Flugzeug-Werke was the Etrich Taube, and
some indication of its influence was apparent in the banana-
shaped wings of DFW's own MD 14 design that appeared in
mid-1914. This was an elegant, stable and pleasant-to-fly
aeroplane, with 3-bay bracing of the modest-span wings and
small, looped skids underneath the lower extremities. Other
characteristics of the MD 14 included the large H & Z side
radiators and a downward-pointing engine exhaust manifold
on the starboard side. Upon the outbreak of war the MD 14
was impressed for military service and given the military
designation B.I. Powered by a 100hp Mercedes D.I engine, it
was employed during the early months of hostilities for observation work on both the Eastern and Western Fronts. Like all B
types, it carried no fixed defensive armament, the only
weapons being a rifle or revolver carried by the observer,
who in the fashion of the time occupied the front seat. With
the arrival in service of armed 2-seaters in 1915, the B.Is were
reallocated to training duties, for which their pleasant flying
qualities made them an excellent choice. The DFW MRD

biplane, which became the military B.II, was externally
similar to the B.I; this may have been a dual-control model
produced especially for the training role. Total production of
B types by the Deutsche Flugzeug-Werke is thought to have
reached about one hundred machines. In 1915 the DFW KD
15 (military designation C.I) entered service in replacement of
the unarmed B types. It was powered by a 150hp Benz Bz.III;
the observer still occupied the front seat, but the centre-
section of the top wing now incorporated a cut-out enabling
him to stand up and operate a free-firing Parabellum machine-
gun mounted over the top wing. Like its predecessor, the C.I
served on the Eastern and Western Fronts, and about one
hundred and thirty of these aircraft are thought to have been
completed. The T 25, or C.II, was a rather smaller aeroplane
with modified tail surfaces, straight-edged staggered wings
and more conventional crew seating with a Schneider ring for
a Parabellum gun in the rear cockpit. Reports indicate that the
C.II was somewhat unstable, and it may not actually have
entered service.

Albatros C.I

Albatros C.I of the Imperial German Military
Aviation Service, late 1915

Engine: One 160hp Mercedes D.III
   water-cooled in-line
Span: 42ft 3⅛in (12·90m)
Length: 25ft 9in (7·85m)
Wing area: 434·9sq ft (40·40sq m)
Take-off weight: 2,624lb (1,190kg)
Maximum speed: 87mph (140km/hr) at
   sea level
Service ceiling: 9,845ft (3,000m)
Endurance: 2hr 30min

For the first few months of World War 1 the opposing forces in France carried out reconnaissance and observation of one another's troop movements and artillery concentrations by means of aircraft that carried no formal armament either for offence or defence. At best, they could defend themselves if attacked only by revolvers or rifles carried by the observer, and since he customarily occupied the front cockpit in tractor-type biplanes, he was prevented by the surrounding engine cylinders, wing struts and bracing wires from making very effective use of such weapons. However, in the spring of 1915 Germany introduced a new category of warplane, the armed 2-seat C class, which not only had more powerful engines but also transferred the observer to the rear position, where he had a much more effective field of fire to the sides, rear and above the aircraft, and armed him with a free-firing machine-gun. One of the first such types to appear in service was the Albatros C.I. This aeroplane was, essentially, a slightly scaled-up version of the unarmed B.II, powered in its prototype form by a 150hp Benz Bz.III engine. Apart from being better defended, by its ring-mounted Parabellum gun, the C.I also offered a better field of view to both crew members by virtue of a distinctive dual-curve cut-out in the upper trailing edge and rectangular cut-outs in the lower-wing roots. Standard production C.Is were 2-bay biplanes with 160hp engines – either the Mercedes D.III or the Argus As.III. They were strongly built, and inherited the same fine stability and flying qualities that had characterised the earlier

B.II. From late spring 1915 the Albatros C.I was used in substantial numbers, both on the Western Front and in Russia, chiefly for photographic or visual reconnaissance and artillery observation duties. It could also be used for light bombing, with a load of some 70kg (154lb) of bombs stowed vertically in a space between the two cockpits. The Albatros C.I's performance, for its time, was sufficiently good to permit it to be used aggressively, as well as on more passive duties, and among those who gathered valuable early fighting experience in Albatros-built C.Is were Oswald Boelcke and Manfred von Richthofen. Albatros-built C.Is could be distinguished by the prominent side radiators flanking the front cockpit; the C.Ia, built by BFW and LFG (Roland), replaced these by a single leading-edge box-type radiator. Comparatively few C.Ias were built, as by this time the improved C.III was ready for production. However, a dual-control variant, the C.Ib, appeared in 1917, built by Merkur for the training role. It is not certain whether these were newly built aircraft or conversions of C.I/Ias, but after their replacement by more up-to-date Albatroses and other C types the C.I series continued to give useful service in the training role. One C.I was built with an experimental 3-bay enlarged wing cellule and a long, communal cockpit; a standard C.I wing unit and undercarriage were also used in the construction of the experimental C.II early in 1916. This was a pusher type with a 150hp Benz Bz.III, but did not go into production.

16

AEG G types

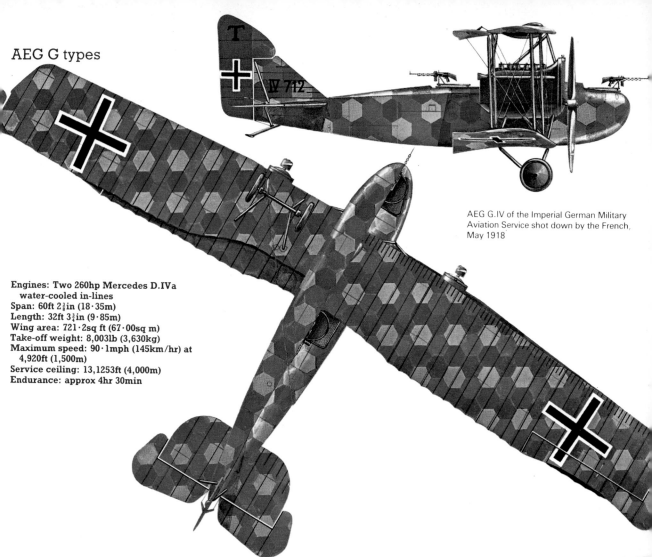

AEG G.IV of the Imperial German Military Aviation Service shot down by the French, May 1918

Engines: Two 260hp Mercedes D.IVa water-cooled in-lines
Span: 60ft 2¾in (18·35m)
Length: 32ft 3¾in (9·85m)
Wing area: 721·2sq ft (67·00sq m)
Take-off weight: 8,003lb (3,630kg)
Maximum speed: 90·1mph (145km/hr) at 4,920ft (1,500m)
Service ceiling: 13,1253ft (4,000m)
Endurance: approx 4hr 30min

The series of twin-engined G types produced by AEG in 1915–18 differed from most other German Grossflugzeuge in having a tractor, rather than a pusher, engine arrangement. The first in the series appeared early in 1915, before the introduction of the Grossflugzeug category, and was given the Kampfflugzeug (combat aeroplane) designation K.I. The K.I, later redesignated G.I, was a 3-seater powered by two 100hp Mercedes D.I engines; comparatively few were built. In July 1915 the G.II appeared, a slightly bigger machine with 150hp Benz Bz.IIIs, two or three defensive machine-guns and a 200kg (441lb) bomb load. It, too, was built in comparatively limited numbers, some G.IIs having two small auxiliary rudders. Both the G.I and G.II were flown by Schlachtstaffeln (Battle Flights) as well as by regular bombing formations. In the early summer of 1916 the G.III, which had first appeared at the end of the previous year, went into service. This had a much increased wing span, balanced and overhung control surfaces and two 220hp geared and handed Mercedes D.IV engines. The G.III was armed with two defensive machine-guns and could carry a 300kg (661lb) bomb load. Again, only small numbers were built, twenty G.IIIs being in service in October 1916; they served in Macedonia as well as on the Western Front. The most widely built G type was the G.IV, which entered service late in 1916. This had a basically similar airframe to the G.III, but utilised the more reliable direct-drive Mercedes D.IVa. A crew of three or four men was carried, and the bomb load was about 350kg (772lb); a Parabellum gun was

installed in each of the front and rear cockpits. Lacking both the range and the lifting power of the Friedrichshafen and Gotha G types, the AEGs were flown mainly as day and night tactical bombers over comparatively short ranges up to about 700km (435 miles). With extra fuel tankage in place of a bomb load, they were also employed on long-range reconnaissance and photographic missions. The AEG G.IV remained in fairly widespread use until the Armistice, appearing on the Western Front, in Salonika, Italy, Romania and Macedonia. Experimental variants included the G.IVb, with a 3-bay extended-span wing cellule, and the G.IVk, with a biplane tail unit, armoured engine nacelles and nose section mounting a 20mm Becker cannon. Final production version was the G.V, which first appeared in May 1918. It retained the same powerplant as the G.IV, but had a much enlarged wing span of 27·24m (89ft 4½in), a 600kg (1,323lb) bomb load and a maximum endurance of 6 hours. The G.Vs were built too late to see any combat service, but a number were employed post-war with Deutsche Luft-Reederei as 6-passenger transports in 1919. Most of them went into commercial service with the minimum of conversion, but a few machines were converted to have passenger cabins. Total wartime production of the G series reached five hundred and forty-two machines; by far the greater proportion of these, perhaps as many as four hundred, were G.IVs, of which fifty were still in service in August 1918.

Friedrichshafen FF types

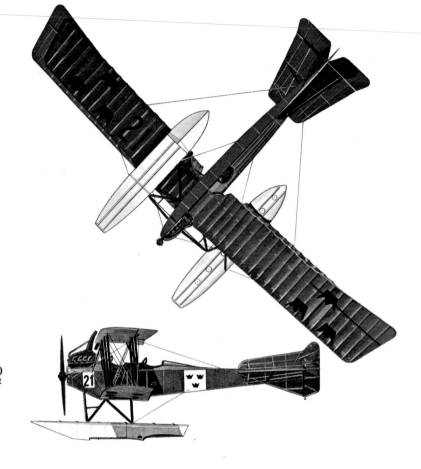

Friedrichshafen FF33J of the Royal Swedish Naval Aviation, 1919

Engine: One 150hp Benz Bz.III water-
 cooled in-line
Span: 54ft 11½in (16·75m)
Length: 34ft 3¼in (10·30m)
Wing area: 565·1sq ft (52·50sq m)
Take-off weight: approx 3,704lb (1,680kg)
Maximum speed: 72·1mph (116km/hr) at
 sea level
Service ceiling: approx 11,485ft (3,500m)
Endurance: 5hr 0min

Serving from the spring of 1915 until the closing stages of World War 1, the Friedrichshafen range of 2-seat patrol floatplanes were probably the most extensively employed German seaplanes of the war period; nearly five hundred examples of the four models listed above were completed. Most of them were armed, and their major duties included coastal and ocean patrol, fleet observation and co-operation and anti-submarine work. Some were based at coastal stations, operating in the North Sea and English Channel areas; others served aboard German seaplane carriers. The best-known example is the FF33E christened *Wölfchen* (Little Wolf), which was carried by the merchant raider *Wolf* in the Indian and Pacific Oceans and helped the German warship to account for twenty-eight Allied vessels. The FF33 went into service in spring 1915 in replacement of another Friedrichshafen design, the FF29A, the first machines being six FF33As with back-to-front seating and 100hp Mercedes D.I engines. They were followed by eleven FF33Bs, six with 120hp D.II engines and five with 160hp D.IIIs, in which the pilot more logically occupied the front cockpit. The first major production model was the FF33E, powered by a 150hp Benz Bz.III, which became the standard installation on all later FF33 variants. The FF33E was also the first model to introduce wireless equipment. One hundred and sixty-two were built, plus a further three armed with a rear-mounted Parabellum machine-gun, which were redesignated FF33Fs. In 1917 the E model was transferred to the training role, its place being taken by the modernised and more efficient FF33J, of which

about a hundred were completed. Thirty modified Js were also built as FF33S trainers. Before the FF33J, however, there had appeared a slightly smaller variant, with 2-bay wings and a ring-mounted Parabellum gun for the observer. This was the FF33H, produced as a seaplane fighter or escort to the unarmed FF33s in 1916; forty-five of these were built, LVG and Sablatnig sharing with the parent company the manufacture of the E and H models. The most effective model of all was the FF33L, which was a slightly smaller development of the H with a spinnered propeller and provision for a forward-firing second gun; it was more manoeuvrable and had a better performance than its predecessors. One hundred and thirty-five FF33Ls were built. The FF39 was an interim design, which appeared in 1917 with a strengthened and refined fuselage, 200hp Benz Bz.IV engine and rear-firing Parabellum; fourteen were completed. The principal Bz.IV-powered model, however, was the FF49, of which twenty-two FF49Bs and two hundred and eighteen FF49Cs were built by Friedrichshafen, LFG and Sablatnig. The Bs were unarmed, but most Cs had a rear-firing Parabellum and at least thirty of the late-production machines in 1918 had two guns fitted. Apart from the more powerful engine, the FF49 broadly resembled the FF33J except that it had balanced control surfaces. Before the war ended twenty examples were ordered of the FF59C, another Bz.IV-engined floatplane with a more compact fuselage and greater range than its predecessors. Friedrichshafen built forty-four seaplanes after the war, in 1918–19, but it is not known what type(s) these were. The only 'in service' figures

V1 *Max* (Friedrichshafen FF49) built and operated *ca* mid-1919 by LuftFahrzeug GmbH

Engine: One 200hp Benz Bz.IV six-
** cylinder in-line**
Span: 56ft 3½in (17·15m)
Length: 38ft 2¾in (11·65m)
Wing area: 766sq ft (71·16sq m)
Take-off weight: 4,718lb (2,140kg)
Maximum cruising speed: 84mph
** (135km/hr)**
Endurance: approx 5hr 30min

available are those for FF33 variants in May 1917: these included one hundred and twenty-one Es, twenty-five Hs, thirty Js and one hundred and fourteen Ls. After the war, in 1918-19, the Flugzeubau Friedrichshafen GmbH built a further forty-four seaplanes of unknown type(s). In addition, a number of FF49s were converted at about the same time to serve in an interim capacity as transport aircraft. These were of somewhat hybrid design, having a forward pilot's cockpit like the FF49C, a new enclosed cabin structure to the rear, and the larger-area rudder of the FF49B. Two cabin sizes are known, the aircraft being designated V1 with a 3-seat cabin

and V11 with a 5-seat cabin. Transport conversions of the FF49 were built by LFG and Sablatnig as well as by the parent company; most of them had Bz.IV engines initially, but the LFG-built V11 is said to have had a 260hp Mercedes D.IVa and some were subsequently re-engined with Junkers L-2 or L-5 powerplants. Operators of passenger/mail-carrying FF49s during the early post-war years included DDL (Det Danske Luftfartselskab) of Denmark, and the German companies DLR (Deutsche Luft-Reederei), LFG (LuftFahrzeug GmbH), LLS (Lloyd-Luftverkehr Sablatnig) and Luftdienst GmbH.

Rumpler C.I

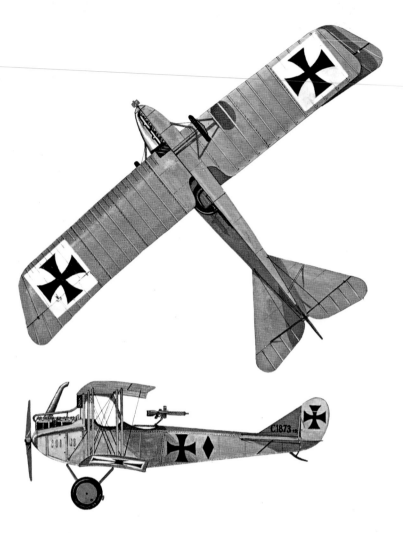

Rumpler C.I of the Imperial German Military
Aviation Service, 1915

Engine: One 160hp Mercedes D.III
  water-cooled in-line
Span: 39ft 10½in (12·15m)
Length: 25ft 9in (7·85m)
Wing area: 384·3sq ft (35·70sq m)
Take-off weight: 2,932lb (1,330kg)
Maximum speed: 94·4mph (152km/hr) at
  sea level
Service ceiling: 16,570ft (5,050m)
Endurance: 4hr 0min

Although mainly concerned with the production of Taube monoplanes in the periods immediately before and after the outbreak of World War 1, the Rumpler Flugzeug-Werke also produced a 2-seat reconnaissance biplane, the B.I, with a 100hp Mercedes D.I engine; about two hundred of these aircraft were built by Rumpler and Pfalz and served on the Eastern and Western Fronts in 1914–15. Early in 1915 Rumpler was one of the first German companies to produce a C type, the C.I, which was to become one of the longest-serving C types of the whole war. It was a well-built aeroplane, and intelligently designed to enable the crew to carry out their various duties with the maximum efficiency. The C.I went into production and service in 1915, its standard engine being the 160hp Mercedes D.III with a semicircular radiator in the centre of the upper leading edge. Its 2-bay wings were slightly swept back, and had cutouts in the lower wing roots to improve the view downward. An extensive production programme was undertaken by the parent company and the Germania, Hannover, Märkische and Albert Rinne factories. Early production C.Is were armed only with a Parabellum gun on a Schneider ring mounting in the rear cockpit, but a synchronised Spandau was fitted on later aircraft on the port side of the front fuselage. A subsequent version designated C.Ia was powered by the 180hp Argus As.III. The Rumpler C.I served on the Eastern and Western Fronts, in Macedonia, Palestine and Salonika. In all theatres it was an extremely efficient machine, both for reconnaissance and for light 'nuisance' bombing raids with up to 100kg (220lb) of small bombs. Visual and photographic reconnaissance was carried out, except in the Middle Eastern theatres where the climate affected the photographic materials. In October 1916 there were two hundred and fifty Rumpler C.Is in service on all Fronts; the type was still in production for part of 1917 and some C.Is were still with front-line units as late as February 1918. Thereafter they were used on training duties, for which their pleasant handling and flying qualities made them eminently suitable; one batch was built especially for the training role by the Bayerische Rumpler-Werke with 150hp Bz.III engines and no gun ring in the rear cockpit. A development, the Rumpler C.II, was projected, but apparently none were actually built.

Ago C Types

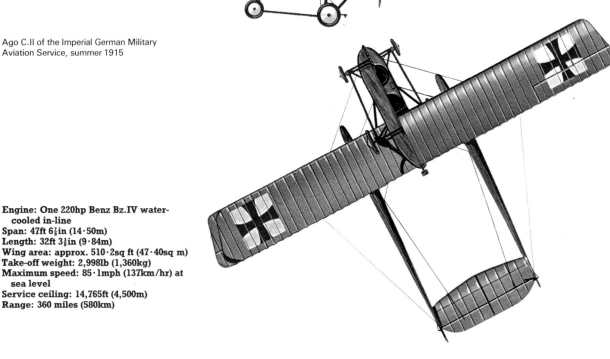

Ago C.II of the Imperial German Military
Aviation Service, summer 1915

Engine: One 220hp Benz Bz.IV water-
cooled in-line
Span: 47ft 6⅛in (14·50m)
Length: 32ft 3⅜in (9·84m)
Wing area: approx. 510·2sq ft (47·40sq m)
Take-off weight: 2,998lb (1,360kg)
Maximum speed: 85·1mph (137km/hr) at
sea level
Service ceiling: 14,765ft (4,500m)
Range: 360 miles (580km)

The Ago Flugzeugwerke, formed in 1912 from the former
Aerowerke Gustav Otto, produced its first C type biplane, the
C.I, in mid-1915. This, and the later C.II and C.III, shared a
similar configuration, being pusher-engined 2-seaters with
two slender oval-section fuselage booms supporting the tail
unit. The C.I, originally powered by a 150hp Benz Bz.III and
later by a 160hp Mercedes D.III, entered service in summer
1915 in small numbers on the Western Front. Designed by the
Swiss engineer August Haefeli, it was characterised by
having small, comma-type rudders and prominent H & Z side
radiators on the nacelle, in the nose of which was mounted a
free-firing Parabellum machine-gun for use by the observer.
For a pusher type the C.I was quite fast and had an operational
endurance of 4 hours. One example of a twin-float version, the
C.IW, was delivered to the German Navy for evaluation. Late
in 1915 the C.I was superseded by the C.II, which had the
more powerful Benz Bz.IV engine with a wing radiator, small
triangular fins and plain rudders and various other
aerodynamic improvements. This remained in service
throughout 1916 and the first half of 1917 and, like its
predecessor, was a useful aeroplane with good handling
qualities. A variant of the Ago C.II was built by Haefeli, at
Thun in 1915-16, as the DH-1 for the Swiss Air Force. For
reasons that remain unexplained, the Ago pushers seem to
have acquired an early reputation for being much larger and

more heavily manned and gunned than in fact they were. A
version did exist, however, with an enlarged wing span of
18·30m (60ft 0½in), and a few of these were built in landplane
and C.IIW floatplane forms for use by the German Navy.
Conversely, the Ago C.III was a smaller edition, powered by
a Mercedes D.III, but only a few of these were built. Ago's
next C type was the C.IV, and this departed completely from
the previous designs in being a tractor biplane with equal-
tapered, equal-span wings of identical pattern, double
ailerons and very slight wing stagger. The C.IV was powered
by a 220hp Bz.IV engine, had a synchronised forward-firing
Spandau gun for the pilot and a ring-mounted Parabellum gun
in the observer's cockpit. The prototype bore a comma-type
rudder only, but a small fixed fin was introduced on
production aircraft, giving a continuously rounded tail
contour. The Ago C.IV was a fast and efficient aeroplane of its
type, but it entailed long and costly constructional methods
that limited the number built. The maximum number of C.IVs
in service at any time was seventy in September 1917; this is
thought to represent little more than a quarter of the total
output, some of which were subcontracted to Schütte-Lanz
and Rathgeber. The C.VII and C.VIII were experimental
developments of the C.IV with, respectively, revised wing
bracing and a different engine installed. Neither went into
quantity production.

Fokker E Types

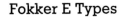

Fokker E.III which force-landed behind British lines in France, 8 April 1916; now in possession of Science Museum, London

Engine: One 100hp Oberursel U.I. rotary
Span: 31ft 2¾in (9·52m)
Length: 23ft 11½in (7·30m)
Wing area: 172·2sq ft (16·00sq m)
Take-off weight: 1,400lb (635kg)
Maximum speed: 83mph (133·6km/hr) at 6,500ft (1,981m)
Service ceiling: 11,500ft (3,500m)
Endurance: 2hr 45min

The air supremacy enjoyed by the Fokker monoplane fighters over the Western Front must have been more than usually galling to the French in particular, for the Fokker E types' design was influenced by the Morane-Saulnier Type H monoplane, and they carried an interrupter gear developed by Fokker's engineers after capturing Roland Garros' Morane-Saulnier Type L. The Fokker M.5 which gave rise to the E types was first flown in 1913. From it were developed the long-span M.5L and the short-span M.5K. Both were powered by the 80hp Oberusel rotary and used in modest numbers early in the war; a few M.5Ls served with the Austro-Hungarian air arm. Following the capture of Garros' Morane L in April 1915, Fokker engineers developed an interrupter gear that was tested on an M.5K. Two other M.5Ks were similarly tested using a Spandau gun, and this version went into urgent production as the E.I; front-line units began to score mounting successes as their E.Is were delivered from June 1915, and production is believed to have totalled sixty-eight. The E.I, essentially a 'rush job', was quickly followed by the E.II in which the 100hp Oberusel was installed. Other E.II modifications included a reduction in wing size, which made it more difficult to fly without any appreciable increase in performance. Deliveries, of about fifty E.IIs, began in July 1915. The most numerous version was the E.III, with wings extended to a span greater than the original E.I. The E.III was normally fitted with a single 7·92mm Spandau gun; a few were flown with twin guns, but the extra weight imposed an unacceptable penalty on performance. Two hundred and sixty E.IIIs are thought to have been completed, being used by the German Army and the Austro-Hungarian Air Service, which had also received a few E.Is. An attempt to produce a viable two-gun fighter resulted in the E.IV, whose prototype appeared in November 1915. This was given a 160hp two-row Oberursel, and the wings were further extended to 32ft 9⅔in (10·00m). However, the E.IV, although faster than the E.III, proved to be much less manoeuvrable, and only about forty-five were built. For a brief period Max Immelmann flew a three-gun E.IV, but he later reverted to a standard two-gun machine. In E types serving with the Austro-Hungarian forces the domestic 8mm Schwarzlose gun was usually substituted for the German weapon. The Fokker E types were in service on the Western Front from mid-1915 until late summer 1916. Their peak period of effectiveness began about October, and from then until January they reigned virtually unopposed in European skies. This lack of opposition led to the almost legendary success of the 'Fokker scourge', which was out of all proportion to the actual numbers in service. Their chief victim was the luckless B.E.2c, which soon earned a reputation as 'Fokker fodder'. From January 1916 the Fokkers began to encounter worthier opposition in the form of the D.H.2, Nieuport 11 and F.E.2b, which had virtually dispelled the Fokker's menace by the spring. The E types continued until the end of 1916 on the Eastern Front and in Mesopotamia, Palestine and Turkey, but thereafter were used almost exclusively for training.

Fokker E.III which force-landed behind British lines in France on 8 April 1916; now in the possession of the Science Museum, London. *Inset:* Inboard profile of E.III structure. Note the spherical fuel tank aft of the pilot's seat

If French pilot Roland Garros had not been shot down near Courtrai on 19 April 1915, or if he had been luckier in his attempts to destroy his aircraft, the world would probably have heard little of the Fokker Eindecker, for it was then in service only in small numbers as a fast communications aircraft. But, with the capture of Garros' special Morane–Saulnier Type L parasol monoplane, Germany gained possession of the first device to be used in air combat that enabled a machine-gun to fire through plates and to deflect those bullets which struck the blades; but Luebbe, Heber and Leimberger, three of Fokker's engineers at Schwerin, went one better. Adopting, in essence, the principle of 'letting the propeller fire the gun', they came up with a mechanical 'interrupter' gear which adjusted the rate of fire to the propeller's rate of turn, i.e. firing was interrupted as a blade passed in front of the gun. In the hands of such leading pilots as Oswald Boelcke, Max Immelmann and others, the Fokker soon became a formidable fighting machine, successes mounting as the number of aircraft in service increased. The hastily-produced E.I was quickly followed by the E.II with powerplant and other improvements, and by the principal service version, the E.III. The first recorded Eindecker victim, probably a B.E.2, fell near Douai on 1 August 1915 to one of the prototype aircraft flown by Immelmann. In October the so-called 'Fokker scourge' began in earnest, and throughout the ensuing winter, against negligible Allied opposition, they gained a reputation for deadliness far in excess of their true military value. Many of their victims were variants of the two-seat B.E.2, an otherwise worthy aeroplane that just did not have the speed or agility to get out of their way. But in January and February 1916 Allied squadrons in France began to re-equip in strength with D.H.2, F.E.2b and Nieuport 11 fighters, and the decline of the Fokkers' reign of supremacy began. The E.III illustrated is the only genuine example of its kind still known to exist, though one has been reported in East Germany.

Siemens-Schuckert R types

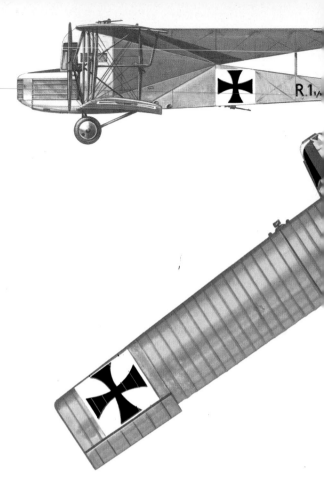

Siemens-Schuckert (Steffen) R.I (R.1/15) of the Imperial German Military Aviation Service, *ca* late 1915/early 1916.

Engines: Three 150hp Benz Bz.III water-cooled in-lines
Span: 91ft 10$\frac{1}{4}$in (28·00m)
Length: 57ft 5in (17·50m)
Wing area: 1,485·4sq ft (138·00sq m)
Take-off weight: 11,464lb (5,200kg)
Maximum speed: 68·4mph (110km/hr)
Service ceiling: 12,465ft (3,800m)
Endurance: 4hr 0min

Marking the opposite extreme in size to its neat little D type fighters (see details of D.III and D.IV on page 62), the Siemens-Schuckert Werke GmbH of Berlin and Nuremberg was also involved in manufacturing some of the largest German aircraft of World War 1. The company, originally noted for airship construction, had closed down its aircraft department in 1911, but reopened it in 1914, at first building small monoplanes. Its first large aeroplane, designed by Forssman, was apparently based upon earlier Sikorsky four-engined biplanes, and was begun in October 1914. Powered by four 110hp Mercedes engines mounted singly on the lower mainplanes, and having a wing span of 78ft 9in (24·00m), it was completed and flown in the spring of 1915. It was, however, considerably under-powered, and the two inner engines were replaced by 220hp Mercedes D.IVs, the outer pair of 110hp engines at the same time being remounted at mid-gap. Thus modified, it resumed trials in September 1915, and in April 1916 was eventually accepted for service use as a training aircraft. Meanwhile, in late 1914 the Idflieg had authorised the development of a new, 3-engined large biplane bomber designed by the brothers Bruno and Franz Steffen. Construction of this aircraft, designated G.I.32/15, began in December 1914, and it made its first flight, from the Steffen works at Neumünster, in the following May. Its configuration was, to say the least, unusual. The unequal-span wings carried ailerons on the upper main-planes only, but secondary ailerons were mounted between the upper and lower wings. The fuselage comprised a nose/cabin structure having polyhedral rear faces, mated to two

triangular-section tapering booms (an upper and a lower) the purpose of which was to allow a wide field of fire to the rear. The lower boom incorporated the customary ventral tunnel, also for a rearward-firing gun. The tail assembly, supported primarily by the inverted-triangular upper boom, consisted of a triangular tailplane and rectangular elevator, beneath which were a central fin, two small outlying rudders, and two auxiliary elevators. All three Benz engines were mounted within the forward fuselage, where minor in-flight repairs or adjustments could be made, and their radiators occupied the entire frontal area of the nose. Power was transmitted via a clutch and gear system to a tractor propeller mounted on each of the inboard bays of interplane struts. Idflieg acceptance of the G.I.32/15, in July 1915, was accompanied by an order for six similar aircraft, to be designated G.33/15 to G.38/15. With the introduction of the Riesenflugzeug (giant aeroplane) category in November 1915 the designations were changed to R.I to R.VII; and again in March 1917 to R.1/15 to R.7/15 respectively. The six new aircraft were intended originally to be powered by a trio of Maybach engines, but development problems with these units led instead to the use of 260hp Mercedes D.IVas in R.II and R.VII, and 220hp Benz Bz.IVs in R.III, IV, V and VI. These being of lower power than the intended installation, wing spans were correspondingly increased, compared with R.I, to 124ft 8in (38·00m) in R.II; 112ft 7$\frac{1}{2}$in (34·33m) in R.III and R.V; 123ft 4$\frac{1}{2}$in (37·60m) in R.IV; 109ft 5$\frac{1}{2}$in (33·36m) in R.VI; and 126ft 1$\frac{1}{2}$in (38·44m) in R.VII. Fuselage design and length also varied to some degree between

the six. The R.II, the heaviest of the six at 18,651lb (8,460kg), was also the slowest, with a maximum speed of 68.4mph (110km/hr); the other five could all manage top speeds of 81–82mph (130–132km/hr). In the event, only four of the SSW R types (R.IV to R.VII) were employed on operational duties, these serving in 1916–17 with Riesenflugzeugabteilung (Rfa) 501, based at Vilna, on the Eastern Front in Russia; R.II and R.III, like R.I, remained in Germany and were employed only for training, a function to which R.IV and R.VII also were later

transferred. In February 1918 construction of two even larger R types was started by SSW, but of these only R.23/16 (R.VIII) was completed. Spanning 157ft 5¾in (48·00m) and powered by six 300hp Basse und Selve BuS.IV engines, it had a gross weight of 35,053lb (15,900kg) and an estimated top speed of 77·7mph (125km/hr); but, while undergoing ground testing in 1919, it was severely damaged by its propellers following a transmission failure, and never flew.

AEG C Types

AEG C.IV of the Imperial German Military
Aviation Service, 1916

Engine: One 160hp Mercedes D.III
    water-cooled in-line
Span: 44ft 1⅛in (13·46m)
Length: 23ft 5½in (7·15m)
Wing area: 419·8sq ft (39·00sq m)
Take-off weight: 2,469lb (1,120kg)
Maximum speed: 98·2mph (158km/hr) at
    sea level
Service ceiling: 16,400ft (5,000m)
Endurance: 4hr 0min

In 1914–15 the Allgemeine Elektrizitäts Gesellschaft built a small series of unarmed reconnaissance and training biplanes under the designations B.I, B.II and B.III. The first C type (armed 2-seater) was the C.I, based on the B.II, powered by a 150hp Benz Bz.III and having a Bergmann machine-gun in the rear cockpit. In autumn 1915 this was followed by the smaller C.II, a more compact aeroplane capable of carrying four 10kg (22lb) bombs. The C.III, which also appeared late in 1915, was apparently influenced by the Roland C.II, for it had a deep, clumsy fuselage that completely filled the interplane gap. No production of the C.III was undertaken. The principal AEG C type to appear was the C.IV, produced in 1916 to meet the need to expand German field reconnaissance and contact patrol units. Externally it generally resembled the C.II, but had wings of much greater span. Its 160hp Mercedes D.III was enclosed in a typical AEG cowling, with the cylinders exposed and a large 'rhino horn' exhaust manifold rising well clear of the top wing. More attention was evidently paid to its structure than to its streamlining, for Allied reports on captured machines commented favourably on the high standard of welding in its steel-tube airframe. The C.IV entered service in early spring 1916, mainly on escort and reconnaissance duties, and a small number were still operational when the war ended. They were armed with a single Spandau gun offset to starboard in front of the cockpit, with a Parabellum gun on a Schneider ring mounting for the observer; the latter could accommodate up to 90kg (198lb) of bombs in his cockpit. The only figures available apply collectively to all AEG armed 2-seaters; these record a total output of six hundred

and fifty-eight C types, and a peak employment of one hundred and seventy at the Front in June 1917. Probably about five hundred of these would have been C.IVs. Variants included the C.IVN night bomber with longer-span wings, a Bz.III engine and a carrying capacity of six 50kg (110lb) bombs; it appeared in 1917. The C.V and C.VII both appeared in 1916, the former having a 220hp Mercedes D.IVa and the latter a Mercedes D.III and sweptback upper wings of smaller span. The C.VIII, appearing in July 1917, had an even shorter span, an improved cowling for its Mercedes engine and redesigned tail surfaces. It was also seen in triplane form later in the year. The major variant, based on the standard C.IV airframe, was that produced for armoured ground-strafing duties from early 1918. The engine and crew positions were encased in some 390kg (860lb) of armour plating, and to power this heavier machine a 200hp Bz.IV was installed. Initial version was the J.I; with small, lower-wing ailerons added this became the J.Ia; and with balanced, overhung top ailerons, elevators and rudder it was known as the J.II. Six hundred and nine AEG J types were built, but they were not an outstanding success. Instead of the normal forward-firing gun, these aircraft had twin Spandaus mounted in the floor of the rear cockpit to fire forward and downward at about 45 degrees; but the guns were difficult to aim properly when the aircraft was flying low. At least one machine flew experimentally as a single-seater, with six of these downward-firing guns. Production of the C.IV was subcontracted to Fokker, who may have built some of the C,IVa machines reported to have had 180hp Argus As.III engines.

LVG C types

LVG C.VI of the Imperial German Military
Aviation Service, 1918

Engine: One 200hp Benz Bz.IV water-
cooled in-line
Span: 42ft 7¾in (13·00m)
Length: 24ft 5⅓in (7·45m)
Wing area: 372·4sq ft (34·60sq m)
Take-off weight: 2,888lb (1,310kg)
Maximum speed: 105·6mph (170km/hr)
at sea level
Service ceiling: 21,325ft (6,500m)
Endurance: 3hr 30min

The Luft-Verkehrs Gesellschaft B type unarmed 2-seaters formed the basis for armed reconnaissance aircraft when the C category was introduced in spring 1915. The C.I, based on the B.I, has the distinction of being the first 2-seat operational German aircraft in which the observer was provided with a Schneider ring mounting and a Parabellum machine-gun. The first four LVG C types were designed by Franz Schneider. Only limited production was undertaken of the C.I (150hp Bz.III), this being followed late in 1915 by the C.II, the basis for which was the unarmed B.II. The LVG C.II was produced in substantial numbers by the parent company, and by the Ago and Otto works, and was powered by a 160hp Mercedes D.III. It was used extensively for visual and photographic reconnaissance work, and also for light bombing. One aircraft of this type made an audacious daylight raid on London on 28 November 1916, dropping six 10kg bombs on Victoria railway station. In spring 1916 some two hundred and fifty C.I/C.II types were in service and some late-production C.IIs had a forward-firing Spandau gun in addition to the usual Parabellum. It is thought that only one example of the C.III was completed, a smaller but slightly heavier version of the C.II in which the observer occupied the front seat. An enlarged C.II appeared in 1916: this was the C.IV, powered by a neatly cowled 220hp Mercedes D.IV and having a balanced rudder. A major step forward in design and performance was made with the appearance in mid-1917 of the LVG C.V. This was later to serve in considerable numbers alongside the DFW C.V (see page 41); the external resemblance of these two types is explained by the fact that the engineer responsible for the LVG machine was formerly the chief designer of DFW.

Among the largest German 2-seaters, the LVG C.V was a neat, compact aircraft with 'libellule' shaped wings and overhung upper ailerons. It had a neatly installed 200hp Benz Bz.IV engine with a leading-edge box-type radiator, and a spinnered propeller. Armament consisted of a single forward-firing Spandau gun and a rear-mounted Parabellum, and up to 115kg (254lb) of bombs could be carried beneath the lower wings. The C.V was in widespread use by autumn 1917, eventually serving in Palestine as well as on the Western Front. It was an excellent all-rounder, being used for artillery observation, photographic reconnaissance and light bombing. It usually operated with an escort, although it was quite able to give a good account of itself in combat when necessary. In 1918 the C.V was joined by the C.VI, of which about one thousand were built by LVG. The C.VI had a deeper, slightly smaller fuselage, in which the engine was less neatly cowled, and the propeller had no spinner. The wings, which were slightly staggered, had plain ailerons and a flush-mounted centre-section radiator. This last feature, which could be hazardous for the occupants if punctured during combat, was replaced in some aircraft by Windhoff radiators on the sides of the fuselage. The crew members' view from their respective cockpits was considerably better in the C.VI than in the C.V, where their outlook was restricted by a confusion of cabane struts, engine cylinders and radiator. Larger and rounder horizontal tail surfaces were also fitted to the C.VI. A variant of the C.VI which appeared in 1918 was the C.VIII; apparently only one was completed, with a high-compression Bz.IVü engine of 240hp, linked double ailerons and other minor improvements.

Lohner Type L

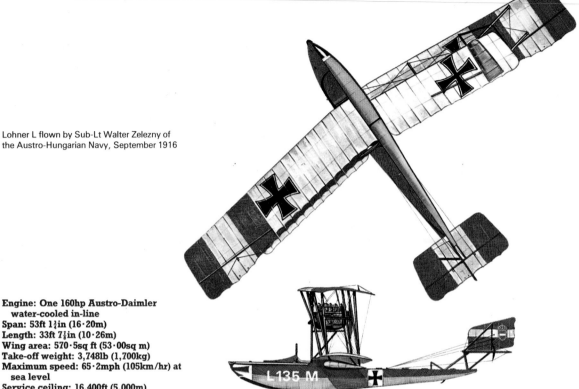

Lohner L flown by Sub-Lt Walter Zelezny of the Austro-Hungarian Navy, September 1916

Engine: One 160hp Austro-Daimler
water-cooled in-line
Span: 53ft 1¾in (16·20m)
Length: 33ft 7½in (10·26m)
Wing area: 570·5sq ft (53·00sq m)
Take-off weight: 3,748lb (1,700kg)
Maximum speed: 65·2mph (105km/hr) at
sea level
Service ceiling: 16,400ft (5,000m)
Endurance: approx 4hr 0min

The first flying-boats produced by the Jakob Lohner Werke of Vienna were the general-purpose E types, built in 1913. They were 2-seaters with 85hp Hiero engines, and in August 1914 one of these aircraft (E18) made the first World War 1 sortie by an Austrian aircraft. The later S types were unarmed training versions of the Type E. About two hundred, some of them converted Es, were in service during 1914–18; most of them had 85hp Hieros, but some were fitted with 80hp Oberursel rotaries. In size and general configuration the Lohner L resembled the Type E, but was powered either by a 140hp Hiero or by an Austro-Daimler of 140 or 180hp. A slender, elegant aeroplane with sweptback sesquiplane wings, the Lohner L seated a crew of two side by side, the observer occupying the right-hand seat and having a Schwarzlose machine-gun on a rotatable mounting. Up to 200kg (441lb) of bombs and/or depth charges could be carried. The Lohner L entered service in the late spring of 1915, and it is thought that one hundred and sixty were completed by the parent company. To these may be added nine or ten similar machines built as Type Ms by the Naval Dockyard at Pola. About thirty-six examples were also completed of the Type R, a 3-seat reconnaissance variant of the Type L with photographic equipment instead of a bomb load. The Lohner Ls were the most widely used flying-boats of the Austro-Hungarian Navy, and operated exclusively in the Adriatic area against Allied shipping and targets on the Italian mainland. It was an aircraft of this type (L40) that fell into Italian hands on 27 May 1915 and eventually gave rise to the long and successful range of Macchi-developed flying-boats. The Austrian Navy's most celebrated pilot, Lt Gottfried Banfield, scored the first of his many aerial victories on 1 June 1916 while flying a Lohner L, and the general effectiveness of the type can be judged from the fact that only thirty of these aircraft were lost during the war, and only one each of the Types E, R and S. (Five Type Rs were owned in 1923 by Alfred Comte, at which time he founded the Luftverkehr und Sportfliegerschule in Zurich.) The illustration depicts one of two Lohner Ls from the Austrian Naval base at Kumbor that attacked the French Laubeuf-class submarine *Foucault* off the coast of Cattaro on 15 September 1916.

Albatros C.III and C.IV

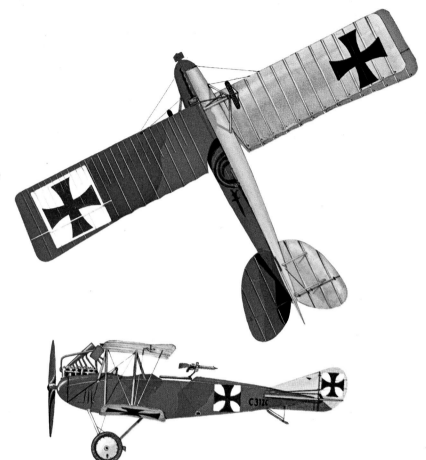

Albatros C.III of the Imperial German Military
Aviation Service, *ca* summer 1916

Engine: One 160hp Mercedes D.III
    water-cooled in-line
Span: 38ft 4½in (11·70m)
Length: 26ft 3in (8·00m)
Wing area: 397·2sq ft (36·90sq m)
Take-off weight: 2,983lb (1,353kg)
Maximum speed: 87mph (140km/hr) at
    sea level
Service ceiling: 11,155ft (3,400m)
Endurance: 4hr 0m

Well and widely as the Albatros C.I series of biplanes served the Flieger Abteilungen, the C.IIIs which followed them were even more successful. As the C.I had been evolved from the B.II unarmed 2-seater, so the C.III was a similarly scaled-up version of the Albatros B.III, repeating the latter's curved tailplane and low-aspect-ratio fin. These revised tail surfaces improved the already excellent flying qualities of the aircraft, making it more stable longitudinally and better able to manoeuvre in combat with Allied fighters. The C.III prototype, like that of the C.I, was powered by a 150hp Bz.III engine, and this unit was installed in some production C.IIIs. The standard powerplant was the well-tried and thoroughly reliable Mercedes D.III of 160hp. The Albatros C.III was the most widely built Albatros C type, the production programme being shared between Albatros, OAW, DFW, Hansa, Linke-Hofmann, LVG and Siemens-Schuckert. The Parabellum gun on a Schneider ring mounting in the observer's cockpit was a standard installation; most C.IIIs were also provided with a synchronised forward-firing Spandau gun on the starboard side of the engine block. The C.III went into service late in 1915, and it continued to serve on the Western Front, in Macedonia and in Russia throughout 1916 and the early part of 1917. Its duties included visual and photographic reconnaissance; it could undertake light bombing duties with about 90kg (198lb) of bombs stowed internally between the cockpits. Without a bomb load, radio equipment could be installed in the C.III for use in artillery co-operation work. In addition to its pleasant handling qualities, the C.III was a compact, sturdily built aeroplane whose ply-covered fuselage enabled it to withstand a considerable amount of battle damage. After its withdrawal from front-line operations early in 1917 it continued to render useful service as a trainer until the end of the war. Single examples were built in 1916 of the C.IV, which was basically a C.III airframe with a completely new single-bay wing cellule, and of the W.2, a twin-float version of the C.III, which was handed over to the German Navy in June. No series production of either version was undertaken. A few Albatros C.VIs were built: these had stronger but lighter C.III-type airframes fitted with 180hp As.III engines, giving a slight improvement in overall performance.

Albatros C.V, C.VII, C.X and C.XII

Albatros C.XII of the Imperial German Military Aviation Service, 1918

Engine: One 260hp Mercedes D.IVa
water-cooled in-line
Span: 47ft 1¾in (14·37m)
Length: 29ft 0½in (8·85m)
Wing area: 459·6sq ft (42·70sq m)
Take-off weight: 3,616lb (1,640kg)
Maximum speed: 108·7mph (175km/hr)
at sea level
Service ceiling: 16,400ft (5,000m)
Endurance: 3hr 15min

Up to and including the C.IV, the early Albatros C types were fundamentally descendants of the unarmed B series designed by Ernst Heinkel. The first entirely newly designed C type was the C.V, the joint handiwork of Thelen and Schubert. Appearing in spring 1916, it utilised a wing cellule resembling, but slightly larger than, that of the Albatros C.III, but the new cigar-shaped fuselage, spinnered propeller and rounded tail unit reflected the same approach to streamlining as that practised on the early Albatros single-seat fighters. The C.V was powered by an almost fully cowled 220hp Mercedes D.IV with, in the original C.V/16 form (i.e. built in 1916), prominent Windhoff radiators on either side of the front fuselage. It was fitted with a synchronised Spandau machine-gun for the pilot, mounted on the starboard side of the engine, with a ring-mounted Parabellum gun in the observer's cockpit. A bomb load of up to 175kg (386lb) could be carried. The C.V/16 was cumbersome to fly; in this respect the C.V/17 was some improvement, having a flush-mounted wing radiator, balanced and tapered ailerons on the top wings and elliptical tips to the lower ones. Four hundred and twenty-four C.Vs were completed by Albatros, but only a fraction of these were in service at any one time between early spring 1916 and the beginning of 1917. They were repeatedly beset by engine crankshaft failures, and when production of the D.IV engine was abandoned, that of the Albatros C.V also came to an end. The next production model was the C.VII, which went into service late in 1916 as an interim measure for long-range reconnaissance and artillery observation. It was powered by a 200hp Benz Bz.IV, installed in typical Germanic fashion with the cylinder heads exposed, and the airframe was a mixture of the lower wings and side radiators of the C.V/16 with the upper wings of the C.V/17. Like other compromise designs before it (and since), the C.VII flew and fought very well, and

was successful enough to be built in considerable numbers. It was still in service late in 1917, its peak period of employment having been in February of that year when three hundred and fifty were in service on all Fronts. Production of the C.VII was shared between Albatros, OAW and BFW. In mid-1917 the fully developed version of the C.V appeared in the form of the C.X, powered by the long-awaited Mercedes D.IVa engine. The C.X was appreciably larger than its predecessors, and showed even greater similarity of outline to the Albatros D types. The flush-mounted wing radiator was reinstated in new wings of increased span with double ailerons. With these aerodynamic improvements and the greater power and reliability of the D.IVa engine, the C.X had an excellent altitude performance and usually carried oxygen equipment for the crew in addition to wireless and/or a light bomb load. Production was shared between the parent company, OAW, Linke-Hofmann, BFW and LFG (Roland), and by October 1917 there were three hundred C.Xs in service. The type remained with front-line reconnaissance and artillery co-operation units until mid-1918. The Albatros C.XII (the C.XI remained a project only) appeared early in 1918 as a successor to the C.X, and continued to serve until the Armistice. In this ultimate form it could probably claim to be the most handsome German 2-seater on the Western Front, its elegant, rakish lines and the addition of a small fin beneath the rear fuselage emphasising still more the design resemblance between the Albatros C and D types. The final production Albatros C type was the C.XV, evolved from the C.XIV prototype of 1917. This was a smaller and much less elegant aeroplane, with a hump-backed fuselage, short-span staggered wings and a 220hp Bz.IVa engine. It went into production in 1918, but only a few had entered service when the war ended.

Hansa-Brandenburg C.I

Hansa-Brandenburg C.I of the Imperial German Military Aviation Service, *ca* spring 1916.

Data for Phönix-built Series 23
Engine: One 160hp Austro-Daimler
 water-cooled in-line
Span: 43ft 0½in (13·12m)
Length: 26ft 10¾in (8·20m)
Wing area: 467·8sq ft (43·46sq m)
Take-off weight: 2,337lb (1,060kg)
Maximum speed: 77·6mph (125km/hr) at
 sea level
Service ceiling: 19,030ft (5,800m)
Endurance: approx 3hr 0min

Although it was employed almost exclusively by the Austro-Hungarian air services during World War 1, the Hansa-Brandenburg C.I or Type LDD was designed by Ernst Heinkel of the parent company in Germany, and may have owed something to the earlier Brandenburg FD (B.I) of 1914, three of which were supplied to Austro-Hungary. A characteristic of both designs was the inward-sloping interplane bracing struts. The Brandenburg C.I was a 2-seat armed reconnaissance biplane of conventional appearance, having the typical communal cockpit favoured in Austrian aircraft at that time, in which the observer occupied the rear position and was provided with a free-firing Schwarzlose machine-gun. On later production C.Is a synchronised Schwarzlose was installed in front of the cockpit on the port side for use by the pilot. From the early spring of 1916 until the end of World War 1 the Brandenburg C.I was employed widely on reconnaissance, artillery observation and light bombing. Its normal war load was 60kg (132lb), but some aircraft were operated with a maximum load of 100kg (220lb), consisting of one 80kg (176lb) and two 10kg (22lb) bombs. Visual and photographic reconnaissance missions were undertaken. The C.I was simple and stable to fly, had good take-off and landing qualities and a gradually improving performance in the air as successive production batches were fitted with engines of increased power. In all, one thousand three hundred and eighteen C.Is were built, in eighteen series, by Brandenburg (eighty-four), Phönix (four hundred) and Ufag (eight hundred and thirty-four). Phönix built C.Is with 160hp Austro-Daimlers (Series 23 and 26), 185hp Austro-Daimlers (Series 27), 210hp Austro-Daimlers (Series 29), 200hp Hieros (Series 29.5, 129, 229 and 329) and 230hp Hieros (Series 429). The Ungarische Flugzeugfabrik AG (Ufag) built Brandenburg C.Is with 160hp Austro-Daimlers (Series 61, 64, 67 and 68), 160hp Mercedes D.IIIs (Series 63), 200hp Austro-Daimlers (Series 269), 200hp Hieros (Series 69), 220hp Benz Bz.IVas (Series 169) and 230hp Hieros (Series 369).

LFG (Roland) C.II

LFG (Roland)-built C.II of an unidentified *Feld Flieger Abteilung*, Imperial German Military Aviation Service, Western Front, late 1916

Engine: One 160hp Mercedes D.III
  water-cooled in-line
Span: 33ft 10¾in (10·33m)
Length: 24ft 8⅛in (7·52m)
Wing area: 279·9sq ft (26·00sq m)
Take-off weight: 2,886lb (1,309kg)
Maximum speed: 102·5mph (165km/hr)
  at sea level
Service ceiling: 13,125ft (4,000m)
Endurance: 4hr 0min

The Roland C.II 2-seater was an extremely advanced design, and one of the best German aircraft on the Western Front during the second half of 1916. It was the smallest C type used by Germany during the war period, being less than 50kg (110lb) over the weight limit for the lighter CL category. The design, by Dipl Ing Tantzen, featured an extremely strong, ply-covered semi-monocoque fuselage, beautifully streamlined and completely filling the interplane gap. The wings had a single 'I' strut and a minimum of external bracing wires. An excellent view of the upper hemisphere was enjoyed by both crew members, but the view downward past the nose, already poor, was restricted further by the large side radiators, and made the C.II a difficult aeroplane to land. The first C.II was flown in October 1915, but the first handful of production aircraft were not delivered until March 1916 and had only a rearward-firing Parabellum gun in the observer's cockpit. Some squadrons met the need for a forward-firing gun by installing captured Lewises above the centre-section, but on later C.IIs a fixed, synchronised Spandau was provided. The first C.IIs in service were flown by the Kampfgeschwadern involved in the fighting at Verdun and the Somme in spring 1916, and their performance was well above that of contemporary German 2-seaters. In fact, the Roland C.II was as fast as the opposing Nieuport and Pup fighters, although it was less

manoeuvrable and took half an hour to reach its fighting altitude of 3,000m (9,845ft). A number were lost in landing accidents due to the poor frontal view, and some weakness was found in the outer wing sections. This led to the introduction, from August 1916, of the C.IIa, with revised and reinforced wingtips. Late in 1916 the C.II was used for night bombing with four 12·5kg (28lb) bombs beneath the fuselage. In mid-year Capt Albert Ball, who scored his first confirmed victory over a Roland C.II, had called it 'the best German machine now', yet it never served at the front in outstanding numbers; the Roland's meticulous streamlining demanded careful and therefore costly constructional methods, which restricted the total built. Peak employment of the C.II/IIa came in December 1916, when sixty-four were at the Front. It was withdrawn slowly during the first half of 1917, after which the majority were employed for training, though some were retained for combat duty on quieter sectors of the Western Front and in Russia. Total production is estimated at between two hundred and fifty and three hundred, some two hundred of these by the parent company and the remainder by Linke-Hofmann. Some late-production aircraft had an enlarged vertical tail. In 1916 a single C.III was produced: this was a C.II development with 2-bay wings, parallel interplane struts, revised tail surfaces and a 200hp Benz Bz.IV engine.

Halberstadt D Types

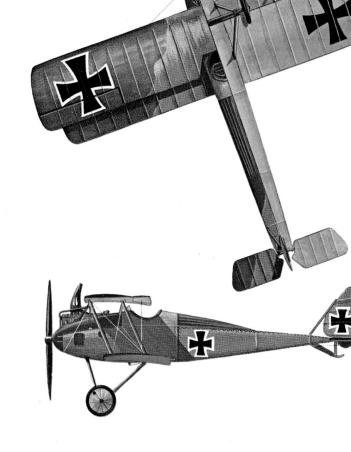

Halberstadt D.II of the Imperial German Military Aviation Service, *ca*. autumn 1916

Engine: One 120hp Mercedes D.II water-
  cooled in-line
Span: 28ft 10½in (8·80m)
Length: 23ft 11¾in (7·30m)
Wing area: approx 244·9sq ft (22·75sq m)
Take-off weight: 1,609lb (730kg)
Maximum speed: 90·1mph (145km/hr) at
  sea level
Service ceiling: approx 13,120ft (4,000m)
Endurance: approx 1 hr 30min

The Halberstadt fighters came after the Fokker E.III had lost its supremacy and before the biplane fighters had fully regained it. Their performance was inferior to the Albatros D.I and D.II, but distinctly better than the indifferent early Fokker D types, and they were probably respected more by their Allied opponents than by their own pilots, who were dubious of the Halberstadts' slender lines and frail-looking tail unit. Such fears were quite unjustified, for the Halberstadt scouts were extremely strong machines that could withstand long, steep dives and tight manoeuvres better than most. The D.I was designed late in 1915, appearing in the following February. In its original form it had unstaggered wings and a 100hp Mercedes D.I engine with side radiators; a single Spandau gun was offset to starboard in front of the cockpit. View from the cockpit was quite good; there was only a small gap between top wing and fuselage, and a semi-hexagonal cut-out in the trailing edge. The D.I was further modified into the D.Ia (120hp Argus As.II in a cleaner cowling and a wing-mounted radiator). In this form, but with the Mercedes D.II, it entered production as the Halberstadt D.II, being built by Aviatik and Hannover in small numbers as well as by the parent company. It was followed by the Argus-powered D.III, which had larger, horn-balanced ailerons, vertical cabane struts and a semi-circular wing cut-out. The D.IV was generally similar except in having a 150hp Benz Bz.III. Final variant was the D.V, which appeared early in 1917. This reverted to the Argus engine, but was considerably better streamlined, had simplified wing bracing and a neatly spinnered propeller. Provision existed to install a second gun in the D.IV and D.V, but as the Halberstadts' performance was already inferior to the Albatros fighters, it is unlikely that advantage was taken of this facility. When it entered service in summer 1916, the D.II was issued in small numbers as an escort for 2-seat reconnaissance aircraft, but from early autumn it joined with the Albatroses in forming the composite equipment of several of the newly formed *Jagdstaffeln*. Peak employment was in January 1917, when a hundred D.II/IIIs were in front-line service in France, but after that winter they started to give way to the later Albatros variants. They were used for a few months longer in Macedonia and Palestine; a few D.IVs were supplied to Turkey.

Sablatnig SF Types

LVG-built SF2 of the Imperial German Navy, late 1916

Engine: One 160hp Mercedes D.III
    water-cooled in-line
Span: 60ft 9½in (18·53m)
Length: 31ft 3½in (9·53m)
Wing area: 602·8sq ft (56·00sq m)
Take-off weight: 3,741lb (1,697kg)
Maximum speed: 80·8mph (130km/hr) at
    sea level
Service ceiling: approx 12,500ft (3,800m)
Endurance: approx 4hr 0min

Dr Josef Sablatnig, an Austrian by birth, built an aeroplane as early as 1903. Moving to Germany, he acquired German nationality and formed the Sablatnig Flugzeugbau in October 1915. In the same month the first Sablatnig-designed seaplane appeared. This was the unarmed SF1, a twin-float biplane with a 160hp Mercedes engine. After it had been tested by the German Navy a modified version was ordered as the SF2, whose prototype differed chiefly in having redesigned vertical tail surfaces. These were revised still further on production SF2s, twenty-six of which were built – six by the parent company, and ten each by LFG and LVG. Delivery took place between June 1916 and May 1917, and they were used chiefly as trainers for Navy pilots. The SF3 was a heavier, scaled-up development of the SF2 intended as an escort and patrol aircraft. It was powered by a 220hp Benz Bz.IV and had a ring-mounted Parabellum gun in the observer's cockpit. The sole SF3 was tested in autumn 1917. The next 2-seat development was the SF5, basically an improved SF2. The SF5 had a 150hp Bz.III; ninety-one were built, fifty by Sablatnig as reconnaissance and coastal patrol aircraft with radio equipment and an observer's gun. It is reported that their performance was poor and they were not a great success. They appeared over the North Sea and the Baltic, and in the latter theatre particularly suffered at the hands of Russian Nieuport

fighters. The remaining SF5s (ten by LFG, thirty by LVG and one 'straggler' from Sablatnig) were delivered as trainers without guns or radio, and it is likely that some of the earlier SF5s were recalled and reallocated to training establishments. Delivery took place between January 1917 and February 1918. One SF5 was converted experimentally to a wheeled undercarriage with the designation SF6. Three examples were ordered of the SF7, a 2-seat fighter development of the SF3. Only one was completed, being delivered in September 1917. It was powered by a 240hp Maybach Mb.IV and had a forward-firing Spandau in addition to the Parabellum gun. Its performance was no more than average. The final Sablatnig design to be built was the SF8. This was evolved expressly as a trainer, reverting to the Bz.III engine and having dual cockpit controls and no armament. Delivery began in spring 1918 of orders totalling thirty-three SF8s, but it is uncertain whether all of these were completed. One single-seat Sablatnig aircraft was also built. This was the SF4, basically a scaled-down version of the SF2 intended for the seaplane station defence role. It was powered by a Bz.III and had a single forward-firing Spandau gun. Two prototypes were completed during the early months of 1917, one as a sesquiplane, the other as a triplane, but neither was very successful.

Fokker D.I to D.V

Fokker D.II of the Imperial German Military
Aviation Service, 1916

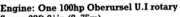

Engine: One 100hp Oberursel U.I rotary
Span: 28ft 8½in (8·75m)
Length: 21ft 0in (6·40m)
Wing area: 193·8sq ft (18·00sq m)
Take-off weight: 1,268lb (575kg)
Maximum speed: 93·2mph (150km/hr)
Service ceiling: 13,120ft (4,000m)
Endurance: 1hr 30min

Produced from mid-1916 to replace the Fokker E.III, the early D types were, on the whole, an undistinguished collection. Designed by Martin Kreutzer, the D.I to D.IV retained a similar basic fuselage to the E.III, allied to a new biplane wing cellule. Comparatively few in-line-engined D.Is and D.IVs were built; production of the rotary-engined D.II and D.III totalled two hundred and ninety-one. The D.I derived from the M.18Z prototype, was powered by a 120hp Mercedes D.II and armed with a single forward-firing Spandau gun offset to port. The pilot's field of view was good, but the D.I, with its warp-controlled wings, was no match in manoeuvrability or climb for Allied Nieuports, and was quickly removed from the Western Front to Russia. At least one (04.41) was completed by MAG in Austro-Hungary. The D.IV, with aileron control, was more manoeuvrable, but the additional output of its 160hp Mercedes was offset to a great extent by the weight of a second gun and it offered little improvement over the D.I. The rotary-engined models were rather better. The D.II, derived from the M.17Z, was probably built before the D.I, and also had warp-controlled wings and a single gun. Span was slightly shorter, but the fuselage was longer and fitted with a 100hp Oberusel U.I in a 'horseshoe' cowling. No German squadrons were equipped fully with D.IIs, which were allocated in small batches to serve primarily as escorts. At least one D.II (04.51) was built in Austro-Hungary by MAG. To take the 160hp U.III two-row rotary, the D.III had a strengthened airframe and the longer-span wings of the D.I, and a deeper-chord cowling and modified undercarriage. It served briefly with a few Western Front *Jastas*, being flown by such pilots as Boelcke, von Richthofen and Udet. However, the U.III engine was an unreliable unit, and with the arrival of more effective fighters the D.III, in company with the other early Fokker D types, was withdrawn to training and miscellaneous duties. The D.III was also built by MAG in Austro-Hungary. Some late-production German D.IIIs, including ten bought by the Dutch Army Air Service in 1917, were fitted with ailerons. Before he was killed in a D.I in June 1916, Kreutzer developed a new prototype, the M.21, from the earlier M.17E. This was taken further by Platz to become the M.22, for which, in October 1916, came a production order as the D.V. This was a more shapely machine, with an entirely new wing cellule, a fully circular cowling for its 100hp U.I engine, and a hemispherical spinner. The D.V handled well, but its performance was inferior to the incoming Albatros fighters and it was transferred to a training role until the end of the war. A few D.Vs were used by the German Navy, possibly also for training.

Gotha G types

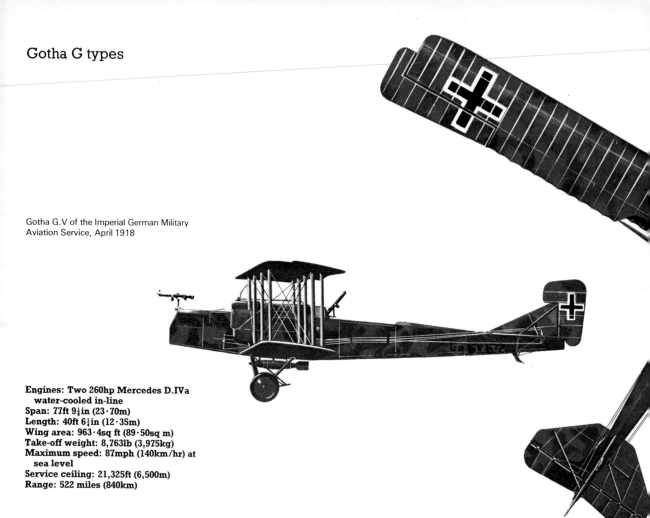

Gotha G.V of the Imperial German Military
Aviation Service, April 1918

Engines: Two 260hp Mercedes D.IVa
water-cooled in-line
Span: 77ft 9½in (23·70m)
Length: 40ft 6¼in (12·35m)
Wing area: 963·4sq ft (89·50sq m)
Take-off weight: 8,763lb (3,975kg)
Maximum speed: 87mph (140km/hr) at
sea level
Service ceiling: 21,325ft (6,500m)
Range: 522 miles (840km)

The first Grossflugzeug (large aeroplane) built by the Gothaer
Waggonfabrik AG was the G.I, evolved by Oskar Ursinus and
Major Friedel of the German Army from a prototype flown for
the first time in January 1915. A few of these were built by
Gotha under licence, in simplified and improved form. They
were intended for ground-attack and general tactical duties
and were employed on the Western and Eastern Fronts. The
G.Is were characterised by a slim fuselage attached to the
upper wings, while the two 160hp Mercedes D.III engines
were mounted close together on the lower wings. Although
following the same basic concept, the Gotha G.II was an
entirely new design, evolved at Gotha under the Swiss
engineer Hans Burkhard and flown for the first time in March
1916. The fuselage and engines (220hp Mercedes D.IVs) were
mounted conventionally on the lower wings; overall span was
increased, and auxiliary front wheels were added to the
landing gear to avoid the risk of nosing over. The Gotha G.II
carried a crew of three and a defensive armament of two
machine-guns; the first production example was completed
in April 1916. The G.II entered service in the autumn, but was
soon withdrawn from operations (on the Balkan Front) after
repeated failures of the engine crankshafts. It was replaced
from October 1916 on the Balkan and Western Fronts by the
G.III, a new model with reinforced fuselage, an extra
machine-gun and 260hp Mercedes D.IVa engines. An initial
twenty-five G.IIIs were ordered, and in December 1916 fourteen were in service at the Front. First major production
model was the G.IV, chosen to carry out raids on the United

Kingdom: an initial fifty G.IVs were ordered from Gotha,
eighty were built by Siemens-Schuckert and about a hundred
by LVG. The G.IV went into service about March 1917, and
began to make daylight raids on southern England towards
the end of May. The G.IV retained the Mercedes D.IVa, but
differed appreciably in having a tunnel hollowed out of the
rear fuselage so that the rear gunner could cover the 'blind
spot' below and to the rear of the bomber. Normally this was
done with the standard rear-mounted gun, but a fourth gun
could be carried for the purpose at the expense of part of the
bomb load. The G.IV, with an all-plywood fuselage, and
ailerons on top and bottom wings, was stronger yet easier to
fly than its predecessors, though its performance remained
much the same as for the G.III, and Germany was obliged to
switch it to night attacks against Britain from September 1917.
By this time it was beginning to be replaced by the new G.V,
which had entered service in August; this version continued
the night bombing of England until the following May. At the
peak of their employment, in April 1918, thirty-six Gotha G.Vs
were in service. Their typical bomb load on cross-Channel
raids was six 50kg (110lb) bombs – about half their maximum
load. Final versions in service were the G.Va/Vb. These
differed from one another only in internal details, but could
be distinguished from the G.V by their biplane tail assembly
and shorter nose. The G.Va/Vb went into production in
March 1918 and into service in June; by August there were
twenty-one G.Vbs at the Front. In general, the Gotha bombers

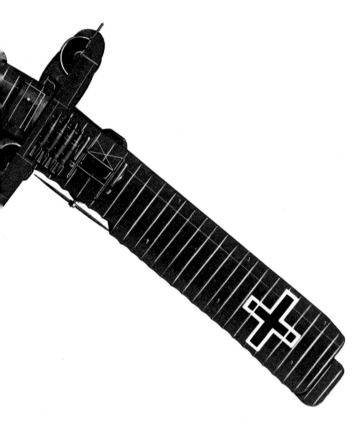

were agile for their size, well defended and difficult to shoot down. More were lost to anti-aircraft fire than in aerial fighting, but far more still were lost in landing accidents. Forty of the Siemens-built G.IVs were completed as trainers, most of them with 180hp Argus As.III or 185hp NAG engines. About thirty of the LVG G.IVs were later transferred to Austro-Hungary, where they were refitted with 230hp Hieros and employed on the Italian Front. A seaplane development of the G.I, the Gotha-Ursinus UWD, was completed late in 1915. It was handed over to the German Navy in January 1916 and used on operations.

Zeppelin (Staaken) R types

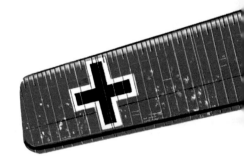

OAW-built R.VI salvaged after crashing at Betz
on 1 June 1918

Engines: Four 260hp Mercedes D.IVa
 water-cooled in-lines
Span: 138ft 5⅜in (42·20m)
Length: 72ft 6⅛in (22·10m)
Wing area: 3,573·6sq ft (332·00sq m)
Take-off weight: 25,265lb (11,460kg)
Maximum speed: 80·8mph (130km/hr) at
 sea level
Service ceiling: 12,465ft (3,800m)
Endurance: 7–10hr according to load

Several German manufacturers produced Riesenflugzeug (giant aeroplane) designs during World War 1, and the most successful of these, though by no means the largest, were those produced by the Zeppelin Werke Staaken. Prior to its move to Staaken in mid-1916 the team responsible for these aircraft was based at the Versuchsbau Gotha-Ost (East Gotha Experimental Works), the first such design being started in November 1914. This was the VGO.I, which flew for the first time on 11 April 1915, powered by three 240hp Maybach Mb.IV engines. One of these, mounted in the nose, drove a tractor propeller, while the other two, mounted midway between the wings, drove pusher propellers. In the front of each of the wing nacelles was a small cockpit mounting twin machine-guns. Redesignated RML 1, this machine was later employed on operations by the German Navy on the Eastern Front, where it was later joined by the VGO.II, a second machine of similar type. Both aircraft served with Rfa 500 (Riesenflugzeugabteilung) late in 1916, but they were seriously underpowered, and the VGO.I later returned to Staaken where it was refitted with five 245hp Maybachs, two in each nacelle; it was later destroyed in a crash. An alternative attempt to provide sufficient power resulted in the VGO.III (later R.III after the introduction of the R category), in which six 160hp Mercedes D.IIIs were installed. Two of these engines were paired in each nacelle to drive single pusher propellers, while the third pair were installed side by side in the nose to drive a tractor propeller. Armament was increased to five machine-guns. The first aircraft in the series to have

an R designation from the outset was the R.IV, which was basically a VGO.III airframe, but with the nacelle engines exchanged for four 220hp Benz Bz.IVs. Up to seven machine-guns were carried by the R.IV, which entered service in July 1917 on the Eastern Front and was later transferred to the Western Front and used in raids on the United Kingdom. Work was also begun in 1916 on single examples of the R.V and R.VII, each powered by five 240hp Mb.IVs – a single one in the nose and a tandem-mounted tractor pair in each outer nacelle, the gun positions of which were relocated at the rear. A fifth machine-gun was carried in a Schwalbenest (swallow's nest) position above the top centre-section. The R.V and R.VII differed chiefly in their tailplane bracing; the former was accepted for service in September 1917 and used against London in 1918, while the latter was lost in a crash in August 1917 during delivery to its unit. The only Zeppelin R type to go into series production was the R.VI, eighteen of which were completed, one by Zeppelin (Staaken), six by Aviatik, four by OAW and seven by Schütte-Lanz. Fifteen of them were powered by four 260hp Mercedes D.IVa engines, in tandem pairs each driving one tractor and one pusher propeller. With the elimination of the nose engine it was possible to install a front gun position with a ring mounting for two Parabellum weapons, and single dorsal and ventral guns were separately manned to the rear of the wings. Between these the two pilots sat side by side in an enclosed cabin. Three of the Aviatik machines, completed in 1918, had four 245 hp Maybachs, the cabin extended to the extreme nose and a large central

vertical tail fin. The Staaken R.VI could carry internally up to eighteen 100kg P.u.W. bombs within the centre of the fuselage. Its maximum load was 2,000kg (4,409lb), though about half of this total was the usual average. Individual bombs of up to 1,000kg (2,205lb) could be carried semi-recessed under the aircraft's belly. Deliveries of R.VIs began in June 1917, and from September they were actively engaged in bombing raids against targets in France and England, operating with Rfa 500 and 501. During their combat career only two R.VIs were shot down by the Allies, but another eight were written off in crashes. Two R.VIs were fitted experimentally with an additional engine, a 120hp Mercedes D.II, driving a compressor to supercharge the main power plant and enable the bomber to sustain its performance at greater heights. Subsequent Zeppelin R types were built in small numbers only. They included three R.XIVs, one R.XIVa and three

R.XVs all powered by five 245hp Mb.IVs and armed with five machine-guns. These had three tractor and two pusher propellers and, therefore, no nacelle gun positions. The R.XVs were probably too late for operational service. Aviatik completed one example (of three ordered) of the R.XVI in October 1918, this having one 220hp and one 550hp Benz in each nacelle. Variants of the R.VI included the Type 8301 seaplane, three or four of which were built using R.VI wings and engine installations with an entirely new fuselage suspended mid-way between the wings and a tail assembly incorporating the large central fin of the final R.VIs. One of these machines was later fitted with a land undercarriage. The Type L seaplane, which was destroyed during trials, was essentially a standard D.IVa-powered R.VI mounted on twin floats some 13m (42ft 7⅞in) long.

Rumpler 6B-1 of the Imperial German Navy,
spring 1917

Engine: One 160hp Mercedes D.III
   water-cooled in-line
Span: 39ft 6¾in (12·05m)
Length: 30ft 10½in (9·40m)
Wing area: 387·5sq ft (36·00sq m)
Maximum take-off weight: 2,513lb
   (1,140kg)
Maximum speed: 95·1mph (153km/hr) at
   sea level
Service ceiling: 16,400ft (5,000m)
Endurance: 4hr 0min

The urgent need by the German Navy during the last two years of war for water-borne fighters to defend its seaplane bases and neighbouring coastal areas was met by three principal aircraft types, all adaptations of existing landplanes. The Albatros W.4 and Brandenburg KDW were evolved from their manufacturers' respective D.I fighters; Rumpler had no single-seat fighter of its own, and so the Type 6B floatplane was based on its 2-seat C.I reconnaissance aircraft. It therefore needed more modification than the other designs, and this took the form of forward stagger for the wings, the elimination of the second cockpit and the fitting of a large plain rudder to offset the additional side area of the twin-step floats. The elevators and triangular tailplane were reduced slightly in area on production 6Bs. The initial version was the 6B-1, first examples of which were delivered in July 1916. By the end of the year about a dozen were in service, and thirty-

eight had been delivered by the end of May 1917. They served mainly with the German seaplane centres at Zeebrugge and Ostend; some were employed in the Black Sea area to defend German bases from attacks by Russian flying-boats. From October 1917 a new version, the Rumpler 6B-2, began to join the 6B-1 in service. These retained the same powerplant, but their airframes were based on the Rumpler C.IV landplane, with bigger dimensions and a 'wing-nut' horizontal tail. Despite a poorer performance, fifty 6B-2s were ordered, delivery taking place between October 1917 and January 1918. For some reason one aircraft was not delivered and its place was taken by an 'extra' 6B-1 delivered in January 1918. Both versions were armed with a synchronised 7·92mm Spandau front gun mounted on the port side of the engine block.

DFW C.V

DFW C.V of the Imperial German Military
Aviation Service, captured by US forces in July
1918

Engine: One 200hp Benz Bz.IV water-
cooled in-line
Span: 43ft 6½in (13·27m)
Length: 25ft 10in (7·87m)
Wing area: 457·5sq ft (42·50sq m)
Take-off weight: 3,153lb (1,430kg)
Maximum speed: 96.3mph (155km/hr) at
3,280ft (1,000m)
Service ceiling: 20,995ft (6,400m)
Endurance: 4hr 30min

The Deutsche Flugzeug-Werke's C.V, one of the finest German 2-seat types to be used during World War 1, was preceded in service by the C.IV of generally similar appearance. Authorities differ in regard to the extent in which the C.IV was produced, and its operational record was certainly overshadowed by that of the more widespread C.V. However, it is certain that among the two thousand three hundred and forty C types produced by DFW during the war period the C.IV and C.V were the predominant models. The basic airframe, designed by Heinrich Oelerich, was common to both aircraft, the C.IV having a neatly installed 150hp Benz Bz.III engine with a radiator mounted flush in the top wing. Its rudder and elevator surfaces were non-balanced, and the fin and tailplane structures were more triangular than those of the C.V. The C.IV first appeared in spring 1916 and was subsequently built by both DFW and Aviatik for both German air services. The C.V (factory designation T 29) was built by Aviatik, Halberstadt and LVG, in addition to the parent company. It differed principally in having the uprated Bz.IV engine (some later aircraft were fitted with 185hp NAG C.IIIs) and was at first fitted with Windhoff side radiators. A single box-type leading-edge radiator was fitted to later C.Vs, and the propeller was fitted with a small spinner. Tail contours were more rounded, and the elevator and rudder surfaces were

balanced. The C.V went into service on the Western Front in late summer 1916, subsequently appearing in Italy, Macedonia and Palestine. It continued to be used in France throughout 1917 and the early part of 1918, and about six hundred C.Vs were still in service on all Fronts when the war ended. The type handled well and was very popular with its crews, and its performance, at high or low level, was excellent for an aeroplane in its class. Its duties included artillery co-operation and infantry contact patrol, and visual and photographic reconnaissance. The C.V possessed a high degree of manoeuvrability, and with an experienced crew aboard could out-manoeuvre even the late-war Allied fighters. Major J T McCudden, VC, in his book *Five Years in the Royal Flying Corps*, admits having to give best to a DFW that evaded his every attempt in his S.E.5a to shoot it down in 1917. Of the C.Vs that fell into Allied hands at the time of the Armistice some twenty-five to thirty were acquired by Belgium, where the type was used for some time for pilot training. On 17 June 1919 a DFW C.V established a world altitude record for an aeroplane of its class by flying to 9,620m (31,561·7ft). The C.VI, which appeared in 1918, remained a prototype only. This aircraft had a 220hp Bz.IVa engine, overhung, balanced ailerons and a redesigned tail unit.

Hansa-Brandenburg KDW

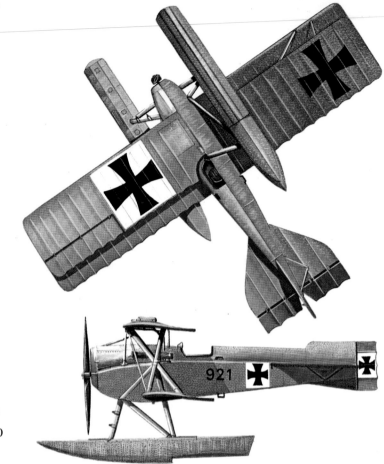

Hansa-Brandenburg KDW of the Imperial
German Navy, February 1917

Engine: One 150hp Benz Bz.III water-
cooled in-line
Span: 30ft 2½in (9·20m)
Length: 26ft 3in (8·00m)
Wing area: 313·8sq ft (29·15sq m)
Take-off weight: 2,293lb (1,040kg)
Maximum speed: 106·9mph (172km/hr)
at sea level
Service ceiling: approx 13,120ft (4,000m)
Endurance: 2hr 30min

The abbreviation KDW, standing for *Kampf Doppeldecker, Wasser* (Fighting Biplane, Water), was a general type classification and not the military designation of any one specific aeroplane: the Hansa-Brandeburg CC flying boat, which was also a single-seat fighter, is often referred to as a KDW. However, the description is generally understood to apply to the W.9 floatplane fighter evolved by Ernst Heinkel in mid-1916. This was basically an adaptation of the landplane D.I 'starstrutter'. Apart from substituting floats for the wheeled landing gear, other alterations included adding a small under-fin and increasing the wing span. View from the cockpit was improved by enlarging the cut-out in the top wing and by leaving small cut-outs in the lower-wing roots; the engine mounting was also revised to give a better view forward. The KDW was brought into being to supplement the Albatros W.4 and Rumpler 6B as a defensive fighter to protect seaplane bases on the Flanders and Adriatic coasts. It is some indication of the KDW's value, and of the priority afforded to German Naval aircraft in general, that the first aircraft was completed in September 1916 and the fifty-eighth was not delivered until February 1918. It is hardly surprising that by

the time all KDWs had been delivered they were outdated, and had already begun to be replaced by later types with better performance and greater versatility. The KDWs were built in five batches. The first three aircraft had 150hp Bz.III engines; the next ten, powered by 160hp Mercedes D.IIIs, had flush-mounted wing radiators that became standard on subsequent aircraft. The third batch, also of ten aircraft, reverted to the Bz.III, but had smaller rudders. The fourth and fifth batches, of fifteen and twenty respectively, were powered by 160hp Maybach Mb.IIIs, had shorter floats, a shallow dorsal fin and a non-balanced rudder. On all except the final batch, armament comprised a single fixed Spandau gun on the port side of the engine block and – like those of the D.I landplane – still out of reach of the pilot. Only on the last twenty aircraft, which had twin Spandaus, were the guns moved back to a position within reach from the cockpit. Variants of the KDW included the W.11, three of which were built with 200hp Bz.IV engines and increased wing span; the W.16 (one built) with a 160hp U.III rotary engine; and the W.25 (one built), which was similar to the Bz.III-engined KDW, but had orthodox wing bracing.

Albatros D.I and D.II

Albatros D.II of the Imperial German Military
Aviation Service, *ca* November 1916

Engine: One 160hp Mercedes D.III
  water-cooled in-line
Span: 27ft 10½in (8·50m)
Length: 24ft 3⅛in (7·40m)
Wing area: 263·7sq ft (24·50sq m)
Take-off weight: 1,958lb (888kg)
Maximum speed: 108·7mph (175km/hr)
  at sea level
Service ceiling: 17,060ft (5,200m)
Endurance: 1hr 30min

Thanks largely to the D.H.2 and the Nieuport 11, the Allies had the measure of the Fokker monoplanes by the late spring of 1916, and Germany clearly needed a new fighter if she was to regain the air supremacy she had enjoyed during the previous winter. Some interim biplane fighters had appeared, with a forward-firing two-gun armament, but in general the weight of the extra gun and its ammunition caused a falling-off in performance. Clearly, more power was needed as well as more guns, and at the Albatros Werke the team under Dipl. Ing. Robert Thelen evolved a prototype known as the D.I which appeared in August 1916. This was armed with twin 7·92mm Spandau guns and was powered by a 160hp Mercedes D.III. The Albatros D.I was the first German fighter to carry a two-gun armament without suffering a corresponding loss of performance, and it quickly entered production, virtually unchanged from the prototype except for the fitting of horn-balanced elevators. It was less manoeuvrable than the Fokker monoplanes, but this factor was more than outweighed by its greater speed, climb and firepower. The appearance of the Albatros D.I coincided with the reorganisation of the German Air Service into *Jagdstaffeln*, and the first operations by D.I-equipped *Jastas* took place in September

1916. In December there were fifty D.Is in service at the Front, but by then they had already been replaced in production by the D.II, which had entered service in October. The D.I's chief limitation had been the rather poor forward view from the cockpit, and the D.II remedied this by having a reduced gap between the fuselage and upper wing and splayed-out 'N' pattern cabane struts. Further improvement was gained by replacing the D.I's side radiators with a flush-mounted wing radiator. By January 1917, their peak period of service, two hundred and fourteen D.IIs were at the Front, where their performance and firepower helped greatly to swing the balance of air superiority back in Germany's favour. The D.II was superseded by the later and even better D.III from January 1917, and by May the January figure of D.IIs at the Front had been exactly halved; by November the total of both D.Is and D.IIs at the Front had dwindled to twenty. German production of the D.II was shared by LVG, and a further twenty D.IIs were built for the Austro-Hungarian Air Service by Oeffag as the Series 53 with 185hp Austro-Daimler engines. After the end of the war, in order to circumvent the terms of the Armistice, all Albatros types were redesignated, the D.I becoming known as the L.15 and the D.II as the L.17.

Hansa-Brandenburg D.I

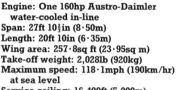

Phönix-built D.I Series 28 of the Austro-Hungarian Air Service, late 1916

Engine: One 160hp Austro-Daimler
  water-cooled in-line
Span: 27ft 10⅝in (8·50m)
Length: 20ft 10in (6·35m)
Wing area: 257·8sq ft (23·95sq m)
Take-off weight: 2,028lb (920kg)
Maximum speed: 118·1mph (190km/hr)
  at sea level
Service ceiling: 16,400ft (5,000m)
Endurance: approx 2hr 30min

Designed by Heinkel early in 1916, the prototype of the aircraft that went into production as the Hansa-Brandenburg D.I was powered by a 160hp Mercedes D.III engine and was given the nickname *Spinne* (Spider). This may have been a reference to the then unique form of interplane bracing, consisting of four small V-struts joined together in a 'star' between each pair of wings. The D.I was not one of Heinkel's better efforts, but it was employed operationally by the Austro-Hungarian Air Service on a fairly wide scale when little else was available. The D.I was ugly and ungainly, with a deep nose whose depth was further accentuated by a radiator mounted directly on top, effectively filling in the gap between the engine and the top wing. The cowling was shaped so that the pilot could see forward along either side of the cylinder block, but his view must have been restricted on the starboard side by the exhaust manifold. With the cockpit roughly in line with the lower trailing edge, and only a small cut-out in the top wing, the view upward and downward must also have left much to be desired. The D.I was armed with a non-synchronised 8mm Schwarzlose gun which seemed to have

been added as an afterthought, for it was mounted in a narrow casing above the top wing, where it added to the aerodynamic drag and was completely inaccessible to the pilot during flight. Production began late in the summer of 1916, deliveries starting in the autumn. The D.I was built in two versions: forty-eight Series 28, built by Phönix with 160hp Austro-Daimler engines, and another forty-eight similarly-powered Series 65·5, built by Brandenburg. Several accidents among early aircraft in service, due to inadequate lateral control, resulted in Phönix adding a small fixed fin and modifying the rudder. Similar alterations were made to the remaining D.Is. Manufacture of the D.I ended early in 1917. One or two D.Is were fitted with 200hp Hiero engines, but the design was really incapable of supporting an engine of this power, and these may have been development machines for the Phönix D.I. This fighter, as its series numbers indicate, was a development of the Hansa-Brandenburg D.I. One Series 28 airframe (28.48) was fitted with unequal-span wings and a modified fuselage to test certain features of the Phönix design.

LFG (Roland) D.I to D.III

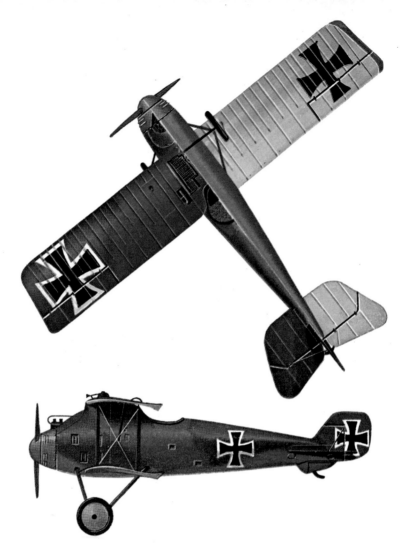

LFG (Roland) D.II of the Imperial German
Military Aviation Service, *ca* spring 1917

Engine: One 160hp Mercedes D.III
water-cooled in-line
Span: 29ft 4in (8·94m)
Length: 22ft 8⅛in (6·93m)
Wing area: 245·4sq ft (22·80sq m)
Take-off weight: 1,753lb (795kg)
Maximum speed: 105mph (169km/hr)
Service ceiling: approx 16,400ft (5,000m)
Endurance: 2hr 0min

The early Roland fighters were designed by Tantzen as progressive single-seat developments of the 1915 C.II. The tubby, fish-like appearance of the C.II had earned it the nickname *Walfisch* (Whale), and the more slender lines of the D.I prototype which was flown in July 1916 inevitably led to it being named *Haifisch* (Shark). The prototype was powered by a 160hp Mercedes D.III, retaining similar hemispherical spinner and side radiators to the C.II. Among differences from the C.II were unstaggered wings and a more angular tail assembly. A small window/escape hatch in the side of the nose was omitted on production D.Is. These were built from late 1916 by the parent company and Pfalz, with only minor changes from the prototype. Standard armament was a single forward-firing Spandau gun. In October 1916 the D.II was flown for the first time, this having a pylon-type cabane for the upper wing in an attempt to improve the view downward past the nose; other modifications having the same object included a wing-mounted radiator, cut-down cockpit sides and a downward-curving engine exhaust. A slightly longer and lighter variant with shorter-span wings and a 180hp Argus As.III was designated D.IIa, and both these types entered service in the early months of 1917. Their standard armament consisted of twin Spandaus. The operational career of these

Roland fighters was undistinguished: the various changes had done little to improve the cockpit view, and they were still tricky to land. They were heavy on the controls and their overall performance was inferior to contemporary Albatros single-seaters. Hence they were generally relegated to fairly quiet sections of the Western Front, to Russia and to Macedonia. The last production version was the D.III, powered by the As.III engine, which introduced a strutted cabane giving a small gap between fuselage and top wing, a reduced-chord lower wing and a longer vertical fin. One hundred and fifty D.IIIs were ordered, but only some twenty-five were delivered to front-line units; the remainder were used as advanced trainers. A development was the sole D.V, completed in 1917 with a D.III wing cellule and a 160hp Mercedes in a slimmer fuselage. A twin-float development of the D.II, flown on 29 June 1917, also had a Mercedes D.III and was designated WD. Two C type machines appeared in 1917, the C.V and the C.VIII. The C.V was based on the D.II, while the C.VIII apparently combined some features of the C.III and D.II and was powered by either a 260hp Mercedes D.IVa or a 245hp Maybach Mb.IV. None of these types achieved production status.

Friedrichshafen G types

Friedrichshafen G.III, possibly of *Bogohl* 2,
Imperial German Military Aviation Service, May
1918

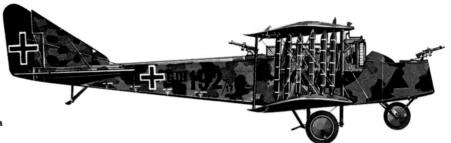

Engines: Two 260hp Mercedes D.IVa
   water-cooled in-lines
Span: 77ft 11in (23·75m)
Length: 42ft 1⅛in (12·85m)
Wing area: 925·7sq ft (86·00sq m)
Take-off weight: 8,686lb (3,940kg)
Maximum speed: 87·6mph (141km/hr) at
   3,280ft (1,000m)
Service ceiling: 14,765ft (4,500m)
Endurance: 5hr 0min

Although better known for its wartime series of naval sea-planes, the Flugzeugbau Freidrichshafen did produce during World War 1 a range of G type twin-engined bombers. They were slightly smaller than the contemporary and more widely used Gotha G types, from which they could be distinguished by the shape of their wingtips and horizontal tail surfaces. The first type to appear was the G.I (FF30), which was completed late in 1914. It was a 3-bay biplane with two 150hp Bz.III pusher engines, a compound tail assembly, and was armed with a single Parabellum defensive machine-gun in the nose. This apparently did not go into production, and it was not until 1916 that the G.II (FF38) appeared, a 2-bay, single-tailed aircraft with two 200hp Bz.IV pusher engines and a Parabellum gun in each of the nose and rear cockpits. The G.II went into limited production by the parent company and the Daimler Motoren-Werke, entering service towards the end of 1916. It continued to serve throughout the following year, but its 150kg (330lb) bomb load was modest by current standards and it was supplanted by the G.III (FF45), a larger aeroplane capable of carrying a heavier load. The G.III first appeared early in 1917, and was again a 3-bay design. All flying surfaces, including the double ailerons, were balanced, but only the elevators were overhung. A 3-man crew was carried, and the defensive armament consisted of single or twin Parabellum guns in each of the front and rear cockpits; the rear gunner was protected from the pusher propellers of the Mercedes D.IVa engines by wire mesh guards on either side of him. Bomb load of the G.III for normal ranges was 500kg (1,102lb), of which 100kg (220lb) was carried internally and the remainder on racks under the fuselage. The Friedrichshafen G.III was in service at about the same time as the Gotha G.V (i.e. from mid-1917 until the end of the war), operating chiefly as a night bomber against targets in France and Belgium, although some accompanied the Gothas in their attacks on the United Kingdom. From early 1918 they were joined by the G.IIIa, which differed principally in having a compound tail unit. Production of the G.III/IIIa was shared by Daimler and Hansa, who built two hundred and forty-five and ninety-three aircraft respectively. Later variants, appearing in modest numbers during 1918, included the G.IVa, G.IVb and G.V. All were short-nosed developments without a front gun position, the G.IVa being a pusher type like the earlier Friedrichshafens, while the G.IVb and G.V had engines driving tractor propellers. The Friedrichshafen G types equipped Bombengeschwadern 1,2 and 5, and served in Macedonia as well as on the Western Front.

Albatros D.III

Albatros D.III of the Imperial German Military
Aviation Service which crashed north of Savoy
in October 1917

Engine: One 160/175hp Mercedes D.IIIa
    water-cooled in-line
Span: 29ft 8½in (9·05m)
Length: 24ft 0½in (7·33m)
Wing area: 220·7sq ft (20·50sq m)
Take-off weight: 1,953lb (886kg)
Maximum speed: 108·7mph (175km/hr)
    at 3,280 ft (1,000m)
Service ceiling: 18,045ft (5,500m)
Endurance: 2hr 0min

The first of the Albatros 'V-strutters', the D.III was the best and most effective of all the Albatros fighters produced during World War I. It resulted from an *Idflieg* request during 1916 for German designers to incorporate in their fighters some of the features that had made the Allied Nieuport scouts so successful on the Western Front. At the Albatros Werke, Dipl. Ing. Thelen decided to retain the basic fuselage of his D.II, with a high-compression version of the Mercedes D.III to give a better altitude performance, and to design an entirely new wing cellule. Following Nieuport practice, though less drastically, he made the lower wings much narrower in chord than the upper pair. The result was an aircraft with an even better speed and climb rate than the Albatros D.II, and when it joined the earlier Albatros fighters in service at the beginning of 1917 it quickly began to establish its superiority. The first *Jastas* to receive the D.III included No. 11 in January 1917, and by that spring all 37 *Jastas* at the Front were fully or partly equipped with Albatros fighters of one kind or another. The D.III remained in service throughout the year, reaching its peak of service in November when four hundred and forty-six were at the Front. During this period it formed the major equipment of the *Jastas*, and was one of the chief agents of destruction in what the Allies came to know as 'Bloody April'. From July the D.III began to be joined in service by the D.V and D.Va, although D.III production did not come to an end until early the following year. In addition to their service on the Western Front, Albatros D.IIIs also operated with the German air service in Palestine and Macedonia, and three Series (53.21, 153 and 253) were built by Oeffag for the Austro-Hungarian air arm, powered respectively by 185, 200 and 225hp Austro-Daimler engines. Modifications introduced during the production life of the D.III included slightly offsetting the wing radiator to starboard – where, if punctured during combat, the scalding water would not fly into the pilot's face – and the fitting of a more rounded rudder, similar to that later used on the D.V; D.IIIs in Palestine were later fitted with twin radiators. During the latter part of 1917 the Albatros D.III was gradually outclassed by later Allied fighters, first by the Sopwith triplane and Spad VII and later by the Camel and S.E.5a. Some German- and some Austrian-built D.IIIs were supplied to the Polish Air Force in 1919. The post-war designation of the Albatros D.III was L.20.

Oeffag-built Albatros D.III (Series 153) flown
by Hauptmann Godwin Brumowski of the Ö.U.
Fliegertruppe, Istrien Sesana, March 1918

Data as opposite except:
**Engine: One 200hp Austro-Daimler in-
line**

**Maximum speed: 102·5mph (165km/hr)
at 3,280ft (1,000m)**

Middle member of the Albatros family of D-type single-seat fighters, the D.III was undoubtedly the best of a good bunch. From mid-1916, first the D.I and then the D.II had begun successfully to wrest back the air supremacy over the Western Front which French and British squadrons had regained at some effort from the Fokker monoplane. One of Britain's leading D.H.2 pilots, Major Lanoe Hawker, succumbed to a D.II flown by Manfred von Richthofen, and other leading lights of the German Air Service – among them Boelcke, Udet and Voss – also played a part in making the presence of the Albatros felt. Compared with the early versions, the D.III exhibited a number of design changes, of which the narrower-chord lower wings and interplane V struts were no doubt the result of studying captured Nieuport scouts. The Albatros D.III was a handsome machine, with an excellently streamlined bullet-shaped body neatly capped by the large propeller spinner. It was also very strongly built: it had a two-spar upper wing and the fuselage structure consisted of six longerons, oval former frames and a plywood skin. With its forward-firing two-gun armament, and high speed, it represented a marked improvement over the slower, more fragile and usually single-gunned Fokker E.III. Its heyday was in the first half of 1917, including a particularly successful period in 'Bloody April' during which a heavy toll was exacted of Allied aircraft – mostly the luckless B.E.2c. The subject of the illustration is one of the Series 153 Albatros D.IIIs, built for the Austro-Hungarian Fliegertruppe by Oeffag and flown by that country's most successful fighter pilot, Hauptmann Godwin Brumowski. This officer had, by the time of the Armistice, accumulated thirty-eight certain victories and three 'probables', and numbered the Iron Cross and the Order of Leopold among his many decorations. The Albatros D.V. and D.Va, which followed the D.III, did not achieve the degree of improved performance expected, although they were equally successful and more widely used. However, two D.Vs, one in Canberra and one in Washington, represent the only examples of the Albatros D types still in being today. The D.V and D.Va are described on page 54.

Albatros W.4

Albatros W.4 from an Imperial German Navy
seaplane base on the Flanders coast, *ca*
autumn 1917

**Engine: One 160hp Mercedes D.III
      water-cooled in-line
Span: 31ft 2⅛in (9·50m)
Length: 27ft 10⅝in (8·50)
Wing area: 340·1sq ft (31·60m)
Take-off weight: 2,359lb (1,070kg)
Maximum speed: 99·4mph (160km/hr) at
      sea level
Service ceiling: 9,840ft (3,000m)
Endurance: 3hr 0min**

The German Admiralty, disturbed by attacks on its seaplane bases along the Flanders coast, issued a specification in the summer of 1916 for a single-seat station defence fighter. The simplest way to meet this quickly was to adapt an existing design, and the Albatros Werke accordingly produced a seaplane fighter based on the D.I landplane. The new fighter, designated W.4, utilised a number of D.I components but had a much larger gap between the fuselage and upper wings, which were of 1m (3ft 3⅜in) greater span; the underfin of the D.I was eliminated, the normal fin and tailplane being increased correspondingly in size, and the aircraft was mounted on twin, square-section floats. In September 1916 the first W.4 (747) was delivered to the German Navy. A second machine followed later that month, and a third in December. Powerplant was the well-tried Mercedes D.III in-line, and the fighter was armed with a pair of 7.92mm Spandau machine-guns on top of the fuselage, firing on either side of the cylinder block. Between February and April 1917 the first ten

production W.4s were delivered. These had better stream-lined floats with revised strutting, and a smaller cockpit. Further batches of twenty, ten, twenty-five, thirty and twenty W.4s brought the total to one hundred and eighteen by December 1917. Some later batches had a wing radiator offset to starboard instead of Windhoff side radiators, and were fitted with ailerons on all four wings. A variety of different float designs were used. The W.4s served principally along the Flanders coast, but some were also reported in action in the Aegean area. By the time the final production batches were being delivered, the W.4 – essentially an interim fighter – was being replaced by the equally fast but better defended Hansa-Brandenburg W.12 2-seater. The W.4 possessed a first-class endurance, good speed, manoeuvrability and fire-power, and gave a good account of itself during its brief operational life against Allied floatplanes, but it found the later RNAS flying-boats somewhat tougher opposition. It could climb to 1,000m (3,280ft) in 5 minutes.

Rumpler C.IV to C.VII

Rumpler C.IV of the Imperial German Military
Aviation Service, late 1917

Engine: One 260hp Mercedes D.IVa
  water-cooled in-line
Span: 41ft 6¾in (12·66m)
Length: 27ft 7⅛in (8·41m)
Wing area: 360·6sq ft (33·50sq m)
Take-off weight: 3,373lb (1,530kg)
Maximum speed: 106·3mph (171km/hr)
  at 1,640ft (500m)
Service ceiling: 21,000ft (6,400m)
Endurance: 3hr 30min

The C.IV, the second of Dr Edmund Rumpler's C type designs to go into large-scale production, was preceded by the generally similar C.III, seventy-five of which were recorded in service in February 1917. The C.III was a 1916 design, powered by a 220hp Benz Bz.IV. When the more powerful Mercedes D.IVa became available it was developed into the C.IV, which was one of the most efficient, as well as most elegant, German 2-seaters to appear on the Western Front. It had the staggered, sweptback wings of 'libellule' planform that characterised subsequent Rumpler C types, and its horizontal tail surfaces were of 'wing-nut' shape. The fuselage was reasonably well streamlined, with attention paid to nose-entry in the neat cowling of the 260hp D.IVa engine and the small conical spinner over the propeller hub. In place of the small, comma-type rudder of the C.III, the C.IV's vertical tail surfaces were of the triangular fin and plain rudder form used on the earlier C.I. The Rumpler C.IV carried the normal 2-seater armament of the period, i.e. a forward-firing synchronised Spandau gun and a ring-mounted Parabellum. The reconnaissance cameras were aimed through a trap in the floor of the rear cockpit. Light 'nuisance' raids were often undertaken, with a small load usually consisting of four 25kg bombs on underwing racks. The C.IV had an excellent performance for an aeroplane in its class, especially at high altitude; it could climb to 5,000m (16,400ft) in 38 minutes, and at its maximum altitude was still fast enough to elude Allied fighters. Rumpler

C.IVs saw service in Italy and Palestine as well as on the Western Front; they were built by the Bayerische Rumpler-Werke and Pfalz Flugzeugwerke, those built by the latter concern having linked double ailerons. The Rumpler C.V was a variant of the C.III airframe fitted with a Mercedes D.IVa, but apparently it did not go into production. There is no record of a C.VI, the next production version being the C.VII, which appeared late in 1917. The C.VII had a 240hp Maybach Mb.IV engine which, although of a lower nominal rating, had a higher compression ratio than the Mercedes D.IVa that enabled it to maintain its output at greater heights. The C.VII was slightly smaller than the C.IV; it was built in two standard forms, the long-range reconnaissance version with radio equipment and a normal 2-gun armament and the C.VII (Rubild). In the latter version the front gun was dispensed with, and instead the aircraft carried additional photographic gear and oxygen breathing apparatus for the crew members, who were also provided with electrically heated flying suits. These assets were extremely necessary, for the C.VII (Rubild) could fly to, and maintain its speed at, even greater heights than those reached by the C.IV. Service ceiling of the C.VII (Rubild) was 7,300m (23,950ft), which it could reach in 50 minutes. At heights in the region of 20,000ft (6,000m) it could fly as fast as such Allied fighters as the S.E.5a. Both the Rumpler C.IV and C.VII remained in German Air Force service until the Armistice.

Hansa-Brandenburg CC

Hansa-Brandenburg CC flown by Lt Gottfried Banfield of the Austro-Hungarian Navy, 1917

**Engine: One 185hp Austro-Daimler
water-cooled in-line**
Span: 30ft 6¼in (9·30m)
Length: 30ft 0¼in (9·15m)
Wing area: 285·2sq ft (26·50m)
Take-off weight: 2,604lb (1,181kg)
**Maximum speed: 99·4mph (160km/hr) at
sea level**
Service ceiling: approx 10,825ft (3,300m)
Endurance: 3hr 30min

The first Brandenburg flying-boat was the 3-seat FB developed by Ernst Heinkel from a Lohner design and built in small numbers for the German and Austro-Hungarian Navies in 1915. In 1916 Heinkel produced an original design for a single-seat wooden-hulled fighter flying-boat, which he named CC after Camillo Castiglioni, financial controller of the Brandenburg company. The CC was characterised by 'star-strut' interplane bracing like that used for the D.I landplane fighter. After flight trials with the prototype a single CC was ordered by the German Navy. This was delivered to Warnemünde in February 1917, powered by a 150hp Bz.III engine and armed with a centrally mounted Spandau front gun. Two CC production batches totalling thirty-five aircraft were delivered during 1917; these had wing radiators and a twin-Spandau armament. Some also had slightly lengthened hulls. Major user of the CC was the Austro-Hungarian Navy, for whom the type was built by Phönix. Designated in the A class in Austrian service, the flying-boats were used up and down the Adriatic in defence of ports and naval bases. Like their German counterparts, they were at first fitted with one, and later with two, machine-guns; it may be supposed that these were the domestic 8mm Schwarzlose weapon. The CC's chief opponent in the Adriatic was the Italian Air Force's Nieuport 11, against which the flying-boats acquitted themselves fairly well, having a slight edge in speed to offset their lesser manoeuvrability. Overall Phönix production of the CC amounted to thirty-five aircraft (A.13–42 and A.45–49). Machine A45 appeared in 1918 as a triplane, but this line of development was not pursued. The 'Phönix A' designation was also applied to sixty-one examples of the Hansa-Brandenburg W.18 seaplane built for the Austro-Hungarian Navy. Examples of the CC in German service included at least one aircraft with a spinner and the engine in a streamlined, egg-shaped nacelle, and another with extra V-struts outboard of the 'star' struts.

Hansa-Brandenburg W.12 and W.19

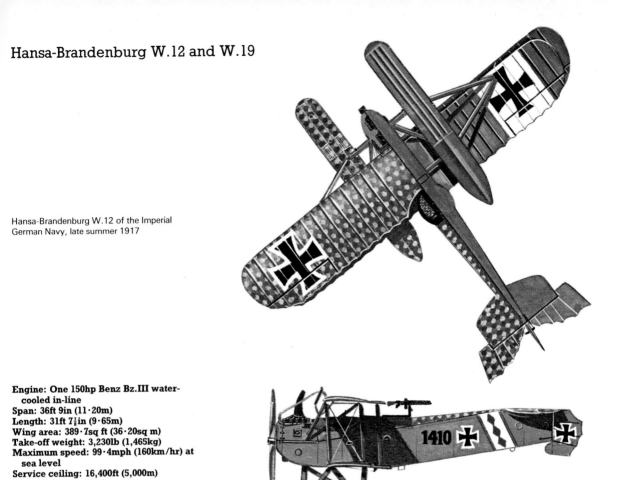

Hansa-Brandenburg W.12 of the Imperial
German Navy, late summer 1917

Engine: One 150hp Benz Bz.III water-
    cooled in-line
Span: 36ft 9in (11·20m)
Length: 31ft 7⅛in (9·65m)
Wing area: 389·7sq ft (36·20sq m)
Take-off weight: 3,230lb (1,465kg)
Maximum speed: 99·4mph (160km/hr) at
    sea level
Service ceiling: 16,400ft (5,000m)
Endurance: 3hr 30min

The Imperial German Navy learned from experience that single-seat seaplanes were vulnerable to attack from the rear, and so in the autumn of 1916 Ernst Heinkel began to design the 2-seat W.12. The prototype was completed in January 1917. Its fuselage maintained an almost even depth from nose to tail, giving plenty of 'keel' to make the W.12 stable in flight without affecting manoeuvrability. The tailplane was mounted on top of the fuselage, with a balanced, comma-type rudder extending behind and below the sternpost. Hence, from the elevated gun-ring in the rear cockpit, the observer commanded a virtually uninterrupted field of fire in the upper hemisphere. Despite an accident to the prototype, the W.12 was ordered into production, one hundred and forty-five being delivered between April 1917 and March 1918. These were in batches as follows: six with 160hp Mercedes D.IIIs and wing radiators; four batches of nine, twenty, twenty and thirty with 150hp Bz.IIIs and frontal radiators, and two final batches of forty and twenty Mercedes-engined W.12s. Minor variations occurred between different batches. The fourth Benz-powered batch had twin forward-firing Spandaus, the remainder a single one to starboard; all W.12s had a Para-

bellum gun in the rear cockpit. The W.12 entered service in April 1917, and as well as giving an excellent account of itself defending German seaplane and naval bases against Allied aeroplanes and airships, it was often used for reconnaissance. From November 1917 it was joined in production by the W.19, fifty-four of which were built, entering service from January 1918. The W.19 had blunter wings, 2.60m (8ft 6⅓in) greater in span; a 1·05m (3ft 5⅓in) longer fuselage; revised tail surfaces; and a 240hp Maybach Mb.IV engine. All except the first three had twin Spandau guns, and one was fitted experimentally with a 20mm Becker cannon in the observer's cockpit. The W.19 had an endurance of 5 hours, and often worked in company with the W.12, patrolling ahead of its smaller companion and returning to fetch it when a target was sighted. The Brandenburg 2-seaters, used in some concentration during spring and summer 1918, were treated by RNAS crews along the Flanders coast and over the North Sea as adversaries worthy of respect. Both types remained in service until the Armistice. The W.27 was a variant with a 195hp Bz.IIIb; it remained a prototype only, but two similar W.32s were completed with Mercedes D.IIIs and used as trainers.

Albatros D.V and D.Va

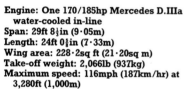

Engine: One 170/185hp Mercedes D.IIIa
   water-cooled in-line
Span: 29ft 8⅛in (9·05m)
Length: 24ft 0⅜in (7·33m)
Wing area: 228·2sq ft (21·20sq m)
Take-off weight: 2,066lb (937kg)
Maximum speed: 116mph (187km/hr) at
   3,280ft (1,000m)
Service ceiling: 20,505ft (6,250m)
Endurance: 2hr 0min

The Albatros D.V was produced in an attempt, not entirely successful, to maintain the edge of superiority gained in 1917 by the excellent D.III, in the face of later Allied types such as the S.E.5a and Sopwith Camel. An interim model, the D.IV, had appeared in 1917, marking a return to the equal-chord wings of the D.II and powered by a fully enclosed geared Mercedes engine. Owing to troubles with this engine the D.IV was not developed, but its fuselage design was retained in the D.V, which resumed the more graceful and more efficient wing form of the D.III. The D.V's fuselage was of oval section (compared with the flat-sided D.III), and the high-compression Mercedes D.IIIa was installed with rather fewer pretensions to careful cowling in order to simplify access and maintenance. The D.V retained the same tailplane as the D.III, but introduced an integral fixed fin, a raked-back underfin and (except for the prototype) a more rounded rudder. Fuselage construction was lighter but stronger than that of the earlier Albatros fighters, although the gross weight of the D.Va was slightly increased over that of the D.V by virtue of additional strengthening. The D.V also differed from the other Albatros fighters in the arrangement of its aileron control wires, and this marked the only visible point of distinction between the D.V and D.Va. Unfortunately, although flying qualities remained good, the D.V and D.Va were no great improvement over the D.III, and achieved their success as much by sheer weight of numbers as by their performance. First D.Vs were delivered to *Jastas* in mid-1917, D.Vas following from late autumn, both versions serving alongside their earlier stablemates. They reached their peak of service in November 1917 and March 1918 respectively, and were the most widely used of all Albatros fighters. Exact production figures are not known, but a minimum of one thousand five hundred and twelve D.V/Vas are known to have served with Western Front units, and this takes no account of aircraft with home establishments or those used in Italy and Palestine. Production was shared by the Ostdeutsche Albatros Werke. Despite limitations on diving manoeuvres, imposed after a series of crashes caused by failure of the single-spar lower wings (also a weakness of the D.III), D.V/Vas remained in service until the Armistice. In the post-war redesignation of Albatros types the D.V/Va became known as the L.24.

Halberstadt CL.II and CL.IV

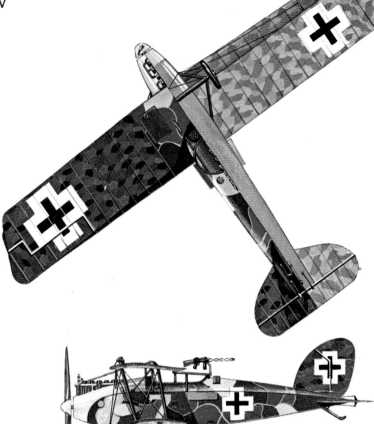

Halberstadt CL.II of the Imperial German
Military Aviation Service. *ca* May 1918

Engine: One 160hp Mercedes D.III
water-cooled in-line
Span: 35ft 4in (10·77m)
Length: 23ft 11½in (7·30m)
Wing area: 296·0sq ft (27·50sq m)
Take-off weight: 2,498lb (1,133kg)
Maximum speed: 102·5mph (165km/hr)
at 16,400ft (5,000m)
Service ceiling: 16,730ft (5,100m)
Endurance: 3hr 0min

Early in 1917 a new class of German 2-seater was introduced: the CL category, a smaller, lighter version of the C type intended to provide protective escort for their heavier brethren and support for the ground forces. The first aircraft to be produced in this category was the Halberstadt CL.II, a neat, compact biplane with its crew seated in a long communal cockpit. Armament consisted of one or two 7·92mm synchronised Spandau guns on top of the front fuselage, and a Parabellum gun of similar calibre on an elevated ring mounting in the rear; four or five 10kg mortar bombs or a number of small grenades were carried in trays attached to the fuselage on either side of the observer. The CL.II entered service in mid-1917, quickly making its presence felt. On 6 September twenty-four CL.IIs, against virtually no air opposition, wrought havoc among Allied troops crossing the Somme bridges. Following this action, increasing use was made of the CL.II in the close support role, and it was largely due to aircraft of this type that the Germans were able to make such an effective counter-offensive at the Battle of Cambrai on 30 November. The expansion of the German *Schlachtstaffeln* (Battle Flights) was made largely with the CL.II and the later CL.IV, and by the spring offensive of March 1918 most of the 38 *Schlastas* then in existence, each with an establishment for six aircraft, were equipped with Halberstadt CL types. They had a marked effect upon the morale of the Allied troops in the trenches who were subjected to their attacks. After the failure of the March offensive they reverted mainly to a defensive role, although some continued to be used for nuisance raids by night on Allied airfields. Other duties included the interception of Allied night bombers and defensive support of the ground troops. A few examples were built of the CL.IIa, with a 185hp BMW IIIa engine in a more streamlined nose; but the only other major variant was the CL.IV, which appeared early in 1918. This retained the Mercedes D.III, though in a blunter cowling, the fuselage was some 2½ft (0·76m) shorter, and had a wider-span tailplane and a more rounded fin and rudder. The CL.IV had much the same overall performance as the CL.II, but it was more manoeuvrable. Production of the CL.II was shared by Bayerische Flugzeug-Werke, and of the CL.IV by LFG (Roland).

Fokker Dr.I

Engine: One 110hp Oberursel UR.II
  rotary
Span: 23ft 7⅛in (7·19m)
Length: 18ft 11⅛in (5·77m)
Wing area (incl. axle fairing): 200·9sq ft
  (18·66sq m)
Take-off weight: 1,290lb (585kg)
Maximum speed: 102·5mph (165km/hr)
  at 13,125ft (4,000m)
Service ceiling: 19,685ft (6,000m)
Endurance: 1hr 30min

The Fokker triplane – or Dr. I (Dreidecker Type I) to give it its more formal designation – was not, as is often said or implied, a 'copy' of the Sopwith triplane which had gone into action with the British air services at the end of 1916. But it was, indisputably, an outcome of the effect which the introduction of the British type had had upon the air fighting over the Western Front; indeed, German and Austro-Hungarian companies had such an attack of 'triplanitis' that no fewer than fourteen of them had produced triple-winged fighter designs by the end of 1917. First and most successful was the Fokker machine, designed in the late spring of that year by the brilliant Reinhold Platz and carrying out its first operations with von Richthofen's Jagdgeschwader I in August. These were performed by the second and third prototypes, the latter being almost exclusively the mount of Leutnant Werner Voss, one of Germany's leading fighter pilots. Voss scored his first victory in the Dr. I on 30 August, and went on to score a further twenty in the next three weeks before, on 23 September, he was shot down and killed by an S.E.5a of No. 56 Squadron, R.F.C. The second prototype had an even shorter

operational life, beginning on 1 September when flown by Manfred von Richthofen in the course of scoring his 60th victory of the war, and ending only a fortnight later when shot down by Sopwith Camels of No. 10 Squadron R.N.A.S., the German pilot on that day being Oblt Kurt Wolff of Jasta 11. Despite these early casualties the Fokker triplane was warmly welcomed by its crews, and would not have gone so early to so eminent a unit as JG I if it had not been so good. Main production deliveries began in October 1917, and the triplane was fully operational by the end of the year, providing pilots of Albatros and Pfalz fighters with a mount that could put them on terms with the S.E.5a, Bristol Fighter and Spad, thanks to its first-class manoeuvrability and a rate of climb that could take it to 13,125ft (4,000m) in 15 minutes or less. One often sees reference to 'Richthofen's triplane' as though to suggest that this was a single aircraft. In fact, the Rittmeister flew several, and became its greatest exponent before his death on 21 April 1918 in the example illustrated. Other famous exponents of the little Fokker included his brother Lothar, Ernst Udet and Hermann Göring.

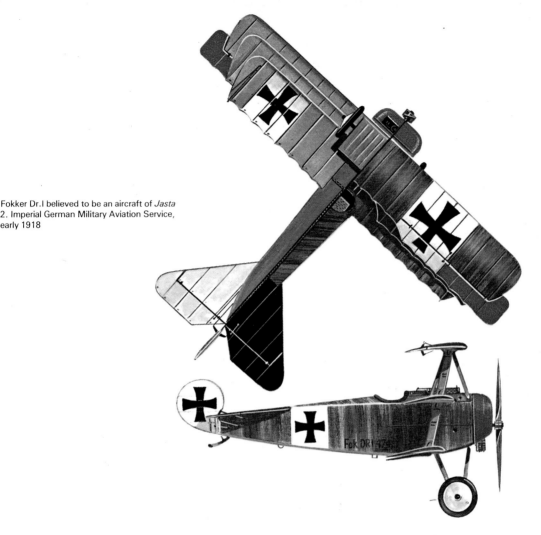

Fokker Dr.I believed to be an aircraft of *Jasta* 2. Imperial German Military Aviation Service, early 1918

Such was the impact created in German military circles by the Sopwith triplane that, apparently believing that the triple-wing arrangement was a magic formula for success, no fewer than fourteen German and Austrian manufacturers produced triplane designs of their own. Most of them did so after inspecting a captured British machine in July 1917, but they were well behind Anthony Fokker, who had seen the Sopwith in action at the Front in April. It has often been implied that the Fokker Dr.I was a copy of the Sopwith triplane, but Reinhold Platz, who designed the Fokker machine at his employer's request, had never seen the British aeroplane, and indeed was quite unconvinced of the merits of a triplane layout. Nevertheless, he produced a prototype known as the V.3 with three sets of cantilever wings, the only struts being those on which the top plane was mounted. Single, thin interplane struts and balanced ailerons, together with two 7·92mm Spandaus, were added after the V.3 had been test-flown by Fokker, and in this form it became the V.4. In virtually unchanged form two further prototypes and three hundred and eighteen Dr.Is were ordered in summer 1917. Following acceptance trials in August, the second and third prototypes became operational with von Richthofen's *Jagdgeschwader I*. The third machine was flown almost exclusively by Leutnant Werner Voss, who scored his first victory with it on 30 August. In the next twenty-four days Voss scored a further twenty victories before being shot down and killed on 23 September

by an S.E.5a of No. 56 Squadron. From mid-October, deliveries of production Dr.Is began to JG.I, but by early November a series of fatal crashes caused them to be grounded. The trouble was faulty workmanship in the wing construction, and for most of the remainder of November the Fokker factory was occupied in repairing or replacing the defective wings. The Dr.I thus did not become fully operational until late November, and its subsequent career at the Front was brief. Nevertheless, it achieved considerable success, due mainly to its excellent manoeuvrability. It was in a Fokker Dr.I that, on 21 April 1918, the legendary Manfred von Richthofen was finally shot down and killed. The Dr.I reached its peak of service early in May 1918 when one hundred and seventy-one were in front-line service. Later that month production ceased, and thereafter the Dr.I was transferred to home defence until the Armistice, at which time sixty-nine were in service. The standard powerplant of the Dr.I was the 110hp Oberursel UR.II or Goebel Goe.II rotary. Some aircraft had the 200hp Goe.III or IIIa engine or the 110hp French-built (captured) or copied Le Rhône; experimental installations included the Sh.III and captured 130hp Clergets. In 1917 Platz produced an alternative triplane prototype, the V.6, which had a 120hp Mercedes D.II stationary engine, but the V.6 proved more clumsy than the rotary-engined Dr.I, and no further examples were built.

Pfalz D.III

Pfalz D.III flown by Vizefeldwebel Hecht of *Jasta* 10 Imperial German Military Aviation Service, September 1917

Engine: One 160hp Mercedes D.III
   water-cooled in-line
Span: 30ft 10⅛in (9·40m)
Length: 22ft 9⅜in (6·95m)
Wing area: 238·6sq ft (22·17sq m)
Take-off weight: 2,055lb (932kg)
Maximum speed: 102·5mph (165km/hr)
   at 9,845ft (3,000m)
Service ceiling: 17,060ft (5,200m)
Endurance: 2hr 30min

The Pfalz Flugzeug-Werke did not produce a biplane fighter of its own design until Rudolfo Gehringer's D.III appeared in the spring of 1917. It clearly owed much to the Roland fighters that Pfalz had been building under licence, but was slimmer, neater and even more shark-like than the Roland 'fish'. The Pfalz D.III was extremely well built, having a semi-monocoque ply fuselage, and the wings were of unequal chord to give a better downward view; Pfalz avoided the structural trap of similar designs by employing a two-spar lower wing. The fuselage-upper-wing gap was kept to a minimum to afford a good all-round view from the cockpit. The prototype D.III was tested in June 1917 and went quickly into production with few modifications. Its twin Spandau guns were completely buried, except for their muzzles, in the front fuselage. The D.IIIa, which followed it into production, had a Mercedes engine offering upward of 175hp, and its guns mounted more conventionally on top of the fuselage, where they were easier to aim and to service. The wingtip shape on later D.IIIs and D.IIIas was altered to a more rounded form. The D.III began to enter service in August 1917, being supplied first to *Jastas* in Bavaria. By 31 December 1917 two hundred and seventy-six D.IIIs and one hundred and fourteen D.IIIas were at the Front. The D.IIIs dwindled thereafter, while D.IIIa numbers rose in proportion. The D.IIIa reached its peak in April 1918 when four hundred and thirty-six were at the Front. Forty-six *Jastas* are known to have had some D.III/IIIas on strength, but the type only fully equipped about a dozen of these. The Pfalz fighters' reputation seems to have suffered in comparison with other late-war German fighters. Certainly they were not as fast as the Albatros D.Va, nor had they the altitude performance of the Fokker D.VII; nevertheless, a prejudice against them seems to have existed among many German pilots, some of whose allegations – e.g. of structural weakness and a lack of manoeuvrability – are difficult to justify. The Pfalz was certainly not weakly constructed – indeed, it could be dived harder and faster than the Albatros, a factor that led to its extensive use on 'balloon-busting' activities. It was also an excellent gun platform and capable of absorbing a great deal of battle damage. The numbers in service, especially in the early spring of 1918, suggest that it played a larger part in retrieving German air superiority than it is generally given credit for. No production total can be quoted with certainty, but it is possible that as many as one thousand were built. The D.IIIa was gradually replaced by the Albatros D.Va and Fokker D.VII from spring 1918, but one hundred and sixty-six were still in service at the end of August.

Aviatik D.I

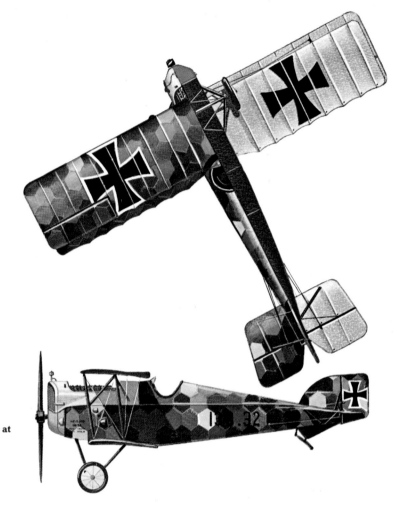

Austrian Aviatik (Berg) D.I of the Austro-Hungarian Air Service, late 1917

Engine: One 200hp Austro-Daimler
   water-cooled in-line
Span: 26ft 3in (8·00m)
Length: 22ft 9½in (6·95m)
Wing area: 234·7sq ft (21·80sq m)
Take-off weight: 1,878lb (852kg)
Maximum speed: 115mph (185km/hr) at
   sea level
Service ceiling: 20,175ft (6,150m)
Endurance: 2hr 30min

The D.I single-seater by Aviatik was the first fighter of Austrian design to enter production during World War I. It was the work of Dipl Ing Julius von Berg, and is often referred to as the Berg D.I or Berg Scout. It had its origins in the 30.14 aircraft which appeared early in 1916, although the true prototype was the 30.21 tested early in 1917. Production D.Is differed only in detail from this machine. Initial contracts were placed with six manufacturers: Aviatik (Series 38), Lloyd (Series 348), WKF (Series 84), MAG (Series 92), Thöne und Fiala (Series 101) and Lohner (Series 115). Repeat orders were placed with Aviatik for Series 138, 238 and 338; with Lohner for Series 215 (not built) and 315; with WKF for Series 184, 284 and 384; and with Thöne und Fiala for Series 201 (not built). Total D.I production amounted to approximately seven hundred, although as many as one thousand two hundred may have been ordered. Standard powerplant was the 200 or 210hp Austro-Daimler, but early and late production batches were fitted with 185 and 225hp engines of the same manufacture. Pilots were not enthusiastic about the D.I when it entered service in autumn 1917, in spite of its excellent flying characteristics and a comfortable, roomy cockpit which gave a good view over and under the top wing. Their dislike was directed chiefly at the Austro-Daimler engine, which easily became overheated; in service the top panels, and occasion-

ally some of the side panels, were left off to assist cooling. The D.I's armament, which originally consisted of a single 8mm Schwarzlose machine-gun mounted over the top wing to fire upward over the propeller, was, by the time the type entered service, replaced by twin Schwarzlose guns, one on each side of the cylinder block; the precise position varied on different batches, frequently being installed with their breeches beyond the reach of the pilot, who was thus unable to clear the gun in the event of a stoppage. A satisfactory location was not achieved until the latter part of the D.I's service. The D.I was used widely until the Armistice by Austro-Hungarian units on the Balkan, Italian and Russian fronts – particularly as protective cover for the *Fliegerkompagnien*'s 2-seaters, and rather less widely with the *Jagdkompagnien*, who in general preferred the German Albatros D.III; by mid-1918 only a few *Jagdkompagnien* were still equipped with Aviatik D.Is. Developments included a prototype Dr.I triplane (30.24) completed in 1917, and the high-altitude D.III with a 230hp Hiero engine, whose prototype (30.30) appeared in 1918. The only other production version was the D.II, generally similar to the D.I except for a cantilever lower wing; production of two Series (39 and 339) began late in 1918, but the D.II was too late for operational service.

Hannover CL types

Hannover CL.IIIa of the Imperial German Military Aviation Service, shot down 2 October 1918 by Capt E V Rickenbacker and Lt Reed Chambers of the 94th Aero Squadron, AEF

Engine: One 180hp Argus As.III water-cooled in-line
Span: 38ft 4½in (11·70m)
Length: 24ft 10¾in (7·58m)
Wing area: 352·0sq ft (32·70sq m)
Take-off weight: 2,381lb (1,080kg)
Maximum speed: 102·5mph (165km/hr) at 1,970ft (600m)
Service ceiling: 24,605ft (7,500m)
Endurance: 3hr 0min

In early 1917 the *Flugzeugmeisterei* introduced a new CL category, for 2-seat aircraft weighing less than 750kg (1,653lb) empty. The first in this category by the Hannoversche Waggonfabrik AG was designed by Hermann Dorner and designated CL.II. It was a small, compact biplane with a 180hp Argus As.III engine and wings resembling the 'Libellule' of the later Rumpler C types. A feature of the design, which remained unique among German single-engined aircraft of the war period, was the biplane tail unit. Production CL.IIs had increased lower-wing dihedral and a more rounded upper tailplane. Four hundred and thirty-nine were built, but it is not certain if this includes CL.IIs built by L F G (Roland) and designated CL.IIa. The CL.IIs entered service from December 1917, armed with a single centrally mounted Spandau front gun and a Parabellum gun on a ring mounting for the observer. Because of the narrow gap between fuselage and upper wing, the pilot had an excellent view forward and upward, and the narrower lower wings extended his view below. The short tailplane span, made possible by using a compound assembly, gave the observer a better-than-usual field of fire to the rear. The CL.II was followed by the CL.III, which had a 160hp Mercedes D.III and overhung ailerons. Because of the demand for Mercedes for fighter aircraft, only eighty CL.IIIs were built; a return was then made

to the As.III, with which the aircraft became the CL.IIIa. Five hundred and thirty-seven CL.IIIas were built. The 'Hannoveranas' were good flying machines and highly manoeuvrable; they were also very strong, and could absorb a great deal of battle damage. Their climb rate was not outstanding, but they possessed an excellent ceiling which enabled them to fulfil their original function of escort fighter. They were equally nimble at low altitudes, and were widely used from spring 1918 for ground attack, carrying stick grenades in small racks on the fuselage sides abreast of the observer's cockpit. About fifty CL.Vs were built during 1918, some with compound tails and others with a single tailplane. These were powered by 185hp BMW.IIIa engines, which raised the speed to 185km/hr (114.9mph) and the ceiling to an outstanding 9,000m (29,530ft). In common with most late-war aircraft designed around this powerplant, the CL.V probably saw little, if any, operational service. Another 1918 variant was the C.IV (sometimes mistakenly called the CL.IV). This was a typical C type, but only one or two were built. It was based on the CL.II/III, but was larger, had simplified bracing and a 245hp Maybach Mb.IV. Experimental conversions of the CL.IIIa were the CL.IIIb (190hp NAG) and the CL.IIIc (extended 2-bay wings).

Junkers J.I

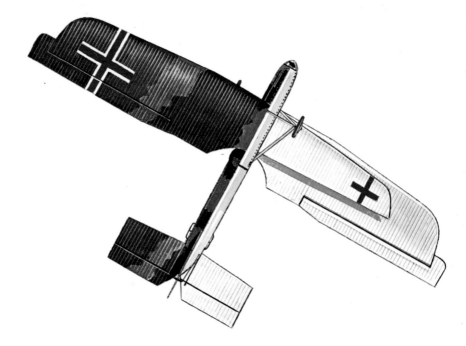

Junkers J.I of the Imperial German Military Aviation Service, *ca* early 1918.

Engine: One 200hp Benz Bz.IV water-
  cooled in-line
Span: 52ft 5¾in (16·00m)
Length: 29ft 10¼in (9·10m)
Wing area: 531·7sq ft (49·40sq m)
Take-off weight: 4,797lb (2,176kg)
Maximum speed: 96·3mph (155km/hr) at
  sea level
Operational ceiling: approx 5,000ft
  (1,525m)
Range: 193 miles (310km)

The J.I, which must vie with the Airco D.H.6 as the most angular aeroplane of World War 1, was the only one of Hugo Junkers' many all-metal aircraft of the war period to be completed as a biplane. It was evolved to replace the interim AEG and Albatros J types for infantry contact patrol and support duties with the Flieger Abteilungen, and made its first flight early in 1917. As such, its function was to fly at low level over the trenches and forward infantry positions to report troop concentrations and movements by means of a W/T link; and its metal construction afforded it excellent protection from ground fire, which was often heavy. The 5mm armoured shell which enclosed the 200hp Benz Bz.IV engine and the crew positions alone weighed some 470kg (1,036lb), and in later examples the rear fuselage section was also metal-skinned. Other distinctive features of the design included the enormous span of the upper wings and the uncommonly short-legged undercarriage. Production J.Is differed from the prototype in having overhung, balanced ailerons and rudder and a redesigned vertical fin. The airscrew spinner was frequently omitted from aircraft in service, some of which carried a camera in the rear of the fuselage. Manufacture of J.Is was shared between the Junkers and Fokker factories: a total of two hundred and twenty-seven were built, the first being completed in October 1917. They entered service at the beginning of 1918, and soon proved efficient at their job. Frequently the J.Is would drop ammunition and food supplies to their own forward troops during the course of a mission. The J.I's size and weight necessitated long take-off and landing runs, and it was rather heavy to handle – factors which led the J.I to be nicknamed Möbelwagen (Furniture Van). Nevertheless, its crews appreciated its strength and the protection it offered, and it was generally regarded as the best German armoured type to appear during the war. Usual armament consisted of two Spandau machine-guns installed under the front engine decking, with a single ring-mounted Parabellum gun in the rear cockpit. Early in their service some J.Is carried, instead of W/T equipment, two extra downward-firing Parabellum guns, manned by the observer, but it was found difficult to aim these successfully at low level while the aircraft was flying fast, and the practice was soon abandoned. At the peak of their employment one hundred and eighty-nine Junkers J.Is were in service at the Front.

Siemens-Schuckert D.III and D.IV

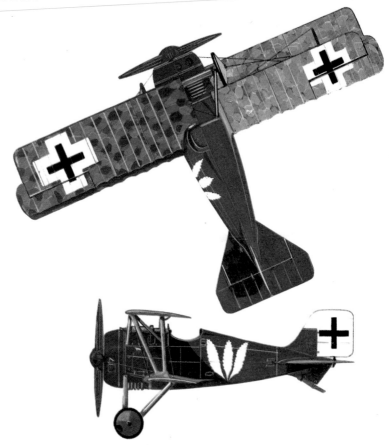

Siemens-Schuckert D.III of *Jasta* 15, Imperial German Military Aviation Service, May 1918

Engine: One 160hp Siemens-Halske
   Sh.III rotary
Span: 27ft 7⅛in (8·43m)
Length: 18ft 8⅜in (5·70m)
Wing area: 202·6sq ft (18·82sq m)
Take-off weight: 1,598lb (725kg)
Maximum speed: 111·8mph (180km/hr)
   at sea level
Service ceiling: 26,575ft (8,100m)
Endurance: 2hr 0min

Although it never achieved the same eminence, the Siemens-Schuckert fighter was, in terms of power, manoeuvrability and rate of climb, the nearest parallel to the Sopwith Camel produced by the German aviation industry during 1914-18. In 1917 another member of the great Siemens combine, the Siemens-Halske engine works, produced a new rotary engine, the 11-cylinder Sh.III, which offered 160hp. Under the direction of Dipl. Ing. Harald Wolff three prototype machines, designated D.II, D.IIa and D.IIb, were built around this powerplant and began flight tests in June 1917. The D.II was not outstandingly fast, but it had an excellent climb. Three more development aircraft were ordered, a short-span and a long-span D.IIc and a standard-span D.IIe. These, completed in October, were later redesignated D.III. Twenty D.IIIs were ordered in December 1917, with smaller, 4-blade propellers and shorter undercarriage legs. Delivery began in January 1918; in February thirty more D.IIIs were ordered, and by the end of May delivery to front-line *Jastas*, notably Nos. 12 and 15, was almost complete. The fully cowled Sh.III had a tendency to overheat, and in the early summer the D.IIIs were returned to the factory for minor airframe alterations and installation of 200hp Sh.IIIa engines. They were returned to service from July onward, having the lower part of the cowling

cut away to facilitate cooling. By this time their primary value was as home defence fighters, in which role they were highly successful. Eighty D.IIIs were built altogether, serving with *Jastas* 2, 12, 13, 15, 19, 26, 27 and 36, with five home defence units and one or two training establishments. Meanwhile the long-span D.IIc had been further refined, and with narrower-chord wings became the forerunner of the D.IV. The D.IV was faster in level flight and even better in a climb than the D.III, and was ordered in March 1918. It became operational in the following August. An eventual two hundred and eighty D.IVs were ordered, but only one hundred and twenty-three were completed. About half of these had reached front-line units (including *Jastas* 11, 14 and 22) by the Armistice. The D.IV was rather tricky to land, but in all other respects was an admirable aeroplane. It had a very short take-off, and at heights above 4,000m (13,120ft) was faster and more manoeuvrable than the Fokker D.VIII. Its outstanding feature was its phenomenal rate of climb – it could reach 6,000m (19,685ft) in less than 14½ minutes. As late as October 1918 it was officially described as 'superior by far to all single-seaters in use at the Front today'. Production of the D.IV did not finally end until summer 1919. In 1918 a 2-bay derivative, the D.V, participated in the Adlershof trials in May/June, but was not built in quantity.

Phönix D.I to D.III

Phönix-built D.III of the Royal Swedish Army Aviation, *ca*. summer 1919, now displayed in the RSwAF Museum, Malmslatt

Engine: One 230hp Hiero water-cooled in-line
Span: 32ft 1⅛in (9·80m)
Length: 21ft 8⅜in (6·62m)
Wing area: 269·1sq ft (25·00sq m)
Take-off weight: 2,097lb (951kg)
Maximum speed: 121·2mph (195km/hr) at sea level
Service ceiling: 22,310ft (6,800m)
Endurance: 2hr 0min

The Phönix D.I was basically a development of the Hansa-Brandenburg D.I with a more powerful engine. Various experimental machines appeared in mid-1917, none offering any significant improvement over the Brandenburg fighter, but eventually aircraft 20.16, with a 200hp Austro-Daimler engine, became in its final form an effective prototype of the Phönix D.I. In autumn 1917 three batches of fifty D.Is (Series 128, 228 and 328) were ordered from Phönix, who later built another forty Series 128s for the Austro-Hungarian Navy. Army D.Is entered service in February/March 1918, initially on escort and reconnaissance. Before being issued to *Jagdkompagnien* in May, it became necessary to reinforce the D.I's wings, which had proved subject to failure under stress. Naval D.Is entered service about June, and remained a serious threat to Italian aircraft over the Adriatic until the end of the war. Although less manoeuvrable than Allied fighters, the Phönix was a speedy machine with a good rate of climb. One serious drawback was the inaccessibility of its twin 8mm Schwarzlose guns. These were fully enclosed by the engine panels, firing through holes in the nose of the cowling – an admirable aerodynamic refinement, but they were completely beyond the pilot's reach in the event of all-too-frequent stoppages. The fault persisted in the D.II and D.IIa. The D.II had the same powerplant as the D.I, but a slightly increased wing span and other changes. Three Series (122, 222 and 322) were ordered, together with a single Series (422)

of the D.IIa, which had a 230hp Hiero and ailerons on both pairs of wings. Little more than half of the D.II/IIas ordered were actually completed, entering service from May 1918. Before the war ended production had begun of the Phönix D.III, an improved D.IIa whose wings were rigged without dihedral, the lower wings having plain ailerons, and the guns at last moved rearward within reach of the pilot. Two prototypes were built of the D.IV, outwardly similar but actually an entirely new design having an oval fuselage and increased vertical tail area. In 1919, after evaluating the D.III prototype (J41), the Royal Swedish Army Aviation purchased seventeen D.IIIs from Phönix. These were originally known in Sweden as Phönix 122s, suggesting that they were laid down as D.IIs but completed as D.IIIs. A further ten D.IIIs were completed by the Swedish Army workshops at Malmen in 1924, having 185hp BMW IIIa engines since Austrian powerplants were no longer available. Swedish D.IIIs could be fitted with ski undercarriages during the winter. With the formation of the *Flygvapnet* in July 1926, nine Phönix 122s (then redesignated J1) were in service with F3 Wing; they remained, latterly with F5 on communications and training duties, until 1930, and one was still carrying out meteorological flights as late as 1936. During their Swedish service some D.IIIs had large aerofoil-section fuel tanks on the upper wings, and increased vertical tail area.

Phönix C.I

Swedish-built C.I *(Phönix-Dront)* of the Royal
Swedish Army Aviation, 1919

Engine: One 220hp Benz Bz.IV water-
 cooled in-line
Span: 36ft 1½in (11·00m)
Length: 24ft 8⅜in (7·52m)
Wing area: approx 249·2sq ft (23·15sq m)
Take-off weight: 2,436lb (1,105kg)
Maximum speed: 110mph (177km/hr) at
 sea level
Service ceiling: 17,715ft (5,400m)
Endurance: approx 3hr 30min

As explained in the description of the Ufag C.I (page 65), that aircraft and the Phönix C.I 2-seaters which appeared in Austro-Hungarian service in 1918 shared a common descent from the Hansa-Brandenburg C.II 'star-strutter' designed by Ernst Heinkel in Germany. Both were chosen for production, the Phönix machine in Series 121, and aircraft 121.01 and 121.02 were utilised as prototypes. They differed principally in their cabane strutting and radiator positions, and 121.02 was subsequently brought up to production standard with a centrally mounted 'Hifa' radiator in the top leading edge. Production Series 121 aircraft were powered by 230hp Hiero engines and, except for the additional crew position, bore a strong resemblance to the Phönix D.I fighter. The unequal-span wings had distinctive, backward-curving tips and were braced by parallel pairs of 'V' struts. The deep, narrow fuselage left a minimum of gap below the top wing, thus giving the pilot an excellent view forward and upward. From the elevated gun position in the rear cockpit the observer also had a first-class field of view and of fire. Armament consisted of a synchronised forward-firing Schwarzlose machine-gun under the port-side engine panels, firing through an aperture in the front of the cowling; a second free-firing Schwarzlose gun was installed in the rear cockpit. A modest bomb load of 50kg (110lb) could be carried beneath the lower wings. The Phönix C.I went into service in spring 1918 and was used until the end of the war on both visual and photographic reconnaissance work. About one hundred and ten were built for the Flieger-kompagnien. They were somewhat slower than the Ufag 2-seaters, but had better take-off characteristics, climbing powers and performance at altitude. After the war thirty aircraft of this type were built in Sweden by the Army Aircraft Workshops at Malmslätt, with 220hp Benz Bz.IV engines in place of the Austrian powerplants. They went into service early in 1919 with the Royal Swedish Army Aviation under the title S 21 Dront and continued to be used until well into the 1920s.

Ufag C.I

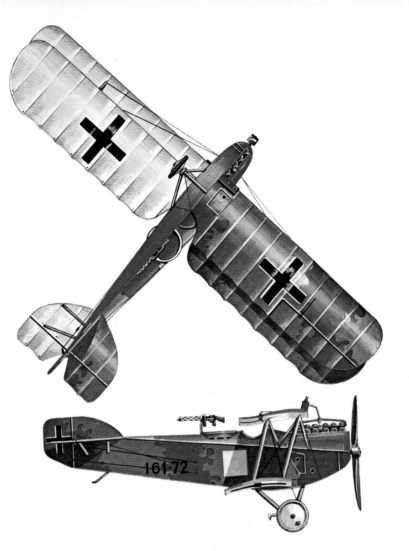

Ufag-built C.I of the Austro-Hungarian Air
Service, *ca*. autumn 1918

**Engine: One 230hp Hiero water-cooled
   in-line**
Span: 35ft 2in (10·72m)
Length: 23ft 7½in (7·20m)
Wing area: approx 290·6sq ft (27·00sq m)
Take-off weight: approx 2,315lb (1,050kg)
**Maximum speed: 118·1mph (190km/hr)
   at sea level**
Service ceiling: 16,075ft (4,900m)
Endurance: approx 3hr 30min

Examples of the Hansa-Brandenburg C.II 2-seat 'star-strutter' designed by Ernst Heinkel were completed in Austro-Hungary in 1916 by both the Phönix Flugzeugwerke and the Ungarische Flugzeugfabrik AG. Each company developed its own C.I derivative of this aeroplane, which were flown in comparative trials in January 1917. Both were powered by 230hp Hiero engines; the Ufag C.I differed from its compatriot in having parallel interplane struts, equal-span, round-tipped wings with a moderate stagger and a squarish, balanced rudder. Each aircraft had an elevated gun ring in the rear cockpit for a single Schwarzlose machine-gun. Flight trials revealed that each aircraft had some features superior to the other, and it was finally decided to put both into production. The Ufag C.I had a somewhat poorer ceiling and take-off than the Phönix, but it was appreciably faster and more manoeuvrable. Consequently, in service, while both types carried out general observation duties, the Ufag was used for lower-level missions such as artillery co-operation, while the Phönix C.I,

with its higher ceiling, was chosen for photographic reconnaissance. In its production form the Ufag C.I had a smaller tailplane, and a plain rudder with a triangular fixed fin that improved the aircraft's directional stability. One or two synchronised forward-firing guns could be mounted in the front of the fuselage. Possibly because of production priority afforded to the Phönix single-seat fighters, the two C types did not go into service much before spring 1918, but for the remaining period of the war they carried out useful work and a small batch of Ufag C.Is were supplied to Romania after the war ended. It may be supposed that the Ufag was considered the better machine, since it was also manufactured under licence by Phönix as well as by the parent company. Phönix-built Ufag C.Is, at least thirty-six of which were completed, were designated Series 123, while Ufag's own machines were known as Series 161; more than one hundred were built by Ufag.

Hansa-Brandenburg W.29 and W.33

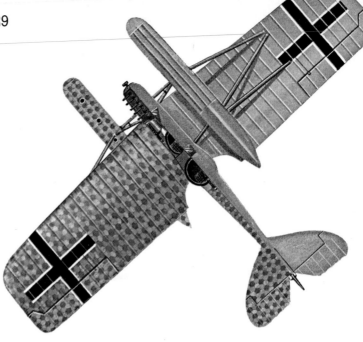

Hansa-Brandenburg W.29 of the Imperial
German Navy, autumn 1918

**Engine: One 150hp Benz Bz.III water-
  cooled in-line**
Span: 44ft 3½in (13·50m)
Length: 30ft 6½in (9·30m)
Wing area: 340·1sq ft (31·60 sq m)
Take-off weight: 3,131lb (1,420kg)
**Maximum speed: 105·6mph (170km/hr)
  at sea level**
Service ceiling: over 9,840ft (3,000m)
Endurance: 4hr 0min

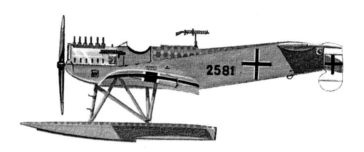

It has been suggested that Oberleutnant Christiansen, commander of the important German Naval air base at Zeebrugge, played a part in urging the development of the W.29: certainly he was invited to fly the prototype, and he may have been allowed to take it back with him to Zeebrugge in February 1918 for operational use. Heinkel's development of the W.29 took the logical form of a monoplane version of the successful W.12, retaining the Benz engine in a shorter but basically similar fuselage. The slightly tapered single wings were increased in span and chord to give a total area almost equal to that of the biplane, and the tailplane was also altered slightly. The first W.29 model to be built could really be regarded as a fighter, being a fast and very manoeuvrable aircraft with twin forward-firing guns and a Parabellum gun in the rear cockpit. It was powered by a 195hp Bz.IIIb. The first six W.29s were to this pattern, as were a further four ordered later in 1918, although there is some doubt whether this second batch was completed. Between these two orders came four other batches totalling seventy aircraft. The first twenty had the standard Bz.III, and radio equipment instead of one of the front guns. A second similar batch of twenty may not all have been delivered. The remaining thirty W.29s, with Bz.IIIs, had two front guns and no radio. Three W.29s were built by Ufag before the Armistice, for the Austro-Hungarian

Navy, but were not delivered. The W.29 entered German Naval service from about April 1918, serving alongside the W.12 and W.19 and often undertaking combined missions with the W.19. Like the earlier Brandenburgs, they were treated with healthy respect by Allied submarines, surface vessels, flying-boats and airships. Most of their successes were achieved by concentrated fire-power, but some W.29s carried a small bomb load. In mid-1918 a still larger version, the W.33, appeared; this had a 15·85m (52ft 0in) wing span. Twenty-six were apparently ordered, but it seems that only six were completed before the Armistice. The first three had two front guns and 260hp Maybach engines; the next two had single front guns and 300hp Basse und Selve engines, but were later refitted with Maybachs. The last of the six (presumably Maybach-powered) had one front gun and a 20mm Becker cannon in the rear cockpit. A later and still larger version, the W.34 (300hp Fiat), was too late for war service, but some were purchased by the Finnish and Latvian Air Forces after the war. Some W.33s and W.29s were also acquired post-war by the Finnish and Royal Danish Air Forces respectively. Not only were the Brandenburg monoplane floatplanes first-class combat machines in themselves, but their general characteristics were also reflected in a number of prototypes from other manufacturers late in 1918.

Fokker D.VI

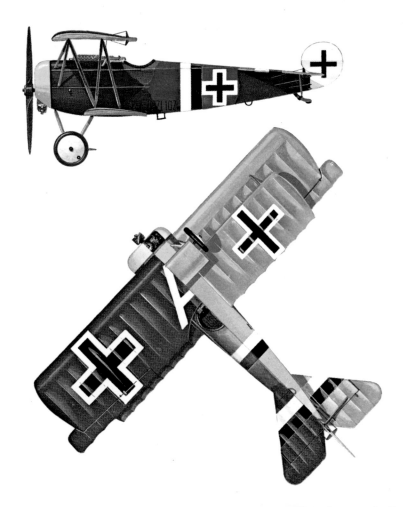

Fokker D.VI of the Imperial German Military
Aviation Service, Russian Front, 1918

Engine: One 110hp Oberursel UR.II
   rotary
Span: 25ft 1¼in (7·65m)
Length: 20ft 5¼in (6·23m)
Wing area: 190·5sq ft (17·70sq m)
Take-off weight: 1,285lb (583kg)
Maximum speed: 121·8mph (196km/hr)
   at sea level
Service ceiling: 19,685ft (6,000m)
Endurance: 1hr 30min

The little D.VI was not a fighter with any outstanding operational significance but it is of interest as a design link between the Dr.I triplane and the later D.VII. It had its origin in the V.9 prototype designed by Platz, which utilised a number of Dr.I components. The V.9 was developed into the V.13, two of which were completed late in 1917. Apart from simplified strutting, the most noticeable changes were to more powerful engines, the V.13/1 having a 145hp UR.III and the V.13/2 a 160hp Sh.III. The fuselage and tail assembly were basically the same as those of the Dr.I, and the wings were a lower-aspect-ratio edition of those fitted to the Fokker D.VII. Despite the fairly wide gap between fuselage and upper wing, the view from the cockpit was quite good. Both V.13s took part in the Adlershof fighter trials in January/February 1918 and, despite the overall supremacy of the D.VII, a small order was also placed for the D.VI. Neither of the intended powerplants was yet fully developed, and so production D.VIs were given 110hp UR.IIs, which were a direct copy of the French Le Rhône. Between April and August 1918, forty-seven UR.II-powered D.VIs were built, together with another dozen which had 200hp Goe.IIIs. Only a few D.VIs saw service with front-line fighter units (including *Jasta* 84), and after the D.VII arrived in service the D.VI was transferred to training duties. The reason for this was certainly not due to any shortcomings in the D.VI, which was a thoroughly man-oeuvrable fighter and at low altitudes was faster than the D.VII. The D.VI was armed with twin forward-firing Spandau guns mounted in front of the cockpit. Seven UR.II-powered D.VIs which were supplied to Austro-Hungary in August 1918 may have been refitted with Schwarzlose guns after their arrival.

Fokker D.VII

Fokker D.VII flown by Oblt Ernst Udet of Jasta 4, 1918

Data as opposite except:
Engine: One 185hp BMW.IIIa in-line

Take-off weight: 2,116lb (960kg)
Maximum speed: 124mph (200km/hr) at
  3,280ft (1,000m)

Unlike the Camel, the Fokker D.VII has been described as an extremely forgiving aeroplane to fly, and one capable of making a good pilot out of a novice. Of the thirty-one contenders in the fighter competition held at Adlershof in January 1918 (nine of which were Fokker designs), Fokker's V.11 prototype was so outstandingly a clear winner that an immediate contract was placed for 400 production aircraft – an unprecedented order, even at that late stage of the war. The first D.VII fighters began to be delivered in April 1918, and by the end of the war between 800-900 had entered service with nearly eighty Jagdstaffeln, about half of them built under licence by the Albatros and OAW factories. Apart from its excellent handling qualities, the D.VII was immensely strong, with two-spar upper and lower wings and a welded steel tube fuselage; its thick-section wings gave useful lift even in relatively thin air, thus maintaining its excellent performance at altitude; even the little aerofoil-type fairing over the main axle, a typical Fokker trademark, gave enough lift to offset the weight of the landing gear. With the 160hp Mercedes D.III engine, for which it was designed, its perfor-

mance was healthy enough, but this was improved immeasurably in the D.VIIF by adopting the 185hp BMW.IIIa, a first-class engine in which the decrease of power with altitude was considerably lower. Rated at 185hp at sea level, it offered only 5hp less at 6,000ft (1,830m), and was still good for 120hp at 18,000ft (5,490m). Such was its reputation that the D.VII was accorded the still-unique distinction of specific mention, by name, in Article IV of the Armistice Agreement, among equipment handed over to the Allies. Fokker, typically, had other ideas, and organised the escape into his native Holland of six train-loads comprising some 220 airframes and more than 400 aircraft engines, among which were some 120 complete or near-complete examples of the D.VII – enough to resume post-war production and export of this remarkable aircraft. Today only a handful survive, including single examples in the RAF Museum at Hendon, the Musée de l'Air in Paris, the Deutsches Museum in Munich, the National Aeronautical Collection of Canada, and the National Air and Space Museum in Washington.

D.VII (possibly Albatros-built), believed to be
an aircraft of *Jasta* 17, Imperial German
Military Aviation Service, *ca*. May 1918

Engine: One 160hp Mercedes D.III
    water-cooled in-line
Span: 29ft 2½in (8·90m)
Length: 22ft 9¾in (6·95m)
Wing area: 220·7sq ft (20·50sq m)
Take-off weight: 1,984lb (900kg)
Maximum speed: 117·4mph (189km/hr)
    at 3,280ft (1,000m)
Service ceiling: 19,685ft (6,000m)
Endurance: 1hr 30min

The Fokker D.VII, widely claimed as the best German fighter of World War I, was evolved to a specification issued late in 1917. Its true prototype was the Fokker V.11, designed by Reinhold Platz. With thirty other machines, six of them alternative Fokker designs, the V.11 was tested at Adlershof in January/February 1918. It proved superior to all other entrants by a wide margin, and with modifications made at the instigation of Rittmeister von Richthofen was immediately ordered for large-scale production: four hundred from Fokker, and substantial quantities from Albatros and OAW. The V.11 was somewhat unstable in a dive, and production D.VIIs therefore had a lengthened fuselage and a fixed vertical fin. There was an excellent view from the cockpit, and the D.VII was armed with twin 7·92mm Spandau guns, with 500rpg, immediately in front of the pilot. It was easy to fly, but its main advance over earlier German fighters was its ability to maintain performance at high altitude. This was enhanced even further from late summer 1918 by the D.VIIF powered by a 185hp BMW IIIa. The D.VIIF was only fractionally faster than the D.VII, but had greater reserves of power above 5,000m (16,400ft), which height the D.VIIF could reach in 14 minutes, compared with the Mercedes D.VII's time of just over 38 minutes. Understandably, the D.VIIF was much sought after. Von Richthofen's *Jagdgeschwader I* (later commanded by Hermann Goering) began to receive the first Fokker D.VIIs in April 1918. Customary practice was to allocate new fighters to *Jastas*, and to pilots within *Jastas*, in order of eminence, and several months elapsed before some lesser *Staffeln* were

able to get D.VIIs. Nevertheless, by the time of the Armistice the ZAK (Central Acceptance Commission) had accepted seven hundred and sixty D.VIIs, and the type had been delivered to forty-eight *Jastas*, although several units operated well below establishment. In all, Fokker built at least eight hundred and forty D.VIIs; seven hundred and eighty-five were ordered from Albatros, and nine hundred and seventy-five from the Ostdeutsche Albatros Werke. In Austro-Hungary the type was built by MAG as the Series 93; a second Series (132) was ordered from the Austrian Aviatik company, but none of the latter were built. Throughout summer and autumn 1918 the Fokker D.VII was treated with a respect afforded to no German fighter since the Fokker E.III three years earlier, and Article IV of the Armistice Agreement paid it a unique tribute by singling it out for specific mention among items of military equipment to be handed over to the Allies. This squashed Anthony Fokker's hopes of continuing in the aircraft manufacturing business in Germany after the war, and precipitated the now-famous smuggling episode in which he succeeded in getting four hundred engines and components of one hundred and twenty aircraft, most of them D.VIIs, out of Germany into Holland. The D.VII continued in production in Holland after the war, and remained in service, first with the Dutch Army Air Service and later in the Nether-lands East Indies, until the late 1920s. Between 1919 and 1926 a number of ex-wartime D.VIIs were used, after conversion to 2-seaters, as trainers by the Belgian *Aviation Militaire*; twenty-seven were supplied to the Swiss *Fliegertruppe*.

LFG (Roland) D.VI

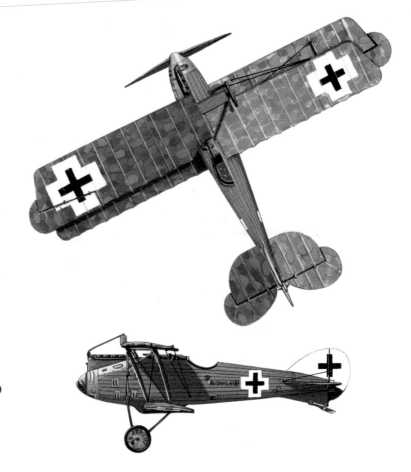

LFG (Roland) D.VIb for the Imperial German
Military Aviation Service, June 1918

Engine: One 150/200hp Benz Bz.IIIa
   water-cooled in-line
Span: 30ft 10¼in (9·40m)
Length: 20ft 8¾in (6·32m)
Wing area: 238·2sq ft (22·13sq m)
Take-off weight: 1,896lb (860kg)
Maximum speed: 113·4mph (182·5km/hr)
   at 6,562ft (2,000m)
Service ceiling: 19,030ft (5,800m)
Endurance: 2hr 0min

The Roland D.VI was one of several excellent German fighters produced in the last year of the war whose careers were eclipsed at least partially by the omnipresent Fokker D.VII. During the summer of 1917 LFG produced a triplane designed by Dipl. Ing. Tantzen. This did not enter production but was noteworthy as the first application to aircraft construction of the *Klinkerrumpf* method of fuselage building. The same method was used in the prototype D.VI which appeared late in 1917. This was powered by a 160hp Mercedes D.III engine and had a small 'keel' on the underside of the fuselage to which the lower wing was attached. A pair of 7·92mm synchronised Spandau guns were mounted in front of the cockpit. The D.VI entered production in two forms. The D.VIa was powered in similar fashion to the prototype, but as Mercedes engines were in short supply, the Benz Bz.IIIa, nominally rated at 150hp, was installed in the D.VIb. On later D.VIbs a high-compression version of this engine delivered 200hp. Both models were evaluated in the fighter competition at Adlershof in January/February 1918 when, like everything else, they were overshadowed by the Fokker D.VII. However, as a precaution against possible failure in the delivery of sufficient Fokkers, limited numbers of the Roland fighters were ordered. As things turned out, there were no delivery delays with the Fokker fighters, and consequently the Roland D.VI saw little operational service. It entered use in the late spring and early summer of 1918, and in some respects was superior to the Fokker. The cockpit was roomy and comfortable, affording an excellent view in most directions, and the controls were said to be easier to operate than those of the D.VII. It had good short take-off characteristics, an excellent rate of climb and at an altitude of 15,000ft (4,570m), which it could reach in 24 minutes, its speed was still in the region of 100mph (161km/hr). Main disadvantages were its tricky landing characteristics (despite a low landing speed) and the tendency of the D.VIb's Benz engine to overheat. The German Navy also used the D.VIa and D.VIb to defend its seaplane bases along the northern European coastline. After the Armistice thirteen aircraft of this type were taken to the United States for evaluation.

Halberstadt C.V

Halberstadt (possibly Aviatik-built) C.V of the Imperial German Military Aviation Service, *ca.* summer 1918

Engine: One 220hp Benz Bz.IV water-
 cooled in-line
Span: 44ft 8½in (13·62m)
Length: 22ft 8½in (6·92m)
Wing area: 462·8sq ft (43·00sq m)
Take-off weight: 3,009lb (1,365kg)
Maximum speed: 105·6mph (170km/hr)
 at sea level
Service ceiling: 16,400ft (5,000m)
Endurance: 3hr 30min

Two principal types were employed by the German Air Force in 1918 for photographic reconnaissance work: of these, the Rumpler C.VII was undoubtedly the superior machine, but its companion, the Halberstadt C.V, was also built and used in substantial numbers. The Halberstadt company's previous C types began with the C.I, a 1916 adaptation, with a rotary engine, of the unarmed B.II. It is doubtful whether this went into production. The C.III, which appeared late in 1917, was the first long-range photographic type designed by Karl Theiss. It was powered by a 200hp Benz Bz.IV and an unusual feature of its design was the attachment of the lower wings to a small 'keel' on the underside of the fuselage. The C.III formed the basis for the C.V, in which a simpler and more conventional attachment was employed for the lower wings. Power-plant of the C.V was the high-compression version of the Bz.IV developing 220hp and giving a much better performance at altitude. The wings were of wide span, with 2 bays of bracing struts and overhung, balanced ailerons on the upper sections. The fuselage was essentially a scaled-up version of that used in the C.IV, but with separate cockpits for the 2-man crew. Reconnaissance cameras were aimed downward through a

trap in the floor of the rear cockpit; the top of the cockpit was built up with the traditional ring mounting for a Parabellum machine-gun. The pilot was furnished with a synchronised Spandau gun immediately in front of his cockpit on the port side; C.Vs also normally carried wireless equipment. The prototype C.V appeared early in 1918, undergoing its official trials in the spring. Its front-line career lasted from summer 1918 until the Armistice. Production was undertaken by the Aviatik, BFW and DFW companies in addition to those built by Halberstadt. Variants appearing during 1918 included the C.VII, C.VIII and C.IX. The C.VII (245hp Maybach Mb.IV) and C.IX (230hp Hiero) remained in the prototype stage, though the latter may have been intended for Austro-Hungarian production. The C.VIII, officially tested in October 1918, was a single-bay biplane, slightly smaller than the C.V and powered by an Mb.IV engine; it had a ceiling of 9,000m (29,530ft), which it could reach in 58 minutes, and was probably intended for series production if the war had continued; however, only the prototype had been completed when the war ended.

Fokker E.V and D.VIII

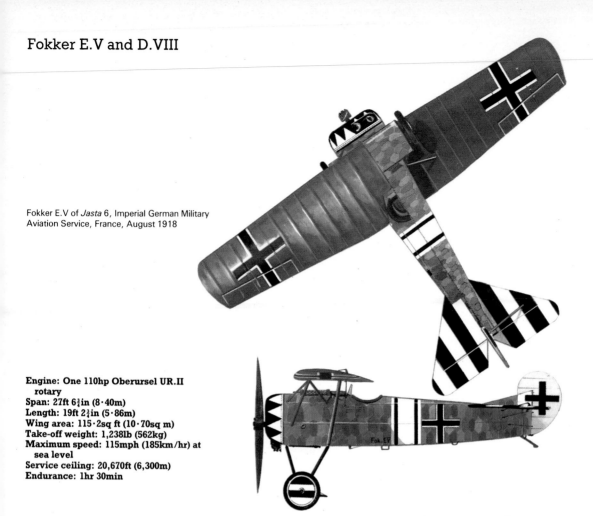

Fokker E.V of *Jasta* 6, Imperial German Military
Aviation Service, France, August 1918

Engine: One 110hp Oberursel UR.II
  rotary
Span: 27ft 6¾in (8·40m)
Length: 19ft 2¾in (5·86m)
Wing area: 115·2sq ft (10·70sq m)
Take-off weight: 1,238lb (562kg)
Maximum speed: 115mph (185km/hr) at
  sea level
Service ceiling: 20,670ft (6,300m)
Endurance: 1hr 30min

Reinhold Platz designed and built several shoulder-wing monoplanes from late 1917. His first parasol monoplanes were the rotary-engined V.26 and V.28 and the stationary-engined V.27, which took part in the second fighter competition at Adlershof in May/June 1918. A refreshingly simple design, it had a one-piece cantilever wing and twin Spandau guns mounted immediately in front of the cockpit. Following their performance at Adlershof, the V.26/28 design was accepted for production and an initial four hundred were ordered with the *Eindecker* designation E.V. It was proposed to use either the 145hp UR.III or the 200hp Goe.III, but since these were not yet available in quantity, the early E.Vs had either Thulin-built Le Rhônes or Oberursel UR.IIs of 110hp. Differing only in rounder wingtips, which slightly increased the span, production E.Vs began to be delivered from July 1918. In August *Jasta* 6, one of the first units to receive E.Vs, experienced three serious crashes due to wing failure, and it looked as if the defects of the Fokker Dr.I were appearing in the E.V. Sixty or so aircraft were withheld pending investigations that ultimately vindicated Platz's design by revealing that the failures were due to poor workmanship and the use of imperfect

timber by the contractor who had built the wing units. With the resumption of production in September 1918 the type was redesignated D.VIII and began to reach the Front towards the end of October. It thus had little chance to prove its worth, but reports indicate that it flew well, was more manoeuvrable than the D.VII and might well have replaced it. Although only eighty-five E.V/D.VIIIs were in service with front-line *Jastas* on 1 November 1918 (plus some with Naval fighter units), it seems that the full four hundred were probably built. Twenty formed part of Anthony Fokker's famous 'salvage act' of aircraft and engines smuggled into Holland, where some later served with the Dutch Army Air Service for several years, eventually with 145hp UR.III engines. Small numbers of D.VIIIs went as spoils of war to Britain, France, Italy and the United States; others went to the Polish Air Force, where they were again used in combat early in 1919 against the Ukrainian forces, and to Japan. At the final Adlershof competition in October 1918 the joint winner was another parasol prototype, the V.29. This was based on the D.VII airframe and powered by a 185hp BMW IIIa.

Junkers CL.I

Junkers CL.I of the Imperial German Military
Aviation Service, summer 1918

Engine: One 180hp Mercedes D.IIIa
  water-cooled in-line
Span: 39ft 6¼in (12·05m)
Length: 25ft 11in (7·90m)
Wing area: 251·9sq ft (23·40sq m)
Take-off weight: 2,326lb (1,055kg)
Maximum speed: 105mph (169km/hr) at
  sea level
Service ceiling: approx 19,685ft (6,000m)
Endurance: 2hr 0min

The CL.I was a 2-seater escort/ground-attack derivative of the D.I fighter. The prototype, which bore the factory designation J.10, had overhung horn-balanced ailerons and was powered by a 160hp Mercedes D.III. It flew for the first time on 4 May 1918. Production of the CL.I started in the summer, and forty-seven had been delivered by the end of the war; not all of these are thought to have reached the Front. They had shorter-span, plain ailerons and 180hp Mercedes D.IIIa engines. Armament consisted of two 7·92mm forward-firing Spandau machine-guns in front of the pilot and a single Parabellum on an elevated ring mounting in the observer's cockpit. Racks were situated on each side of the fuselage, abreast of the rear cockpit, in which stick grenades or other anti-personnel weapons could be carried when the CL.I was used for ground attack. The Junkers CL.I was probably the best ground-attack type produced in Germany during the war, but it arrived at the Front too late to make any impact. It was fast, manoeuvrable and very strongly built, and could

climb to 3,000m (9,840ft) in 14 minutes. The type did see some post-war combat service in Finland and one or two Baltic states, and at least one machine was used in a civil capacity. This was fitted with a canopy over the rear seat and used on a commercial basis by Junkers in 1919 – in all probability the first all-metal aircraft ever to operate an air service. It may have been the same aircraft that later became D-78 on the German civil register. Three examples were built late in 1918 of a twin-float variant, the CLS.I. The substitution of floats increased the overall length to 29ft 4½in (8·95m), the additional side area being compensated by the addition of a small, triangular fixed fin; span was increased by 2ft 3½in (0·70m). Despite its greater all-up weight, the CLS.I, powered by a 195hp Bz.IIIb, had a better level speed – 180km/hr (111·8mph) – than the landplane. However, some troubles were encountered with the tail design and the CLS.I did not go into production.

Junkers D.I

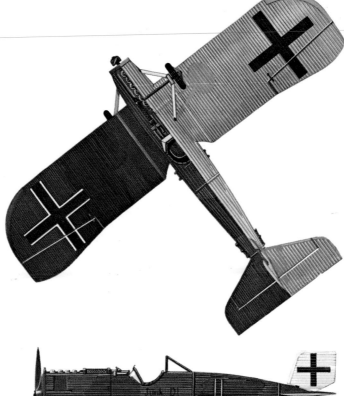

Junkers D.I of the Imperial German Military
Aviation Service, summer 1918

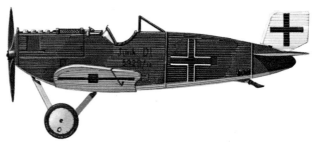

Engine: One 160hp Mercedes D.IIIaü
    water-cooled in-line
Span: 29ft 6¼in (9·00m)
Length: 23ft 9¾in (7·25m)
Wing area: 159·3 sq ft (14·80sq m)
Take-off weight: 1,839lb (834kg)
Maximum speed: 136·7mph (220km/hr)
    at sea level
Service ceiling: 21,980ft (6,700m)
Endurance: 1hr 30min

The evolution by Dr Hugo Junkers of all-metal monoplanes with cantilever wings began in 1915, the first to be built being the J.1, which flew for the first time on 12 December that year. (This should not be confused with the military J.I, which was a 2-seat biplane and had the factory designation J.4) A number of other monoplane prototypes followed, but the true precursor of the D.I fighter was the J.7 of October 1917. This appeared in at least three forms, but whether these were separate machines or successive modifications to the first is uncertain. The J.7 was powered by a 160hp Mercedes D.III, whose radiator was mounted, as if as an afterthought, on top of the cylinder block: a frontal radiator was fitted later. A novel feature was the use of pivoting wingtips instead of conventional ailerons, but these were found to create wing flutter and were later replaced by ailerons. The direct prototype of the D.I was the J.9, which appeared in March 1918 and was basically a refined J.7 with slightly bigger dimensions. Accounts of the production and service record of the D.I are conflicting. The machine that took part in the second D types competition at Adlershof in May/June 1918 was described as a J.9, and at that time was powered by a Mercedes D.IIIa of 180hp. In a list of types evaluated by leading German pilots in July, the only Junkers product was referred to as a D.I and had

a standard Mercedes D.III: this seems to imply that the first production order was placed at about this time. The powerplant intended for production Junkers D.Is is believed to have been the 185hp BMW IIIA, and a D.I with this engine took part in the third D types competition in October 1918; but it is thought that the 160hp Mercedes powered at least some of the early production aircraft. Many authorities refer to a total of forty-one D.Is at the Front when the Armistice was signed, but it seems more likely that this figure represented the number of machines actually built at that time, with only a comparative handful having reached front-line *Jastas*; some notice would surely have been taken of larger quantities of such a fast and manoeuvrable fighter, especially one of such distinctive appearance, in the closing stages of the war. This supposition is strengthened by reports that the D.I's flying qualities were unsatisfactory in some respects. An alternative explanation may be that early production aircraft delivered with Mercedes D.IIIs were recalled later for refitting with more powerful BMWs. At least one D.I had a Vee-type in-line engine: this could have been the Daimler D.IIIb, which had a similar output to the BMW IIIa. The D.I was armed with twin forward-firing synchronised Spandau machine-guns and with the BMW engine could climb to 5,000 m (16,400ft) in 22¼min.

Pfalz D.XII

Pfalz D.XII (*Jasta* unidentified) of the Imperial German Military Aviation Service, captured by the French in October 1918

Engine: One 180hp Mercedes D.IIIa water-cooled in-line
Span: 29ft 6½in (9·00m)
Length: 20ft 10in (6·35m)
Wing area: 233·6sq ft (21·70sq m)
Take-off weight: 1,978lb (897kg)
Maximum speed: 105·6mph (170km/hr) at 9,843ft (3,000m)
Service ceiling: 18,535ft (5,650m)
Endurance: 2hr 30min

In the early months of 1918 Pfalz produced a prototype, believed to have been the D.XI, with a 180hp Mercedes D.IIIa, a similar fuselage to the Pfalz D.III and wings resembling those of the Fokker D.VII. This did not enter production, and it seems reasonable to infer that the all-conquering Fokker had a marked influence on the Pfalz design team, for its successor, the D.XII, had contours even more like the Platz fighter. However, despite this strong external likeness, the constructional methods of the Fokker D.VII and Pfalz D.XII were quite different. The D.XII was a sound design, and a strong one, but by the latter part of 1918 German ground crews had become accustomed to the canti-lever Fokkers and other types with little or no external bracing, and resented the additional work involved in rigging the much-braced Pfalz fighter. Two prototypes, one with a Mercedes D.IIIa and the other with a 185hp BMW IIIa, were evaluated at Adlershof in May/June 1918. The Mercedes version was chosen for production, to augment supplies of Fokker D.VIIs. There is a popular belief that the Pfalz company, which enjoyed the support of the Bavarian govern-ment, may have used bribery to secure these contracts. Pfalz D.XIIs entered service in September 1918, being delivered during the remaining months of the war to ten *Jagdstaffeln*,

including four Bavarian *Jastas* of JG IV. German units had been conditioned by extensive publicity for the Fokker D.VII into believing that anything else must be inferior, and the Pfalz machines were not given a warm welcome. Nevertheless, once pilots had become acquainted with them they found them fast, manoeuvrable aircraft that could cope adequately with Allied S.E.5as and Camels. Their climb was poor – they took twice as long as the Fokker to reach 5,000m (16,400ft) – but their stronger construction enabled them to be dived harder. They were armed with twin forward-firing Spandau guns. Like other good German fighters that appeared in 1918, their reputation was dwarfed by the exploits of the far more numerous Fokkers; had the war continued a little longer the Pfalz D.XII would probably have made a greater impact. It is believed that about a hundred and seventy-five D.XIIs were surrendered at the Armistice, and for a year or two after the war some were used by civilian private owners in several European countries. Wartime variants included the D.XIV, with enlarged fin and 200hp Benz Bz.IVü; and the D.XV, which was tested a week before the Armistice. Powered by a 185hp BMW IIIa, the D.XV had its lower wings separated from the fuselage and simplified interplane bracing. It is believed that it was earmarked for series production.

Dornier Do J (Do 15) Wal (Whale)

Dornier-built Do J II b Bos *Grönland-Wal* of Deutsche Luft Hansa, *ca* 1933 (the aircraft flown by von Gronau across the Atlantic in August 1930). Military designation Do 15

Engines: Two 600hp BMW VI twelve-cylinder Vee-type
Span: 76ft 1½in (23·20m)
Length: 59ft 8½in (18·20m)
Wing area: 1,033·3sq ft (96.00sq m)
Take-off weight: 17,637lb (8,000kg)
Maximum speed: 140mph (225km/hr)
Operational ceiling: 9,845ft (3,000m)
Endurance: 1,365 miles (2,200km)

When World War 1 ended in 1918 the German Zeppelin-Werke at Lindau, headed by Prof Claude Dornier, had under construction a twin-engined all-metal flying-boat known as the Gs I. After the Armistice the design was modified for commercial operation, and it first flew on 31 July 1919, but the terms of the Armistice prohibited German manufacture and the Gs I was sunk at the Allies' request in April 1920. Similarly the completion of two 9-seater Gs II developments was banned, but between them the two designs provided the basis for a subsequent German flying-boat that was to become widely known. This was the Do J, or Wal, whose prototype flew for the first time on 6 November 1922. Restrictions on German production of such an aircraft were still in force, but Dornier had circumvented these in 1922 by establishing an Italian company, Società di Costruzioni Meccaniche di Pisa, at Marina di Pisa, to build its products under licence. This company became a Fiat subsidiary in 1929, and changed its title in 1930 to Costruzioni Meccaniche Aeronautiche SA (CMASA). More than 150 Wals were built in Italy, including a number by Piaggio. First customer for the Wal was the Spanish Navy, whose initial order, for six with 300hp Hispano-Suiza engines, was completed in 1923. Overall production of the Wal totalled about three hundred aircraft, produced in a multiplicity of variants with a score or more of alternative powerplants and wing spans ranging from 73ft 9¾in (22·50m) to 89ft 2¾in (27·20m), which makes a detailed record virtually impossible. The Dornier company itself began Wal production in 1932, at Friedrichshafen, and other manufacturers included CASA in Spain (forty), Aviolanda in Holland (about the same number) and Kawasaki in Japan (three). In 1933 CMASA built a version known as Marina Fiat MF.5; those built by Dornier were designated Do J II and known as 8 ton or 10 ton Wals according to their metric gross weight. The latter version had a fully-enclosed crew cabin. The *Luftwaffe* designation Do 15 was applied to a military version of the 8 ton Wal ordered in 1933. Other military users of the Wal included the *Regia Aeronautica* and the Spanish and Netherlands navies. Commercial Wals were operated for many years, on passenger or mail-carrying services, by European and other airlines, among them Deutsche Luft Hansa and Aero Lloyd in Germany, Aero Espresso and SANA in Italy, Condor and Varig in Brazil, SCADTA in Colombia and Nihon Koku in

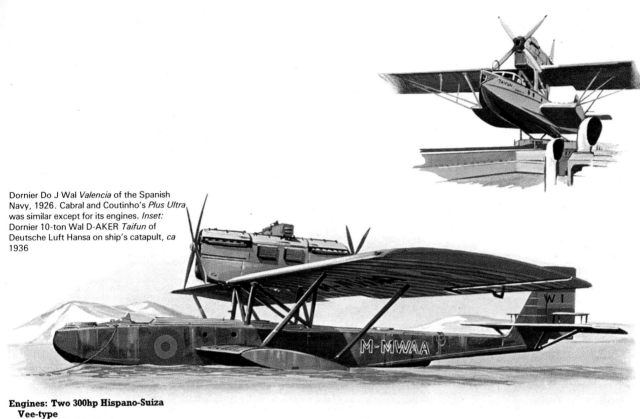

Dornier Do J Wal *Valencia* of the Spanish Navy, 1926. Cabral and Coutinho's *Plus Ultra* was similar except for its engines. *Inset:* Dornier 10-ton Wal D-AKER *Taifun* of Deutsche Luft Hansa on ship's catapult, *ca* 1936

Engines: Two 300hp Hispano-Suiza Vee-type
Span: 73ft 9¾in (22·50m)
Length: 58ft 2¾in (17·25m)
Wing area: 1,033.3sq ft (96·00m)
Take-off weight: 12,566lb (5,700kg)
Maximum cruising speed: 96mph (155km/hr)
Service ceiling: 11,480ft (3,500m)
Range: approx 1,245 miles (2,000km)

Japan. A number of Wals featured in other noteworthy flights during the inter-war period. Two CMASA-built aircraft (N24 and N25) were purchased by Norway in 1925 for Roald Amundsen's attempt to reach the North Pole by air. The former aircraft had to be abandoned after reaching 87° 43′ N, the farthest north then reached by aeroplane, on 21 May 1925; N25 was later purchased by Englishman F T Courtney, re-registered G-EBQO and refitted at Pisa with 450hp Napier Lion engines for an attempted trans-Atlantic flight. After two failures it was resold to Germany where, as D-1422 *Amundsen Wal* and fitted with 600hp BMW VI engines, it was successfully flown to Chicago via Iceland, Greenland and New York by Wolfgang von Gronau between 20-26 August 1930. This was the first east-west crossing of the Atlantic by a flying-boat. This remarkable airman made a similar trip in 1931 in the *Grönland Wal* (D-2053), and a round-the-world flight in 1932. Well before von Gronau's exposition of the Wal's abilities, however, a Spanish crew had taken one of the very first Wals on an equally notable flight across the South Atlantic. Spain had been the first customer for the Wal, initially buying six, and on 22 January 1926 the fifth of these (M-MWAL *Plus Ultra*,

almost identical to the Wal illustrated, but with 450hp Napier Lions instead of the standard 300hp Hispano-Suiza engines) left Palos de Moguer, the port from which Columbus had sailed for America. On board were Commandant Rámon Franco (pilot), Captain Julio Ruiz de Alda (navigator), Lt Juan Durán, engineer Pablo Rado, and a photographer, Leopoldo Alonso. Flying via Las Palmas, Porto Praia, Fernando de Noronha, Pernambuco, Rio de Janeiro and Montevideo, they arrived in Buenos Aires on 10 February 1926, after a 6,258 mile (10,072km) journey completed in 59½ hours' flying. King Alfonso XIII of Spain subsequently donated *Plus Ultra* to the Argentine government, and it is today in the possession of the Lujan Museum in Argentina – the only surviving Wal in the world, so far as is known. On 30 September 1926 the prototype was flown of an enlarged development, the Do R Super Wal, which was powered by two 650hp Rolls-Royce Condor engines. Comparatively few twin-engined Super Wals were built, however, the majority of production aircraft having four engines (two tandem pairs) mounted above the wing. First flight of the four-engined version was made on 15 September 1928.

Dornier Do X

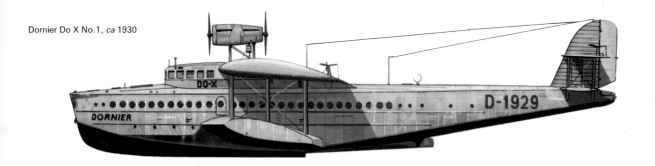

Dornier Do X No.1, *ca* 1930

**Engines: Twelve 600hp Curtiss
  Conqueror twelve-cylinder Vee-type**
Span: 157ft 5¾in (48.0m)
Length: 131ft 4¾in (40·05m)
Wing area: 4,886·8sq ft (454.0sq m)
**Maximum take-off weight: 123,459lb
  (56,000 kg)**
Maximum speed: 134mph (216km/hr)
Operational ceiling: 1,640ft (500m)
Typical range: 1,056 miles (1,700km)

Although it is only in comparatively recent times that plane-loads of 150 or more passengers have become an accepted standard, one aircraft with such a capacity was flown more than fifty years ago, and the fact that it was not an unqualified success cannot detract from the engineering feat which it represented. Design of the Do X, which began in 1916 under the leadership of Professor Claude Dornier (1884-1969), was aimed at producing a transport aircraft capable of carrying large payloads over trans-oceanic distances. The project was the subject of considerable scepticism, but Prof Dornier and his team remained undaunted, completing a full-size mock-up of the giant aeroplane and carrying out static testing of the proposed engine installation. This, in its original form, comprised twelve 525hp Siemens-built Bristol Jupiter air-cooled radial engines, mounted in back-to-back pairs in six nacelles and driving four-blade propellers. The entire installation rested on an auxiliary 'over-wing' supported on six faired-in pylons. The Do X (a stopgap designation, later retained officially and signifying 'unknown quantity'), was primarily of metal construction, though large areas of wing and the wing and tail control surfaces were fabric-covered. Small metal auxiliary balancing surfaces were mounted above the ailerons and elevators. The first Do X (sometimes referred to as the Do-X1) was completed in mid-1929 and made its first flight on 25 July of that year. At this time it was by far the largest aeroplane in the world, and its load-carrying ability was amply demonstrated on 21 October 1929 when it made a 1-hour flight with 169 people on board – a 10-man crew, 150 passengers

and 9 stowaways. This flight, although excellent for publicity purposes, gave a somewhat exaggerated picture of the Do X's intended operational capacity, for the standard interior layout was for 66-72 passengers. The maximum fuel load of 3,520 Imp gallons (16,000 litres) was an indication of the aircraft's potential range. The passengers, accommodated on the main deck of the three-deck hull, were offered the travelling luxury of a bar, smoking and writing rooms, lounge and sleeping quarters in addition to the normal seating facilities. Early test flights of the Do X soon revealed a serious engine problem: the inadequate cooling of the six rear-facing Jupiters. A solution was found by substituting a completely new installation of twelve liquid-cooled Curtiss Conqueror engines; at the same time, replacement of the over-wing and 'solid' pylons by an open, strutted structure reduced the total wing area by 32·2sq m (346·6 sq ft). On 2 November 1930 the flying-boat left Friedrichshafen for a world-wide demonstration tour which took it by way of Amsterdam, Calshot, Bordeaux, Lisbon, the Canary Islands, Bolama, the Cape Verde Islands, Fernando de Noronha, Natal (Brazil), Rio de Janeiro, Antigua and Miami to New York, where it arrived on 27 August 1931. Some of the time during the 10-month trip was taken up with repairs, after fire had burnt part of the wing at Lisbon and the hull had sustained damage when taking off from the Canaries. After its return to Germany the Do-X1 was owned briefly by Deutsche Luft Hansa before being transferred to the DVL (Deutsche Versuchsanstalt für Luftfahrt) for experimental work. Eventually it went on display in the Aircraft Museum in Berlin, where it was destroyed in an Allied air attack during World War 2. While the Do-X1 was making its world tour, two examples of the Do-X2 were being completed for Italy. These were basically identical to the first aircraft but were powered by 550hp Fiat A.22R liquid-cooled engines, mounted on 'solid' pylons but retaining the horizontal tubular support struts. Identified as I-REDI *Umberto Maddalena* and I-ABBN *Alessandro Guidoni*, they had been ordered originally by SA Navigazione Aerea for operation in the Mediterranean area, but were not after all so used. They were, however, used for a time by the *Regia Aeronautica* for experimental flying before being broken up.

Heinkel He 59

Heinkel He 59B-2 of the 1st Staffel, K.Fl.Gr. 106, *Luftwaffe, ca* 1937

Engines: Two 660hp BMW VI 6·0 ZU
    twelve-cylinder Vee-type
Span: 77ft 9in (23·70m)
Length: 57ft 1in (17·40m)
Wing area: 1,649sq ft (153·2sq m)
Take-off weight: 19,842lb (9,000kg)
Maximum speed: 137mph (220km/hr) at
    sea level
Operational ceiling: 11,480ft (3,500m)
Maximum range: 1,085 miles (1,750km)

Intended originally for the torpedo-bomber/reconnaissance role, and designed at a time when the secretly-forming *Luftwaffe* was still very much in an embryo state, the Heinkel He 59 stayed in service, performing a variety of duties, for more than ten years. All production He 59s were floatplanes, although when designed by Reinhold Mewes in 1930 provision had been made for the aircraft to operate from either wheels or floats and the second of the two prototypes was indeed completed as a landplane. This aircraft (D-2215) was the first of the type to fly, in September 1931; it was followed by the twin-float prototype, D-2214, in the following January. In the spring of 1932 production was initiated with an evaluation batch of fourteen He 59A floatplanes and a generally similar batch of sixteen He 59Bs, all of which were unarmed and carried a crew of two. The first armed version was the He 59B-1, in which a single 7.9mm ring-mounted MG 15 machine-gun was installed in an open cockpit in the nose; similar guns were installed in dorsal and ventral positions in the four-seat He 59B-2, in which glazed positions were introduced in the nose and ventral step for bombardier and gunner. Weapon load comprised a single torpedo or up to 2,204lb (1,000kg) of bombs. Large orders were placed for the B-2, which went into

operational service in the Spanish Civil War from 1936, and a proportion of these were undertaken by the Arado company. (One Arado-built B-2 was used in 1937 to flight-test the nose section of a new and larger twin-float seaplane, the He 115. The He 59 was first used in Spain for night-bombing, but a later application was in the role of anti-shipping aircraft, for which some B-2s were given a reinforced nose mounting a movable 20mm MG FF cannon. Subsequent production versions included the He 59B-3 (a long-range reconnaissance model, built by the Walter Bachmann company and omitting one of the 7.9mm guns); the He 59C-1 with a 'solid', rounded nose, also employed for reconnaissance or training; the unarmed air/sea rescue He 59C-2, which carried six dinghies and additional radio; the He 59D aircrew trainer and He 59E-1 torpedo trainer; and the He 59E-2 photographic reconnaissance version, of which six were completed. Some He 59Ds, fitted out with special radio equipment as navigation trainers, were designated He 59N in this form. During World War 2, until their replacement by Dornier flying-boats in 1943, He 59s remained active on a variety of duties which included those of convoy shadowing, mine-laying, coastal reconnaissance and transport as well as in a training capacity.

Focke-Wulf Fw 44 Stieglitz (Goldfinch)

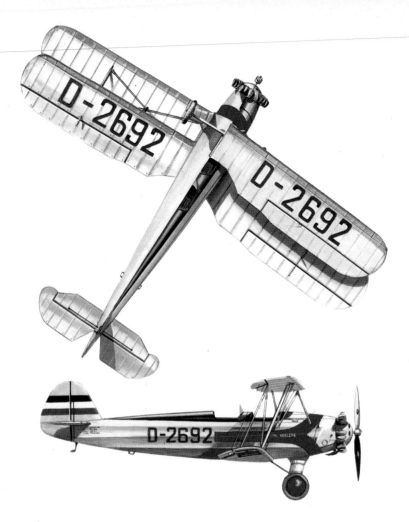

Focke-Wulf Fw 44 of the *Luftsportverband, ca* 1933

Engine: One 150hp Siemens Sh 14a 7-cylinder radial
Span: 29ft 6¼in (9·00m)
Length: 23ft 10¾in (7·285m)
Height (tail down): approx 9ft 2⅛in (2·80m)
Take-off weight: 1,896lb (860kg)
Maximum speed: 118mph (190km/hr) at sea level
Operational ceiling: 14,435 ft (4,400m)
Range: 335 miles (540km)
Armament: None

Flown for the first time in the late summer of 1932, the Fw 44 was the first aircraft to be designed by Dipl-Ing Kurt Tank after his appointment as Technical Director of Focke-Wulf Flugzeugbau GmbH at Bremen. It was to become one of the most widely-used aircraft in its class during the 1930s, several hundred being built in Germany for the home market and for export; many were built abroad under licence. The Fw 44A was the prototype for the Fw 44C major production version, the first model to go into production being the Fw 44B. This was powered by a 120hp Argus As 8 in-line engine, but a relatively small quantity were built before being superseded by the Fw 44C. The change to a 160hp BMW-Bramo/Siemens Sh 14A radial engine resulted in a shorter nose configuration, reducing the overall length by 1ft 4⅛in (0·41m); gross weight remained the same, but the performance was marginally improved with the radial engine. The Fw 44 seated two occupants in tandem, with dual controls, and was one of the standard types employed for the basic training of pilots for the emergent *Luftwaffe*. Home production of the Stieglitz was shared by several firms in the German aircraft industry, and substantial numbers were also built for export to Bolivia, Chile, China, Finland, Romania and Turkey. The Fw 44 was also built under licence in several other countries. Those manufactured by the Bulgarian State Aircraft Factory were designated DAR-9, while eighty-five were built as Sk 12s for the Royal Swedish Air Force by ASJA and the RSwAF Workshop, and forty more by Fábrica do Galeao for the Brazilian Air Force. Largest overseas production was in Argentina, where five hundred were built by the FMA factory at Córdoba, and in Czechoslovakia, where six hundred were completed by the SKD works at Prague. The Stieglitz was employed both as a military trainer and at civilian flying clubs in many parts of the world, and substantial numbers continued to be in service as elementary trainers during World War 2.

Junkers Ju 52/3m

Junkers Ju 52/3m g3e of I./KG 152
'Hindenburg', Greifswald, mid-1936. Its career
as a bomber was short-lived, but it became one
of the most famous transport aircraft ever built.
Inset: The retractable ventral gun/bomb-
aiming 'dustbin' of the Junkers Ju 52/3m
bombers

Engines: Three 600hp BMW 132A-3
    radials
Span: 95ft 11½in (29·25m)
Length: 62ft 0in (18·90m)
Wing area: 1,189·4sq ft (110·50sq m)
Take-off weight: 20,944lb (9,500kg)
Maximum speed: 172mph (277km/hr) at
    3,280ft (1,000m)
Service ceiling: 19,360ft (5,900m)
Range: 620 miles (1,000km)

Sometimes described as Germany's counterpart of the Ford 'Tin Goose', the Junkers Ju 52/3m went by many other names during her long life: Pava (turkey) to the Nationalists in the Spanish Civil War, 'Iron Annie' or 'Corrugated Coffin' to the Allies in World War 2, and Toucan to the French in the early post-war years; but most often, and most affectionately, as 'Tante Ju' to her Luftwaffe crews and the Parachute and Wehrmacht troops who flew in her. Winner of no prizes for aesthetic appeal, she was roomy, noisy, draughty, docile, rugged and, above all, reliable. The sound of her three engines, of whatever type (and she had many) has been variously likened to a collection of unsynchronised lawn-mowers or half a dozen motor-cycles racing downhill in bottom gear. Yet she was easy (if laborious) to handle, and demanded a field length of only some 750m (2,460ft) from which to operate with full load. A tri-motor development by Dipl Ing Ernst Zendel of the single-engined Ju 52 of 1930, the Ju 52/3m first flew in April 1931 and remained in steady production in Germany from 1932 to 1944; including foreign manufacture, the total built was close on 5,000, and Hitler chose one of the early production aircraft (D-2600 *Immel-mann*) as his personal transport. First commercial services, by DLH, began in June 1932, and two years later the first bomber-

transports were delivered to the still-clandestine Luftwaffe. Career as a bomber was short-lived, but in the transport role the Ju 52/3m became one of the most adaptable and best-known types ever built. Nearly 200 entered service with some thirty airlines before World War 2, and during the war the Luftwaffe made prolific and prodigal use of the 'Tante Ju' as troop and Fallschirmjäger transport and supply aircraft, ambulance, glider tug, mine clearer and for many other tasks. More than 570 took part in the invasion of Norway and Denmark in April 1940, and almost as many in France and the Low Countries a month later. In due course the Ju 52/3m appeared in the campaigns in Greece, North Africa, Crete and Russia, and is credited by some with playing a larger part in shaping the course of the air war than any Axis combat aircraft. It was the last of a long line of Junkers corrugated aircraft, and a few examples could still be found in service in the mid-1970s, after an operational life of almost forty years. The original Ju 52 was a single-engined aircraft, designed as a cargo transport and having a 590 cu ft (16·7 cu m) cabin capable of accommodating a 4,067lb (1,845kg) payload. The prototype (D-1974), which first flew on 13 October 1930, was powered initially by an 800hp Junkers L 88 engine, but among

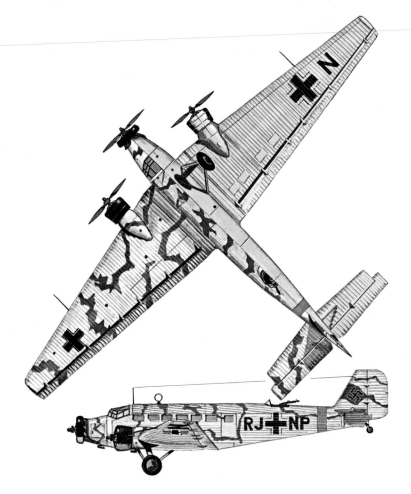

Junkers Ju 52/3m ge *Werner Voss* of Deutsche Luft Hansa, *ca* 1933

Engines: Three 660hp BMW 132A-1 nine-
  cylinder radials
Span: 95ft 11½in (29·25m)
Length: 62ft 0in (18·90m)
Wing area: 1,189·4sq ft (110·50sq m)
Normal take-off weight: 20,282lb
  (9,200kg)
Cruising speed: 152mph (245km/hr)
Service ceiling: 17,060ft (5,200m)
Range: 568 miles (915km)

the five Ju 52s known to have been built numerous alternative engines were fitted at different stages of their careers. The seventh Ju 52 was fitted with three 575hp BMW (Pratt & Whitney) Hornet radial engines, with which it flew for the first time in April 1931, and all subsequent aircraft were completed as tri-motor Ju 52/3ms. The characteristic corrugated-metal skinning was a typical trade mark of Junkers aircraft of the 1920s and 1930s, and was designed to give great structural strength and resistance to torsional loads. Other unmistakable recognition features of the Ju 52/3m includes the Junkers double flaps and elevators, and the toeing-out of the two wing-mounted engines. Accommodation was for a crew of 2 or 3 and up to 17 passengers, with a toilet and a baggage/freight compartment at the rear of the passenger cabin. Production of the Ju 52/3m began in 1932, the first two examples being delivered to Lloyd Aereo Boliviano. Most pre-war Ju 52/3ms were powered by one version or another of the Hornet engine or its German counterpart, the BMW 132, but other powerplants included Pratt & Whitney Wasp or Bristol Pegasus radials and Hispano-Suiza Vee-type engines. Predictably, the largest single commercial operator was Deutsche Lufthansa. By the end of World War 2 no fewer than

two hundred and thirty-one Ju 52/3ms had appeared in the DLH inventory, although the majority of these were operated in wartime on behalf of the Luftwaffe. The highest known DLH peacetime total is fifty-nine, the number taken on charge by the Luftwaffe prior to the outbreak of war in 1939. Some, fitted fitted with a twin-float landing gear, were designated Ju 52/3mW (for *Wasser = water*). With the creation of the *Luftwaffe*, the aircraft was adopted for military service as interim equipment for the first bomber squadrons, and several hundred were built as interim 4-seat bombers. The first major bombers, known as Ju 52/3m g3e's, saw their first operational service in the late summer of 1936 when twenty of them were among the first German aircraft sent to Spain after the outbreak of the Civil War. By the end of the following year, however, the Junkers type had been superseded as a *Luftwaffe* bomber by such later types as the He 111 and Do 17, and was largely transferred to troop transport duties, which were more appropriate to its capabilities. In this latter role the aircraft customarily retained its dorsal-mounted 7·9mm MG 15 machine-gun, but more often than not the second gun and its retractable ventral 'dustbin' mounting were omitted. Successive military variants were distinguished by suffixes

Junkers Ju 52/3m g3e of *Grupo 2-G-22*,
Spanish Nationalist Air Force, *ca* 1936

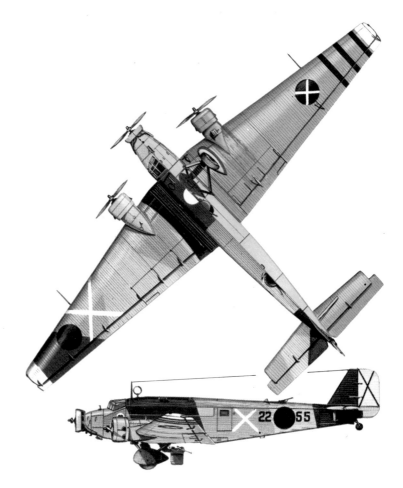

Engines: Three 600hp BMW 132A
  (licence Pratt & Whitney Hornet)
  9-cylinder radials
Span: 95ft 11½in (29·25m)
Length: 62ft 0in (18·90m)
Height (tail down): 14ft 9½in (4·50m)
Take-off weight: 20,944lb (9,500kg)
Maximum speed: 180mph (290km/hr) at
  sea level
Operational ceiling: 20,670ft (6,300m)
Range: 795 miles (1,280km)
Armament: Two 7·9mm MG 15 machine-
  guns, one in dorsal position and one in
  ventral 'dustbin'; up to 2,205lb
  (1,000kg) of bombs internally

from g3e to g14e, signifying either the specific role of a
particular model (e.g. transport, ambulance, mine clearance),
the installation of later variants of the BMW 132 engine
(licence version of the American Hornet) or miscellaneous
structural alterations. The early production models were
powered by 600hp BMW 132A engines; the first version to
introduce the higher-powered BMW 132T was the
Ju 53/3m g5e. Principal production model was the
Ju 52/3m g7e, with enlarged cabin doors, autopilot, and other
detail improvements; this could be fitted out either as an
18-seat troop transport or as an ambulance with provision for
12 stretchers. Its best-known action came with the invasion of
Norway and Denmark in April 1940, in which nearly six hundred of these transports were engaged. Almost as many were
in action during the invasion of France and the Low Countries,
and in both campaigns well over a quarter of the Junkers
transports involved were lost. Nevertheless, they continued
to figure prominently in such subsequent Nazi campaigns as
those in Greece, Libya and Crete. Other duties undertaken by
the Ju 52/3m during its *Luftwaffe* career included those of
supply transport and glider tug, and some aircraft were fitted
with electromagnetic 'degaussing' rings for clearing mine

fields. Most models had provision for interchangeable wheel,
ski or float landing gear. Overall production of the Ju 52/3m
between 1934 and 1944, including civil models, amounted to
just over four thousand eight hundred and fifty aircraft. Many
pre-war commercial Ju 52/3ms were impressed for military
service, and when the war was over several hundred were
allocated to many foreign airlines, assisting them to re-
establish their pre-war services until more modern types
became available. There were also a hundred and seventy
Spanish CASA-built aircraft, and more than four hundred
completed in France by the Ateliers Aéronautiques de
Colombes as the AAC. I. In the immediate post-war years, the
Ju 52/3m was in commercial service with operators in
Norway, Sweden and Denmark; ten, converted by Short &
Harland Ltd, were employed by BEA from November 1946 to
August 1947. The Ju 52/3m was most numerous, however, in
France, being supplied to several domestic operators and to
the national carrier, Air France, which at one time had a fleet
of eighty-five of these veteran aircraft. Some of the
Scandinavian machines were later sold to customers in Spain
and elsewhere. Post-war military operators included the
Swiss and Spanish air forces.

Junkers Ju 52/3m of *Kampffliegerschüle*
Thorn, winter 1942-43

Engines: Three 830hp BMW 132T radials
Span: 95ft 11½in (29·25m)
Length: 62ft 0in (18·90m)
Height: 14ft 9½in (4·50m)
Maximum take-off weight: 24,317lb
   (11,030kg)
Maximum speed: 190mph (305km/hr) at
   8,200ft (2,500m)
Operational ceiling: 18,045ft (5,500m)
Range with 2,205lb (1,000kg)
   payload: 808 miles (1,300km)
Armament: One 13mm MG 131 machine-
   gun in dorsal position and two 7·9mm
   MG 15 guns firing through passengers'
   windows

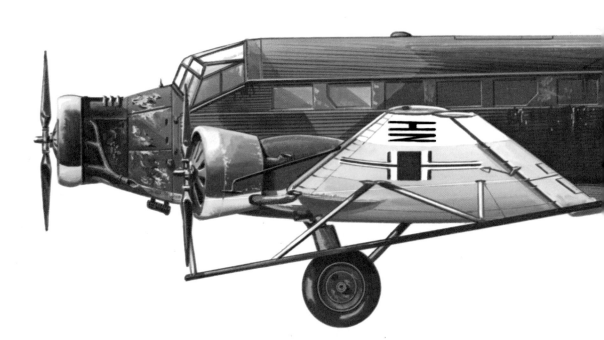

Junkers Ju 52/3m g4e (MS) (NJ + NH) of Minensuchgruppe 1, *ca* 1942

Gruppe emblem of **Minensuchgruppe 1**

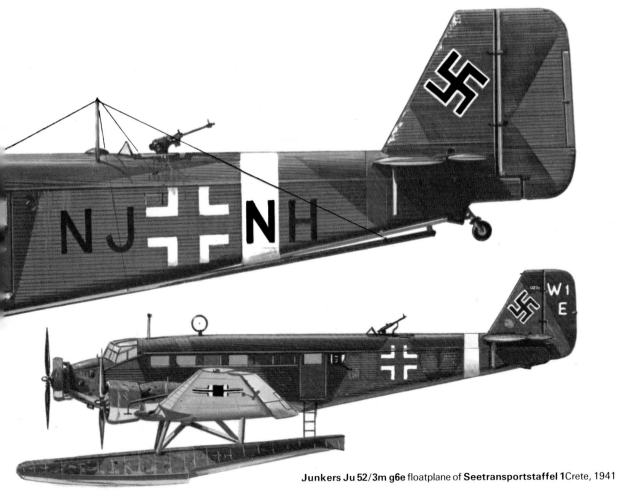

Junkers Ju 52/3m g6e floatplane of **Seetransportstaffel 1** Crete, 1941

Dornier Do 23

Dornier Do 23G of the 5th *Staffel*, II *Gruppe*, 2nd *Geschwader, Luftkreiskommando* III (Dresden) 1936

Engines: Two 750hp BMW VI U
    12-cylinder Vee type
Span: 83ft 11¾in (25·60m)
Length: 61ft 7¼in (18·775m)
Height: 17ft 8½in (5·40m)
Normal take-off weight: 19,290lb
    (8,750kg)
Maximum speed: 162mph (260km/hr) at
    985 ft (300m)
Operational ceiling: 19,030ft (5,800m)
Normal range: 746 miles (1,200km)
Armament: One 7·9mm MG 15 machine-
    gun in each of nose, dorsal and ventral
    positions; up to 2,205lb (1,000kg) of
    bombs internally

Despite its later numerical designation, the Dornier Do 23 actually preceded its more illustrious stablemate, the Do 17, into production and service with the *Luftwaffe*. In fact its origins go back to 1931, to an aircraft then known as the Do F which flew for the first time on 7 May 1932. This was powered by two 550hp Siemens-built Bristol Jupiter radial engines, and featured a retractable main landing gear. A less obvious feature, at least prior to the official disclosure of the *Luftwaffe*'s existence in 1935, was that the gun emplacements, bomb racks and other military items were delivered separately and secretly, while the Do 11C (as the production version was known) was itself delivered as an 'innocent' civil aeroplane ostensibly intended for freight transport duties with the German railways. The Do 11C was contemporary with the Ju 52/3m in forming the initial equipment of *Luftwaffe* bomber squadrons, but was a much less satisfactory aeroplane. Attempts to eliminate some of its worst characteristics led to the Do 11D, with modified, shorter-span wings, and the

Do 11Cs in service were also converted to this standard. The Do 13, whose prototype flew on 13 February 1933, was a simplified version with 750hp BMW VI engines which went into production as the Do 13C; but this continued to suffer from deficiencies in the wing structure and was in turn replaced by the Do 23. The Do 23 offered a strengthened airframe, a further reduction in wing span, and small auxiliary fins mounted below the tailplane. Production began in 1934 with the Do 23F, and was quickly followed by the Do 23G, which became the principal service version built. However, the Do 23 was not destined for a long service life as a bomber, being replaced by the Do 17, Ju 86 and He 111 from 1937, after which it was relegated to second-line duties, including training. On these it remained in use during the early years of World War 2, when one of its tasks was the 'degaussing' of Allied sea minefields. Wartime use was also made of some of the earlier Do 11Ds, transferred by Germany to the Bulgarian Air Force.

Heinkel He 70 and He 170

Heinkel He 70F-1 of the 2nd *Staffel*,
Aufklärungsgruppe I, *Luftkreiskommando* II
(Berlin), *ca* 1935

Engine: One 750hp BMW VI 7·3
  12-cylinder Vee type
Span: 48ft 6¾in (14·80m)
Length: 38ft 4½in (11·70m)
Height: 10ft 2in (3·10m)
Take-off weight: 7,540lb (3,420kg)
Maximum speed: 224mph (360km/hr) at
  13,123ft (4,000m)
Operational ceiling: 17,225ft (5,250m)
Range: 497 miles (800km)
Armament: One 7·9mm MG 15 machine-
  gun in rear cockpit

The highly advanced aerodynamic and structural design exhibited by the He 70 would compare favourably enough even with some aircraft of the present day; that it should have been designed and built in little over six months, and flown at as early a date as 1932, is remarkable indeed. It was on 1 December of that year that the He 70V1 prototype, whose design had been inspired by Siegfried and Walter Günter, was flown for the first time, and during the early months of 1933 this aircraft and the first pre-production He 70A machine had set up a series of impressive new closed-circuit speed and speed-with-payload records which earned the aircraft the name *Blitz* (Lightning) from Deutsche Lufthansa, for whose use it had been designed. These early He 70s were powered by 630hp BMW VI Vee-type engines, successive variants of which became the standard powerplant for the commercial He 70B, C, D and G models, of which a total of twenty-eight were built. In 1933 the He 70E model was evolved for light attack duties with the *Luftwaffe*, being based on the 750hp He 70D and having underwing racks for small HE or incendiary bombs. Only a single rearward-firing MG 15 machine-gun was provided for defence, the aircraft relying upon its speed to

escape attack. Its performance also made the He 70 potentially a most useful reconnaissance aircraft, and this requirement resulted in the appearance of the He 70F-0 and F-1 in 1934–35. Over long ranges, however, the twin-engined Dornier Do 17 proved a more practical choice, with the result that the He 70F was reallocated to a short-range communications role after a comparatively short period of first-line *Luftwaffe* service. During this time some eighteen He 70Fs performed active reconnaissance and bombing duty with Germany's Condor Legion taking part in the Spanish Civil War of 1936–39. Seven were lost during that war but the survivors continued to serve for many years afterwards, the last not disappearing until the early 1950s. The He 170 was an export version, about twenty of which were completed in 1937–38 for the Hungarian Air Force. These differed from the standard He 70 in having 910hp Gnome-Rhône 14K radial engines in place of the Vee-type BMW VI, and remained in Hungarian service until mid-1941. A prototype was flown in 1938 of the He 270, with a 1,175hp DB 601A engine, but this version did not enter production.

Bücker Bü 131 Jungmann and Bü 133 Jungmeister

Bücker Bü 131A Jungmann of the *Luftsportverband, ca* 1934

Engine: One 80hp Hirth HM 60R
    4-cylinder inverted in-line
Span: 24ft 3½in (7·40m)
Length: 21ft 10½in (6·66m)
Height: 7ft 4½in (2·25m)
Take-off weight: 1,323lb (600kg)
Maximum speed: 109mph (175km/hr) at
    sea level
Operational ceiling: 13,125ft (4,000m)
Range: 405 miles (650km)
Armament: None

Herr Carl Bücker, a German Navy pilot during World War 1, became a test pilot for the Swedish Navy in 1920 and later became managing director of Svenska Aero AB in Stockholm. He returned to Germany in 1932, and a year later formed the Bücker Flugzeugbau GmbH at Johannisthal, near Berlin. In October its chief designer, A J Andersson, began developing the first of what was to become a world-famous series of aerobatic light aircraft. This was the prototype (D-1350) of the Bü 131A Jungmann (Young Man), which made its first flight on 27 April 1934 powered by an 80hp Hirth HM 60R inverted in-line engine. A clean-looking 2-seat biplane, with sweptback outer wings and a divided-axle main landing gear, it was placed in series production later in 1934 and deliveries began before the end of the year. In particular, it was ordered in substantial numbers by the *Luftsportverband*, which ostensibly was a civilian flying organisation but which in reality existed primarily to train pilots for the embryo *Luftwaffe*. From the Jungmann, which was a tandem-seat basic trainer, Bücker developed in 1935 the Bü 133A Jungmeister (Young Champion), a single-seater intended for advanced training, including aerobatics. The prototype Jungmeister (D-EVEO), with a 135hp Hirth HM 6 engine, was the only German-built example to have an in-line engine, although others were built elsewhere with this type of powerplant. Two German pro

duction models were proposed, that with a 160hp Hirth HM 506 being designated Bü 133B, and that with a 160hp Bramo-Siemens Sh 14A radial engine being the Bü 133C. The former was not after all built in Germany, but *circa* 1941–42 CASA in Spain built a total of fifty Jungmeisters which included a few Hirth-engined Bü 133Bs; the remainder were Bü 133Cs. Licence manufacture of the Bü 133C was also undertaken in Switzerland. Dornier's Altenrhein factory built forty-seven for the Swiss Air Force, which acquired four others direct from Germany. Production of the Bü 133C in Germany was extensive, and included machines built for export. By the end of 1937, Jungmanns and Jungmeisters were flying, in civil and military guise, in nearly twenty countries. Meanwhile, in 1936 Bücker had introduced a new version of the 2-seat Jungmann, the Bü 131B. Powered by a 105hp Hirth HM 504 in-line engine, this was adopted by the now officially extant *Luftwaffe* as its standard primary training aircraft, the Bü 133C Jungmeister being standardised for advanced and aerobatic training. A few Bü 131Bs were completed, as the Tatra T-131, in Czechoslovakia during the late 1930s. A large number of Jungmeisters are still flying in the world today (many now with different powerplants), and continue to testify to the fundamental excellence of what one present-day pilot at least has called 'the finest precision aerobatic machine ever built'.

Heinkel He 51

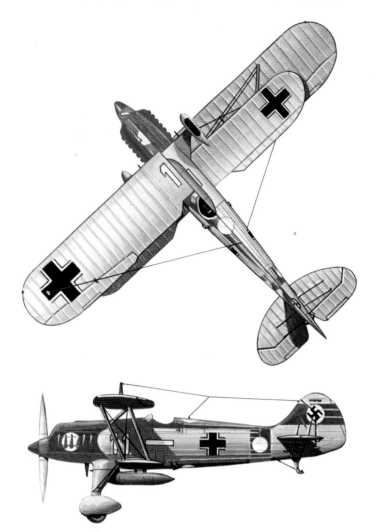

Heinkel He 51B-1 of *Staffel* 6, II/JG 132
Richthofen, *Luftwaffe*, Döberitz 1936

Engine: One 750hp BMW VI 12-cylinder
　　Vee type
Span: 36ft 1in (11·00m)
Length: 27ft 6¾in (8·40m)
Height: 10ft 6in (3·20m)
Take-off weight: 4,189lb (1,900kg)
Maximum speed: 205mph (330km/hr) at
　　sea level
Operational ceiling: 25,260ft (7,700m)
Normal range: 354 miles (570km)
Armament: Two 7·9mm MG 17 machine-
　　guns in upper front fuselage

The origins of the He 51 fighter are traceable back through a series of small, streamlined fighters, beginning with the He 37 evolved in the late 1920s and continuing via the He 38, He 43 and He 49. It was the He 49a, designed by Siegfried and Walter Günter and flown for the first time in November 1932, which effectively became the prototype for the He 51a, the fourth He 49a embodying sufficient modifications to justify the allocation of the later designation. This aircraft (D-ILGY) first flew in mid-1933; later that year construction began of nine pre-series He 51A-0s for service trials, and delivery of these began in the summer of 1934. Delivery of the first production model, the He 51A-1, started in April 1935 to JG 132, and later to JG131 and 134. Early in 1936 the next production model began to enter service. This was the He 51B-1, preceded by twelve pre-production B-0s and differing from its predecessor in having modified landing gear bracing and provision for an auxiliary ventral fuel tank. He 51B production included a number built as twin-float He 51B-2s for service at coastal fighter stations. At the end of July 1936 six He 51s, the first of many, were sent to Spain to support the Nationalist forces in the Civil War fighting under General Franco. Eventually, one hundred and thirty-five He 51s served either with the

Nationalist Air Force or Germany's *Legion Condor* in the Civil War. Flown by Spanish pilots, the first He 51s achieved some early success, but when, a few months later, Soviet I-15 fighters began to appear in the Republican ranks, the German fighter found itself completely outclassed and suffered extensive losses. By the end of the war almost two-thirds of the He 51s fighting in Spain had been lost. Formations of He 51s continued to operate with some effect as ground-attack aircraft, a role for which the He 51C was built from the outset. Those supplied to the Franco forces were He 51C-1s, while those built for use by the *Luftwaffe* in Germany featured some equipment changes and were designated He 51C-2. But the disappointing results achieved as a fighter in Spain – which were reinforced by the He 51's poor showing in comparative trials at home with the Arado Ar 68 – led to its withdrawal from first-line *Luftwaffe* fighter units to close-support or training roles in 1938, after a comparatively short career. A total of seven hundred He 51 production aircraft were built. This included seventy-five A-1s by Heinkel, two hundred and twenty-five (including seventy-five A-1s) by Arado, two hundred by Erla and two hundred (at least half of which were He 51Cs) by Fieseler.

Focke-Wulf Fw 56 Stosser
(Falcon Hawk)

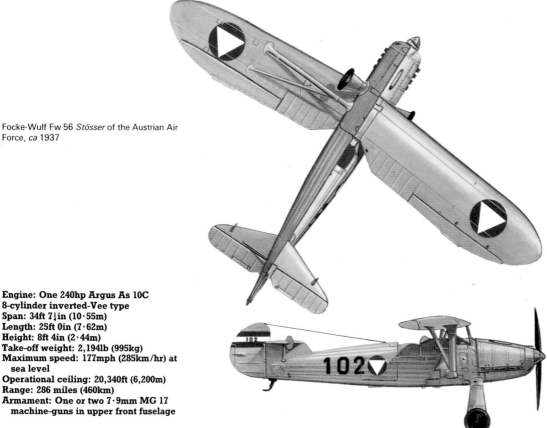

Focke-Wulf Fw 56 *Stösser* of the Austrian Air Force, *ca* 1937

Engine: One 240hp Argus As 10C
8-cylinder inverted-Vee type
Span: 34ft 7¼in (10·55m)
Length: 25ft 0in (7·62m)
Height: 8ft 4in (2·44m)
Take-off weight: 2,194lb (995kg)
Maximum speed: 177mph (285km/hr) at
  sea level
Operational ceiling: 20,340ft (6,200m)
Range: 286 miles (460km)
Armament: One or two 7·9mm MG 17
  machine-guns in upper front fuselage

The Fw 56 single-seat parasol monoplane was among the first aircraft to be designed for the Focke-Wulf Flugzeugbau by the now-famous Dr Kurt Tank. It first appeared in 1934, and was an extremely clean-looking aircraft, of mixed wood and metal construction with fabric covering. The primary purpose of the Fw 56 was that of an advanced trainer, but one of the early machines gained the distinction of first demonstrating the dive-bomber concept to the German High Command. This followed a visit to the USA by the celebrated German flier Ernst Udet, who was so impressed by the displays he had seen by American dive-bombers that he asked Focke-Wulf to fit bomb racks and an elementary release gear to an Fw 56 for

demonstration to *Luftwaffe* officials. The Fw 56 was itself too modestly-powered and not structurally strong enough to fulfil a serious dive-bomber role, but this application of aerial warfare materialised in due course in Germany's first *Sturzkampfflugzeug*, the Junkers Ju 87. The Fw 56 was built in substantial numbers, not only for the emergent *Luftwaffe* but for German civil flying clubs and for export. The Stösser was supplied to the air forces of Austria, Bolivia, Bulgaria, Holland and Hungary, in many cases remaining in service until the end of World War 2. It was highly popular with pilots, was fully aerobatic, and in the fighter-trainer role could be armed with one or two 7·9mm MG 17 machine-guns.

Focke-Wulf Fw 58 Weihe (Kite)

Focke-Wulf Fw 58C of the 1st *Staffel*, 1st *Gruppe*, II/KGzbV.1, *Luftkreiskommando* (Königsberg), displayed at the Munich Air Show late 1936

Engines: Two 240hp Argus As 10C 8-cylinder inverted-Vee type
Span: 68ft 10¾in (21·00m)
Length: 49ft 11¼in (14·00m)
Height: 12ft 9½in (3·90m)
Take-off weight: 7,934lb (3,600kg)
Maximum speed: 162mph (260km/hr) at sea level
Operational ceiling: 18,375ft (5,600m)
Range: 497 miles (800km)
Armament: None

First flown in prototype form (D-ABEM) in 1935, the Focke-Wulf Fw 58 was one of many designs to be produced for the German company by Dipl Ing Kurt Tank, later famous as the originator of the Fw 190 wartime fighter. One Fw 58 (D-ALEX) was used by Dr Tank as his personal transport. It was built in considerable numbers, and besides being adopted by the *Luftwaffe* was produced for civil or military use in Argentina, Austria, Brazil, Bulgaria, China, Denmark, Hungary, the Netherlands, Romania and Sweden. A substantial number of prototypes was built, and the two initial production models were the civil Fw 58A 6-seat aerial taxi and the initial *Luftwaffe* series, the Fw 58B. The latter could be used as a communications or light transport aircraft, but with appropriate modifications and equipment changes was also employed extensively as a pilot, bombing, gunnery or radio trainer or for photographic reconnaissance. These derived from the Fw 58V2 second prototype, which was built with a cut-down rear cabin and single 7·9mm machine-guns on ring mountings above the nose and behind the crew cabin. Production Fw 58B trainers had detachable alternative nose sections, one 'solid' and the other a glazed section mounting a single 7·9mm gun. In the bombing training role, the Weihe could carry twelve 22lb (10kg) bombs. The rearward-retracting main landing gear of the standard Fw 58B landplane could be replaced by twin floats, in which form the aircraft was designated Fw 58W. One aircraft (D-OXLR) was also flown experimentally during the war with a non-retractable tricycle undercarriage. Production continued during World War 2, when the principal version built was the Fw 58C for ambulance, crew training or communications duties; apart from the appropriate operational equipment, this differed in detail only from the Fw 58B. Standard powerplant of the Fw 58 was the 240hp Argus As 10C in-line engine, but a number were completed also with 260hp Hirth HM 508D engines.

Heinkel He 111

Heinkel He 111B-1 prior to delivery to KG 154 of the *Luftwaffe*, autumn 1936

Engines: Two 1,000hp Daimler-Benz DB 600Aa 12-cylinder inverted-Vee type
Span: 74ft 1¾in (22·60m)
Length: 57ft 5in (17·50m)
Height: 14ft 5¼in (4·40m)
Maximum take-off weight: 20,536lb (9,315kg)
Maximum speed: 248mph (400km/hr) at 13,125ft (4,000m)
Operational ceiling: 22,965ft (7,000m)
Range: 559 miles (900km)
Armament: Three 7·9mm MG 15 machine-guns, one each in nose and dorsal positions and one in retractable ventral 'dustbin'; up to 3,307lb (1,500kg) of bombs internally

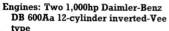

Altogether, the Heinkel He 111 was in service in one form or another somewhere in the world for some thirty years following its first appearance in the early months of 1937. The origin of its design actually dates from 1934, when the brothers Siegfried and Walter Günter began to evolve it as an all-metal twin-engined monoplane of unusually clean lines. The He 111V1 prototype first flew on 24 February 1935, powered by a pair of 660hp BMW VI inverted-Vee engines and equipped for a medium bomber role with three defensive 7·9mm machine-guns and an internal bomb load of 2,205lb (1,000kg). Three other prototypes were completed; of these, the V2 and V4 were completed as 10-seat commercial passenger and mail transports. Some efforts were made to interest Deutsche Lufthansa in purchasing the aircraft, and the German airline did, later, operate six He 111Cs and four He 111Gs. The He 111V3 meanwhile served as the prototype for the first military pre-production version, the He 111A-0. Manufacture of this version began in mid-1935, and by the following spring aircraft of this model were being delivered for service trials to the *Luftwaffe* test centre at Rechlin. The He 111 was found to possess good handling qualities, and its handsome lines were clearly inherited from its single-engined pre-

decessor, the He 70. It was, however, somewhat underpowered with the BMW engines, and for this reason the early-production He 111A-1s with these engines were rejected for squadron service. The ten He 111A-0s were sold to China. Production therefore, continued with the He 111B-0 and B-1, in which two DB 600 engines were adopted as the powerplant. These in turn were followed by improved models, the He 111B-2 (DB 600C) and the He 111D-1 (DB 600G). In 1937 the He 111B-2 was among several modern German aircraft to participate in the Spanish Civil War, where it was one of the types flown regularly by Germany's Condor Legion. In Spain, the He 111's performance was such that it could outpace most of the interceptor fighters sent up to destroy it, and could thus carry out unescorted raids with comparative impunity. (The belief that it could continue to do so against Britain in 1939–40 was very quickly dispelled, and the He 111 was soon given an increased defensive armament and a fighter escort.) To conserve supplies of the DB 600 engine for the Bf 109 fighter programme, the He 111E was produced next, with a powerplant of two 1,010hp Junkers Jumo 211A engines. Meanwhile a further civil version, the He 111G, had been developed by

Heinkel He 111H-3 of III/KG.53 during the Battle of Britain, summer 1940

Engines: Two 1,200hp Junkers Jumo
   211D-1 inverted-Vee type
Span: 74ft 1¾in (22·60m)
Length: 53ft 9½in (16·40m)
Height: 13ft 1½in (4·00m)
Normal take-off weight: 24,912lb
   (11,300kg)
Maximum speed: 258mph (415km/hr) at
   16,400ft (5,000m)
Operational ceiling: 25,590ft (7,800m)
Range with maximum bomb load:
   758 miles (1,220km)
Armament: One 20mm MG FF cannon in
   ventral gondola, and five 7·9mm
   MG 15 machine-guns in nose, dorsal,

ventral and beam positions; up to
4,409lb (2,000kg) of bombs internally

Heinkel. Instead of the semi-elliptical wings used on earlier versions, the He 111G introduced new, straight-tapered wings which were easier to manufacture. Few customers appeared for this model, but the new-style wings were introduced on the He 111F bomber variant which was the next to enter production. Both the E and F versions saw service in the Spanish Civil War, bringing to seventy-five the total number of He 111-type aircraft to take part in this conflict. Twenty-four F-1s and five G-5s were supplied to Turkey; the Luftwaffe F model was the F-4. About ninety He 111Js, similar to the F-4 but with DB 600CG engines and their bomb bays deleted, were built as torpedo-bombers, but in the event were delivered for standard bombing duties. Just before the outbreak of World War 2, the new He 111P had begun to enter service. This had a completely redesigned nose section, of continuous-curve contours (i.e. with no 'step' for the cockpit) and mounting a ball-type gun turret in the extreme nose, offset slightly to starboard. By 3 September 1939 total output of He 111 variants had reached almost a thousand aircraft, and production was to mount rapidly during the war years. The He 111P was built in comparatively small numbers, again because of the use of

Daimler-Benz engines, but its Jumo-powered counterpart, the He 111H, became the most widely used series of all, well over five thousand being built before production ended in 1944. Reflecting their rough reception during the Battle of Britain, successive H and subsequent types appeared with progressive increases in defensive armament, the number of crew members being increased to five or six according to the number of guns. Although most extensively used in its intended role as a medium bomber, the He 111H carried a variety of operational loads during its service. The H-6 was particularly effective as a torpedo bomber, carrying two of these weapons usually, while other H sub-types became carriers for the Hs 293 glider bomb and the FZG-76 (V1) flying bomb. More bizarre variants included the H-8 fitted with balloon-cable cutters, and the He 111Z *Zwilling* (Twin) glider tug, a union of two H-6 airframes linked by a new centre-section supporting a fifth Jumo engine. The H-23 was an 8-seat paratroop transport. German production, of all versions, was well in excess of seven thousand. Licence-built He 111H-16's, designated C.2111, were built in Spain by CASA, and served with the Spanish Air Force until well into the 1960s.

Geschwader emblem of
KG 4 'General Wever'

Geschwader emblem of
KG 55

Gruppe emblem of
III./KG 53
'Legion Condor'

Personal emblem painted
on **He 111H-6 of St G 3**

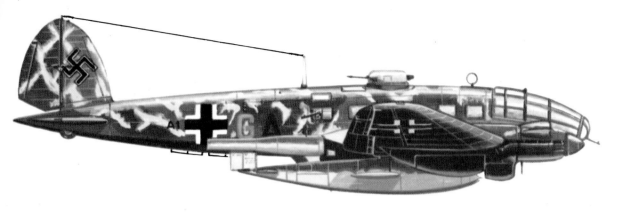

Heinkel He 111H-22 (A1 + GA) of Stab./KG 53 (the Netherlands, *ca* October/November 1944), with Fieseler Fi 103 mounted beneath the starboard wing root

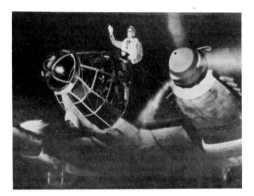

An **He 111** about to take off for a night mission during the Battle of Britain

An **He 111** bomber bearing the diving eagle emblem of **KG 30 'Adler'**

Heinkel He 111H-16 (5J + GN) of 5./KG 4 in temporary use as a transport, Stalino, winter 1942/43

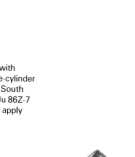

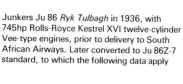

Junkers Ju 86 *Ryk Tulbagh* in 1936, with
745hp Rolls-Royce Kestrel XVI twelve-cylinder
Vee-type engines, prior to delivery to South
African Airways. Later converted to Ju 86Z-7
standard, to which the following data apply

**Engines: Two 800hp Pratt & Whitney
  Hornet S1E-G nine-cylinder radials**
Span: 73ft 9¾in (22·50m)
Length: 57ft 5in (17·50m)
Wing area: 882·6sq ft (82·00sq m)
Take-off weight: 17,637lb (8,000kg)
Maximum cruising speed: 224mph
  (360km/hr) at 11,480 ft (3,500m)
Service ceiling: 25,590ft (7,800m)
Range: 932 miles (1,500km)

Although it achieved greater prominence in its military guise
(see next page), the Ju 86 also achieved some status as a
commercial transport during the 1930s, nearly fifty seeing
service with eight operators in as many countries. Like its
contemporary, the Heinkel He 111, the Ju 86 was designed in
1934 to a joint Lufthansa/RLM specification for a multi-
engined aircraft for use both as a bomber and as a commercial
transport. The design team was led by Dipl Ing Ernst Zindel,
and the two civil prototypes were the Ju 86 V2 (D-ABUK) and
V4 (D-AREV), which made their first flights on 22 March and 24
August 1935 respectively. From the outset, the Ju 86's development was affected by problems with the Jumo engines
selected to power it, but production began in 1935 of the
initial commercial version, the Ju 86B, equipped with two
600hp Jumo 205C-4 engines. At least eight examples were
built of the pre-production Ju 86B-0, of which HB-IXI, in April
1936, was the first to be delivered to a customer airline
(Swissair); five others were delivered to Deutsche Lufthansa,
which put them into service in mid-1936 from Berlin to
Gleiwitz, Bremen and Cologne and from Cologne to Breslau.
The Swissair example, used for a night mail service between
Zurich and Frankfurt, was damaged in a crash-landing in
August 1936, but six months later was replaced by the Ju 86Z-1
HB-IXE (redesignated Ju 86Z-2 and re-registered HB-IXA after
being re-engined with BMW 132 engines). Standard accom-
modation was for a flight crew of 3, and 10 passengers in
individual seats, with a baggage compartment aft of the main
cabin. DLH became one of the two major airline operators of

the Ju 86. In addition to accepting the V2, V4 and five B-0s, it
also received six Ju 86C-1s, two Ju 86Z-2s and the Ju 86 V24, to
make a total of sixteen altogether. By 1937 they were serving
on 18 Lufthansa routes, and the Ju 86 fleet remained in service
until 1939. In 1940 it was disposed of, probably for use by the
Luftwaffe. The C-1 version retained the Jumo 205C powerplant, but featured an extended rear fuselage. The 'Z' designation suffix for civil variants, introduced in 1936, was
allocated to three models: the Jumo-engined Z-1 (corresponding to the former B-0 or C-1), sold to Swissair (one, as
described above), Airlines of Australia (one) and LAN-Chile
(three); the BMW 132H-engined Z-2 for Lufthansa (two) and the
para-military Manchuria Air Transport (five or more); and the
Hornet-engined Z-7, delivered to AB Aerotransport of
Sweden (one, for use on mail services), Lloyd Aereo Boliviano
(three) and South African Airways (seventeen). The ABA aircraft was later transferred to the Swedish Air Force, with
which it served, under the designation Tp 9, until 1958. SAA's
original intention had been to have its Ju 86s powered by
745hp Rolls-Royce Kestrel Vee-type engines. Six aircraft for
SAA, flown with these engines, were refitted with Hornets
before being delivered, and the remainder also were Hornet-
powered. The fleet was impressed for service with the South
African Air Force in 1939, joining an eighteenth aircraft (a Ju
86K-1 bomber) already acquired by the SAAF for evaluation.
In addition to the forty-eight known airline examples described above, at least ten other Ju 86s bore German civil
registrations. Some were military development aircraft, but

96

Junkers Ju 86

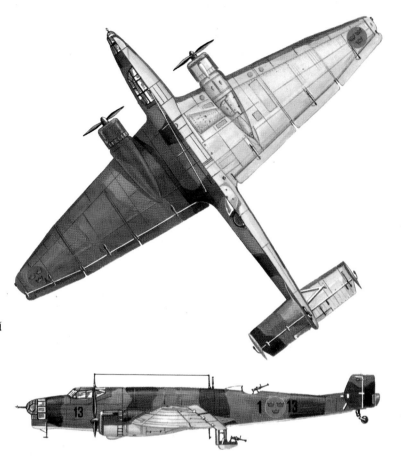

Junkers Ju 86K-4 (B 3A) of F1 Wing Royal
Swedish Air Force, Västeras *ca* autumn 1938

Engines: Two 820hp Swedish-built Bristol
  Mercury III 9-cylinder radials
Span: 73ft 9in (22·48m)
Length: 58ft 8in (17·88m)
Height: 15ft 8¼in (4·78m)
Take-off weight: 18,078lb (8,200kg)
Maximum speed: 224mph (360km/hr) at
  13,125ft (4,000m)
Operational ceiling: 22,965ft (7,000m)
Maximum range: 1,243 miles (2,000km)
Armament: Three 7·9mm MG 15
  machine-guns, one each in nose and
  dorsal positions and one in ventral
  'dustbin'; up to 2,205lb (1,000kg) of
  bombs internally

they included three owned by Hansa Luftbild, an aerial photography company, and D-AXEQ, a Ju 86A Junkers demonstrator. The Ju 86 was a contemporary of the He 111, both aircraft being designed in 1934 to a joint military and civil requirement for a multi-engined aircraft capable of serving both as a bomber and as a commercial transport. Five prototypes were ordered initially, of which the first made its maiden flight on 4 November 1934, powered by two Siemens radial engines pending the availability of the Junkers Jumo 205 engines for which it had been designed. These were installed in the Ju 86V2 (D-ABUK), which flew for the first time in April 1935. A pre-series batch of thirteen Ju 86-A-0s, for service trials, was followed by the first deliveries of the Ju 86A-1 model to KG 152 in May/June 1936. These aircraft (about twenty of which were built) had 600hp Jumo 205C-4 engines and an internal bomb load of 1,764lb (800kg). From the A model was developed the Ju 86D-1 (the B and C series having been commercial transports), with increased fuel capacity and an extended fuselage tail-cone to improve stability; but the Jumo engine proved to be unsuitable for the type of operations the bomber was to perform. Installation of the Pratt & Whitney Hornet radial engine or its German licence-built counterpart, the 810hp BMW 132F, in two Ju 86Ds led to the adoption of a version with the latter engines (the Ju 86E) to supersede the D model in production. The Ju 86E began to enter service in the late summer of 1937; about fifty were built, some of them with 865hp BMW 132N engines. A further forty aircraft, begun as Ju 86Es, were

completed as Ju 86Gs, having redesigned front fuselages with the cockpit further forward to improve the pilot's view for take-off or landing. From the autumn of 1938 (when there were two hundred and thirty-five Ju 86A/D/E/G bombers in service) the type began to be withdrawn from first-line *Luftwaffe* units in favour of the He 111 and Do 17. However, before this, the aircraft had also been the subject of foreign military orders. Three Hornet-engined bombers (designated Ju 86K-1) were evaluated by Sweden in the winter of 1936-37, these trials beings followed by the delivery of twenty (designated B 3A) with Swedish-built Bristol Pegasus III engines and a further seventeen (B 3B) with Pegasus XIIs. The German designations for these were Ju 86K-4 and K-5 respectively. The Swedish Saab company then built under licence sixteen Ju 86K-13s, these being either B 3Cs (with Pegasus XXIV engines) or B 3Ds (Pegasus XIX). Small batches of Hornet-engined Ju 86Ks were also supplied to Chile and Portugal, and twenty-four with 870hp Gnome-Rhône 14K-series engines were built under licence in Hungary; in addition, eighteen Ju 86 airliners of the South African Airways fleet were taken over by the SAAF in 1939 and re-equipped as bombers. After the outbreak of World War 2 Junkers evolved the Ju 86P, a high-altitude bomber and photographic reconnaissance version with redesigned nose, extended-span wings and Jumo 207A engines; and the Ju 86R, which had a further-increased wing span and 1,000hp Jumo 207B engines. Most P and R series aircraft were produced by converting existing airframes of earlier models.

Focke-Wulf Fw 61

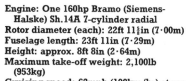

Focke-Wulf Fw 61V12, 1937

Engine: One 160hp Bramo (Siemens-Halske) Sh.14A 7-cylinder radial
Rotor diameter (each): 22ft 11½in (7·00m)
Fuselage length: 23ft 11in (7·29m)
Height: approx. 8ft 8in (2·64m)
Maximum take-off weight: 2,100lb (953kg)
Cruising speed: 62mph (100km/hr) at sea level
Operational ceiling: 8,600ft (2,620m)
Range: 143 miles (230km)

As a class of vehicle the helicopter had no single inventor, any more than the fixed-wing aeroplane did. Much of the credit for the modern helicopter goes, deservedly, to Igor Sikorsky; but in Britain, France, Italy, Germany and the USSR contemporaries of Sikorsky all produced significant designs well before the historic VS-300 had left the ground. High on the short list of helicopter pioneers must come the name of Professor Henrich Karl Johann Focke, whose Fw 61 made its first free flight, lasting 45 seconds, on 26 June 1936. This was, coincidentally, exactly one year after the less publicised flight of the Breguet-Dorand machine, which can thus claim to have been the first really practical helicopter to have flown in Europe. But the Fw 61, once it had begun to fly, rapidly proved itself a much superior machine to the Breguet, not only as regards performance but as a practical basic design capable of much further development. Focke's first experience of rotorcraft construction and operation was gained from building the Cierva C.19 and C.30 Autogiros under licence, and then in 1934 he built and flew successfully a scale model helicopter that rose to a height of some 18m (59ft). There followed a period of research into, and testing of, rotor and transmission systems before, in 1936, the Fw 61 prototype made its appearance. Registered D-EBVU, the Fw 61V1 utilised the fuselage and Sh.14A engine of a Focke-Wulf Fw 44 Stieglitz basic trainer, with the tailplane mounted on top of the fin and the propeller cut down to the diameter of the engine cylinders to serve purely as a cooling fan. It gave no assistance to the aircraft in forward flight, though its presence may have led the Hungarian engineer von Asboth to believe that the Fw 61 was really an autogyro, for he vehemently challenged the helicopter records (see below) set up by the German machine. Focke confirmed, however,

that not only were these all genuine helicopter flights, but that every landing was made vertically. The twin rotors, mounted on steel-tube outriggers on either side of the cabin, were fully articulated 3-blade assemblies whose blade angle could be increased or decreased so as to provide lateral movement of the aeroplane by creating a lift differential between one side and the other. In May 1937, some months before a similar feat was accomplished by the Breguet-Dorand helicopter, the Fw 61 made its first landing using autorotation, and in February 1938 the aircraft's controllability was convincingly demonstrated by Germany's celebrated aviatrix Hanna Reitsch, who flew the machine inside the Deutschlandhalle sports stadium in Berlin. Meanwhile a second prototype, D-EKRA, had been completed, and from mid-1937 the Fw 61 established the following list of FAI world records for helicopters: 25/26 June 1937 (pilot Ewald Rohlfs): 2,439m (8,001·95ft) altitude; 1hr 20min 49sec endurance; 80·604km (50·085 miles) distance in a closed circuit; 122·553km/hr (76·151 mph) speed over a 20km closed circuit; 16·40km (10·19miles) distance in a straight line. 25 October 1937 (pilot Hanna Reitsch): 108·974km (67·713 miles) distance in a straight line. 19 June 1938 (pilot Karl Bode): 230·248km (143·069 miles) distance in a straight line. 29 January 1939 (pilot Karl Bode) 3,427m (11,243.44ft) altitude. Before any of these were established, Prof Focke had left to form the Focke-Achgelis company to develop Fw 61 derivatives. The obvious promise in the Fw 61's basic design led to a development contract for a 6-passenger aerial taxi helicopter, the Fa 266 for Deutsche Lufthansa. War intervened, however, before this machine could be flown, and it was subsequently developed for a military role with the type number Fa 223 (See page 129).

Henschel Hs 123

Henschel Hs 123A-1 of 8/SG.1 Eastern Front, spring 1942

Engine: One 880hp BMW 132Dc radial
Span: 34ft 5⅜in (10·50m)
Length: 27ft 4in (8·33m)
Height: 10ft 6⅜in (3·21m)
Normal take-off weight: 4,894lb (2,220kg)
Maximum speed: 211mph (340km/hr) at 3,940ft (1,200m)
Operational ceiling: 29,530ft (9,000m)
Maximum range: 534 miles (860km)
Armament: Two 7·9mm MG 17 machine-guns in upper engine cowling; provision for two 20mm MG FF cannon, four 110lb (50kg) bombs or canisters of smaller bombs beneath lower wings

The Henschel Hs 123, the *Luftwaffe's* first production dive bomber (and also its last combat biplane), first flew in the spring of 1935 , making its public debut on 8 May in the hands of General Ernst Udet, the man primarily responsible for its existence. Two of the first three prototypes broke up during high-speed diving tests, but the structural weaknesses were successfully eliminated in the Hs 123V4, which underwent service trials in the autumn of 1935. Apart from the substitution of the more powerful BMW 132Dc radial for the 650hp BMW 132A-3 of the prototypes, the Hs 123A-1 production model differed little from the V4, and began to enter service with *Luftwaffe* units in mid-1936. In December, five Hs 123s were despatched to Spain to join the Condor Legion and gain genuine battle experience. Others followed in 1938 and, in the event, were used in Spain more for ground-attack duties than for dive-bombing, proving notably successful in their changed role. The decision of the *Luftwaffe* to standardise on the Ju 87 for dive-bombing led to the cessation of Hs 123 production in the autumn of 1938 after only a comparatively small number (by current German standards) had been produced. By 1939 the Hs 123 was virtually obsolete by world standards, but in the early campaigns in Poland, France and the USSR, where the *Luftwaffe's* air superiority provided a protective umbrella for its activities, it continued to be used with marked success as a close-support aircraft and did not finally disappear from combat units until the summer of 1944; after this it was utilised chiefly for supply dropping or glider towing. Prototypes were flown before the war for proposed Hs 123B and C models, the former with a 960hp BMW 132K engine and the latter a specialised ground-attack version with two extra guns mounted in the wings; but neither of these went into production.

Dornier Do 18, Do 24 and Do 26

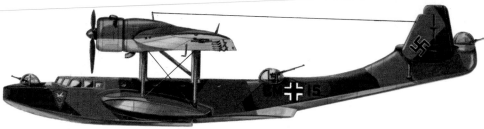

Dornier Do 18D of the 2nd Staffel,
K.Fl.Gr.506, *Luftwaffe* 1938

Engines: Two 600hp Junkers Jumo 205C
  six-cylinder double-opposed diesels
Span: 77ft 9in (23·70m)
Length: 63ft 1½in (19·25m)
Wing area: 1,054·9sq ft (98sq m)
Maximum take-off weight
  (Do 18G): 23,810lb (10,800kg)
Maximum speed (Do 18G): 165mph
  (265km/hr) at 6,560ft (2,000m)
Operational ceiling (Do 18G): 13,780ft
  (4,200m)
Range (Do 18G): 2,175 miles (3,500km)

Continuing in the same basic configuration as the Wal, from which it was developed, the Dornier Do 18 originated in a DLH requirement of 1934 for a replacement for the former type on the German airline's mail routes across the Atlantic. The first of three prototypes (D-AHIS *Monsun*, D-AANE *Zyklon* and D-ABYM *Aeolus*) made its initial flight on 15 March 1935; all three, with two other essentially similar aircraft (D-AROZ *Pampero* and D-ARUN *Zephir*), were delivered to the airline under the collective designation Do 18E. The standard powerplant comprised two tandem-mounted 600hp Junkers Jumo 205C engines, although the Do 18V1 had been fitted originally with 540hp Jumo 5s. The Do 18Es entered service with Deutsche Luft Hansa in the autumn of 1936 over the North Atlantic route to New York, but were later switched to the South Atlantic service to Brazil, on which they continued until the outbreak of World War 2 (except for *Pampero*, lost in October 1938). A sixth civil machine was also delivered. This was the unnamed D-ANHR, first flown in June 1937 and intended for experimental rather than scheduled flights. It was designated Do 18F, and had enlarged wings with a span of 86ft 3½in (26·30m) and area of 1,196·95sq ft (111·2sq m). On 27–29 March 1938 the Do 18F set a new seaplane record for distance flown in a straight line, when it flew 5,215 miles (8,392km) from the English Channel to Caravellas in Brazil. It was later re-engined, making its first flight on 21 November 1939 as the Do 18L with a pair of 880hp BMW 132N radial engines. Major production of the Do 18, however, was for the *Luftwaffe*, for whom the first model was the Do 18D, which entered service in 1938. In dimensions and powerplant

this was essentially similar to the E model, but carried a four-man crew and a defensive armament of two 7·9mm machine-guns, one each in open positions in the bow and mid-upper fuselage. Four 110lb (50kg) bombs could be carried beneath the outer wing panels. It was built in Do 18D-0 (pre-production), D-1 and D-2 versions, which were superseded in production in 1939 by the Do 18G-1. The G model, though dimensionally similar to the D, had more powerful (880hp) Jumo 205D engines, a 13mm MG 131 gun in the bow, and the dorsal gun replaced by an enclosed turret mounting a 20mm MG 151 cannon. Some G-1s were later converted (as Do 18N-1s) for air/sea rescue, and an unarmed training version was produced as the Do 18H-1. Overall Do 18 production, including prototypes and civil examples, totalled slightly more than one hundred. A broadly similar structural layout was followed in the Do 24, designed in 1935 to the requirements of the Royal Netherlands Naval Air Service for use in the East Indies. The major design changes were apparent in the power installation and tail assembly, the Do 24 having three radial engines mounted separately in the wing leading-edge, and twin fins and rudders. Three prototypes were completed, of which the first to fly, on 3 July 1937, was the Do 24V3, powered by 890hp Wright Cyclone radial engines. The Do 24V1 and V2 had 600hp Jumo 205C diesel engines, but the Cyclone was chosen for the eleven initial production aircraft. These, designated Do 24K, were delivered to the Dutch government from 1938, joining the Do 24V3 which had been handed over in the previous year.

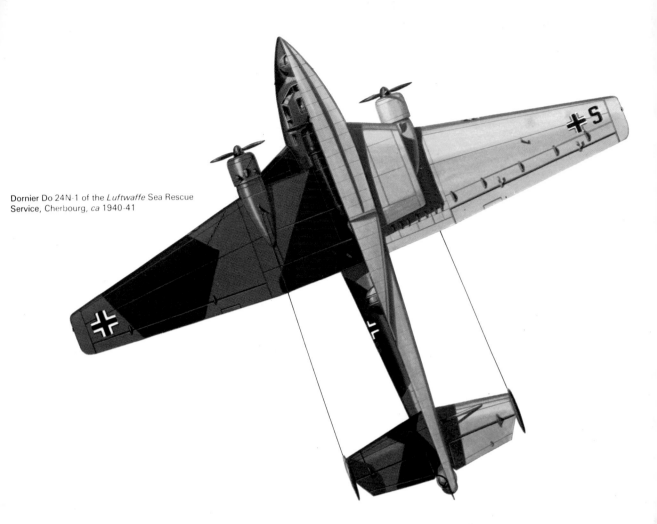

Dornier Do 24N-1 of the *Luftwaffe* Sea Rescue
Service, Cherbourg, *ca* 1940-41

The Aviolanda and de Schelde factories in Holland then
continued to build the type under licence, twenty five (of
forty-eight ordered) having been completed before Holland
was overrun by the Nazis in 1940. Several were casualties
during the early months of the war in the Pacific, but others
escaped to Australia and were employed by the RAAF. Those
Do 24Ks unfinished when Holland was invaded were completed in Germany and operated by the *Luftwaffe* as Do 24N-1
air/sea rescue flying-boats. After the occupation of Holland
and France production continued with Do 24T-1 reconnaissance and Do 24T-2 transport models (1,000hp Bramo 323R-2
radial engines, mostly for the *Luftwaffe*; one hundred and
fifty-four were built in Holland and forty-eight at the CAMS
plant in Occupied France. After the German withdrawal
twenty-two of the latter aircraft were delivered to the
Aéronavale and operated by *Flottille* 9F (later renamed
Escadrille 30S). One Do 24T, interned during the war, was
operated under the designation Tp 24 by the Royal Swedish
Air Force until 1951, when it was claimed by the USSR as spoils
of war. The Spanish government purchased twelve Do24Ts in
1944, and in 1953 acquired a further number after their retire-
ment from service with the French Navy. Armament of the
Do 24T-1 consisted of a 20mm MG 151 cannon in a dorsal
turret and single 7·9mm MG 15 guns in the nose and tail; up to
twelve 110lb (50kg) bombs could be carried externally. The
Dornier Do 26, which combined many advanced structural
and aerodynamic features with the best aspects of the Do 18
and Do 24, did not reach the production stage, and its six

prototypes proved to be the last flying-boats manufactured by
the German company. Like the Do 18, the Do 26 was evolved
originally as a trans-Atlantic mail carrier for DLH. It had
cantilever gull wings, with four 600hp Jumo 205E engines in
tandem pairs, and the extension shafts which drove the two
pusher propellers could be elevated 10 degrees during take-
off to raise the propeller blades clear of spray. Retractable
stabilising floats were located approximately at mid-span,
replacing the hull sponsons which had performed this function in earlier designs. Three civil-registered prototypes were
completed (D-AGNT *Seeadler*, D-AWDS *Seefalke* and
D-ASRA *Seemöwe*), and the first of these made its maiden
flight on 21 May 1938. The first two aircraft, which carried a
mail payload only, were operated by the airline across the
South Atlantic under the collective designation Do 26A; the
third, which seated four passengers, was intended as a Do 26B
production prototype. The outbreak of war, however, caused
it instead to be converted for the *Luftwaffe* as a transport/
reconnaissance aircraft with an armament of three 7·9mm
MG 15 guns (two in waist blisters and one in the rear floor of
the hull) and one 20mm MG 151 cannon in a bow turret. The
Do 26V4 to V6, which had 700hp Jumo 205Ea engines and
were intended as Do 26C prototypes, underwent similar conversion as 10/12-seat transports. All six Do 26s (as well as the
Do 24V1 and V2) were employed operationally during the
German invasion of Norway, during which two of them were
destroyed; the survivors continued for as long as spares were
available and then withdrawn.

Arado Ar 68

Arado Ar 68F of *Staffel* 2, I/JG 131 at Jesau, *ca* late 1936

**Engine: One 675hp BMW VI 12-cylinder
    Vee type**
Span: 36ft 1in (11·00m)
Length: 31ft 2½in (9·50m)
Height: 10ft 10in (3·30m)
**Maximum take-off weight: 4,409lb
    (2,000kg)**
**Maximum speed: 205mph (330km/hr) at
    sea level**
Operational ceiling: 24,280ft (7,400m)
Range: 311 miles (500km)
**Armament: Two 7·9mm MG 17 machine-
    guns in upper front fuselage**

The Ar 68 was the second major biplane fighter to go into service with Hitler's *Luftwaffe*. It flew for the first time in 1934, having been redesigned by Ing Rethel of Arado as a replacement for the unpopular Heinkel He 51. Five prototypes were completed, the first (D-IKIN) and fourth machines each being powered by a 750hp BMW VI engine and the remainder by the 610hp Junkers Jumo 210A. Despite its lower power, the latter engine conferred a much better performance, and it was hoped to instal this in the first series production version, the Ar 68E. In the event, however, development and delivery delays of the Jumo resulted in the BMW-powered Ar 68F being produced first, to bridge the gap until the Ar 68E became available. Deliveries of the Ar 68F began at the end of 1936, but a comparatively small number were built, supplies of Jumo 210D and 210E engines permitting the first deliveries of Ar 68E fighters to be made in the following spring. At about this time the new Bf 109 monoplane fighter was undergoing service trials, but this did not immediately spell the foreseeable end of the Ar 68's front-line career. Indeed, a number were still in *Luftwaffe* service at the outbreak of World War 2, when some were pressed into use as emergency night fighters, although by that time most Ar 68s had been transferred to a training role. The Ar 68E and F remained the only series-built variants, but two other experimental models were designed. These were the Ar 68G, a projected high-altitude version abandoned for lack of a suitable powerplant, and the Ar 68H. The latter was a much-modified development, with an enclosed cockpit, four machine-guns instead of the normal two, and an 850hp BMW 132 radial engine. Its performance was more than satisfactory, but by then the Bf 109 had established itself as the *Luftwaffe*'s standard fighter type and the Ar 68H was not produced in quantity. The Ar 167, which appeared in 1937, was evolved from the basic Ar 68 design for use aboard the German aircraft carrier *Graf Zeppelin*, but development was abandoned after only three prototypes (one with a Jumo 210 engine and two with BMW 132s) had been completed.

Junkers Ju 87

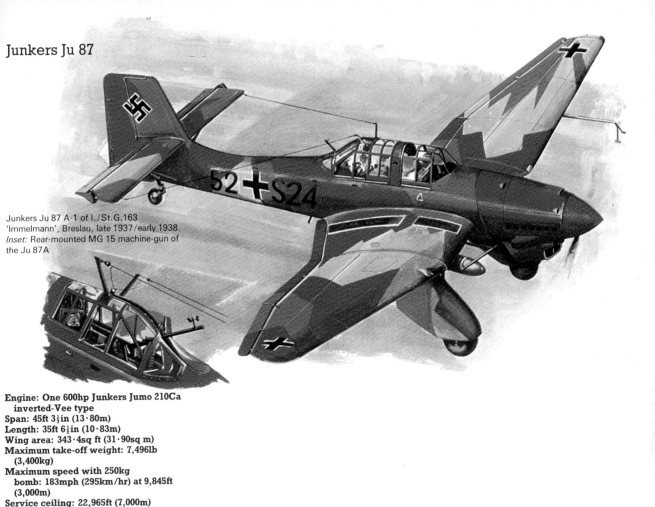

Junkers Ju 87 A-1 of I./St.G.163
'Immelmann', Breslau, late 1937/early 1938.
Inset: Rear-mounted MG 15 machine-gun of
the Ju 87A

Engine: One 600hp Junkers Jumo 210Ca
    inverted-Vee type
Span: 45ft 3½in (13·80m)
Length: 35ft 6½in (10·83m)
Wing area: 343·4sq ft (31·90sq m)
Maximum take-off weight: 7,496lb
    (3,400kg)
**Maximum speed with 250kg
    bomb:** 183mph (295km/hr) at 9,845ft
    (3,000m)
Service ceiling: 22,965ft (7,000m)
Maximum range: 621 miles (1,000km)

In the mid-1940s the McDonnell Aircraft Company in the USA built a carrier-based jet fighter which it named the Banshee. It is a name that might with considerably greater aptness have been bestowed upon a much less attractive warplane of a decade earlier; but the Junkers Ju 87 gave rise to a name of its own that was to have far more terrifying connotations to millions of Europeans. For the Ju 87 was a Sturzkampf-flugzeug, the German word for dive-bomber, and with deadly effect it was to personify the stern 'Stuka' for the rest of its career. Development of the dive-bomber in Germany was fostered by Ernst Udet, after seeing a demonstration by the American Curtiss Helldiver in 1933, and the Ju 87, designed by Dipl Ing Hans Pohlmann of Junkers, made its first flight in the early part of 1935. Even today it would still be in any 'top ten' awards for ugliness, but beauty was hardly its business. To put it as generously as possible, its design was strictly functional, and there is no doubt that this objective was achieved. The initial Ju 87A version, blooded in the Spanish Civil War from December 1937, was soon superseded by the improved Ju 87B with (though it may not have looked like it) aerodynamic improvements and a substantially more power

ful engine. Able to carry up to 1,000kg of bombs, according to version, the Ju 87B also was fitted with small sirens near the tops of the main undercarriage leg fairings, to add a devastating and demoralising scream to the whine of its engine and the whistle of its falling bombs. Hailed as the 'supreme weapon' by the German propaganda machine, it did indeed appear to justify this title as it screamed and bombed its way through Poland, Norway, France and the Low Countries during World War 2, against little or no effective fighter opposition. Then, at Dunkirk and in the Battle of Britain, it came up against the Hurricane and Spitfire – and was quickly proved to be clumsy, poorly armed and extremely vulnerable. Before the end of August 1940 it had been withdrawn from major operations against Britain, though later, in conditions more favourable to it, it succeeded again in Greece, in Crete and on the Russian Front. But the 'supreme weapon' myth had by then been exploded, and even its quite successful use as a tank-buster (Ju 87D) and anti-shipping aircraft (Ju 87R) was not enough to restore fully its tarnished reputation. (*continued on page 106*)

Junkers Ju 87G-1 of 10.(Pz)/St G1, Eastern Front, October 1943

Gruppe emblem of **I./St G 1**

Emblem of **10.(Pz)/St G 1**

Junkers Ju 87B-2/Trop. (A5 + HL) of 3./St G1, Libya, late 1941

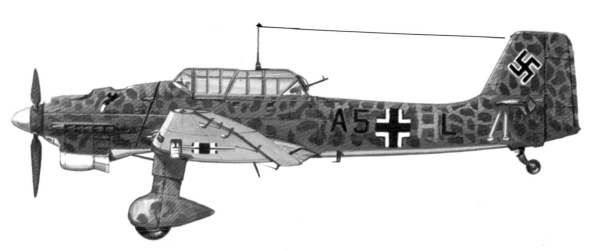

Junkers Ju 87B-2 (A5 + KH) of 1./St G 2,
Polish campaign, September 1939

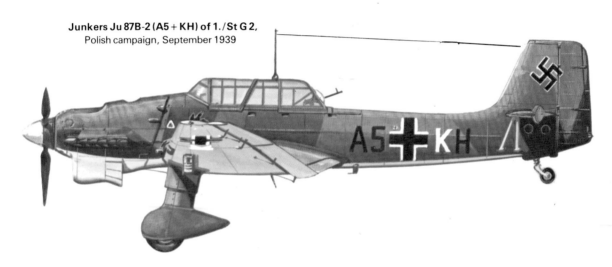

Junkers Ju 87D-1/Trop. (S7 + AA) of St G 3, Libya, June 1942 (aircraft of the Geschwaderkommodore,
Oberstleutnant Walter Sigel)

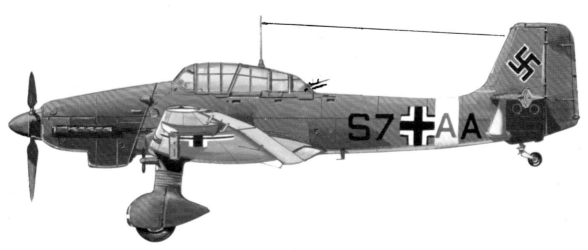

Junkers Ju 87B-1 of *Geschwader Stab/St. G. 2 "Immelmann"*, France, *ca* summer 1940

Engine: One 900hp Junkers Jumo 211A-1
    inverted-Vee type
Span: 45ft 3¼in (13·80m)
Length: 36ft 5in (11·10m)
Height: 12ft 8½in (3·87m)
Normal take-off weight: 9,370lb (4,250kg)
Maximum speed: 242mph (390km/hr) at
    13,410ft (4,400m)
Operational ceiling: 26,250ft (8,000m)
Range with 1,102lb (500kg) bomb
    load: 342 miles (550km)
Armament: One 7·9mm MG 17 machine-
    gun in each wing and one 7·9mm
    MG 15 gun in rear of cabin; one 1,102lb
    (500kg) or 551lb (250kg) bomb beneath

fuselage and up to four 110lb (50kg)
bombs beneath the wings

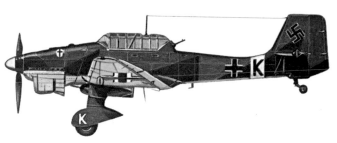

The United States and Germany, in particular, were enthusiastic proponents of the dive bomber during the later 1930s and the early part of World War 2. This particular species of warplane seemed to be typified in the Ju 87, whose ugly lines and wailing engine struck an especial note of terror in the skies above Poland, France and the Low Countries in 1939–40. Design of the Ju 87, by Dipl-Ing Pohlmann, started in 1933, and the first prototype flew early in 1935. This was powered by a Rolls-Royce Kestrel engine and had rectangular twin fins and rudders, but the Ju 87V2, flown in the following autumn, had a single tail and a 610hp Junkers Jumo 210A engine, and was more representative of the production aircraft to follow. A pre-series batch of Ju 87A-0s was started in 1936, and in the spring of 1937 delivery began of the Ju 87A-1 initial production model, followed by the generally similar A-2. About two hundred A series were built before, in the autumn of 1938, there appeared the much-modified Ju 87B. Powered by the Jumo 211, this had an enlarged vertical tail, redesigned crew canopy and new-style cantilever fairings over the main legs of the landing gear. Both the A and B models were sent for service with the Condor Legion in Spain in 1938, but by the outbreak of World War 2 the A series had been relegated to

the training role, and the three hundred and thirty-six aircraft in front-line service were all Ju 87B-1s. The fighter superiority of the *Luftwaffe* ensured the Ju 87 a comparatively uninterrupted passage in 1939–40, but opposition during the Battle of Britain was much sterner, and losses of the Ju 87 were considerably heavier. Nevertheless, production of the B series continued into 1941, and substantial numbers were supplied to the *Regia Aeronautica*, and to the air forces of Bulgaria, Hungary and Romania. In production alongside the B series was the long-range Ju 87R, which from 1940 was used for anti-shipping and other missions. Before the war small numbers were also completed of the Ju 87C, a version of the B with arrester hook, folding wings and other 'navalised' attributes. This was planned for service aboard the carrier *Graf Zeppelin*, but the ship was never completed, and the few Ju 87C-0s built served with a land-based unit. Others laid down as C-1s were completed as B-2s. After the setbacks in the Battle of Britain the Ju 87B continued to serve in the Mediterranean and North Africa. Its subsequent development and employment was mainly in the close-support role or as a trainer. Next major variant was the Ju 87D, whose evolution had begun in 1940. Several sub-types of this model

Junkers Ju 87D-3 of 2/St. G. 77, Eastern
Front summer 1943

Engine: One 1,400hp Junkers Jumo 211J-1
  inverted-Vee type
Span: 45ft 3½in (13·80m)
Length: 37ft 8¾in (11·50m)
Height: 12ft 9½in (3·89m)
Maximum take-off weight: 14,550lb
  (6,600kg)
Maximum speed: 255mph (410km/hr) at
  13,500ft (4,115m)
Operational ceiling: 15,520ft (4,730m)
Maximum range: 954 miles (1,535km)
Armament: One 7·9mm MG 17 machine-
  gun in each wing and two 7·9mm
  MG 81 guns in rear cockpit; typical
  warload of one 1,102lb (500kg) bomb

beneath fuselage and one pack of
ninety-two 4·4lb (2kg) SC-2 anti-
personnel bombs beneath each wing

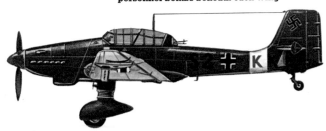

were built, their chief characteristics being the use of a more powerful Jumo engine, increased fuel tankage similar to that of the Ju 87R, and a considerably refined airframe with reinforced armament and extra armour protection for the crew. Most D variants were evolved for a ground-attack role, and could carry a variety of different weapon loads ranging from a single 3,968lb (1,800kg) bomb beneath the fuselage to a pair of underwing pods each containing six 7·9mm machine-guns. The dive brakes fitted to the earlier Ju 87s were usually omitted. The Ju 87D-5 introduced an extended wing of 49ft 2½in (15·00m) span, and the D-7 was a specialised night-attack version. Variants of the Ju 87D served in the Mediterranean, North Africa and on the Eastern Front, equipping units of the Hungarian and Romanian air forces as well as those of the *Luftwaffe*. Proposals to replace the D model by developments of it designated Ju 87F and Ju 187 were abandoned in 1943, but

one other variant was encountered operationally. This was the Ju 87G, which entered service in 1943 as an anti-tank aeroplane with a 37mm BK 3.7 cannon mounted in a stream-lined fairing attached beneath each wing. These could be replaced by bombs for more general ground-attack missions. The Ju 87G was essentially a conversion of the long-span D-5, and aircraft of this type were quite successful in knocking out Soviet tanks along the Eastern Front until the appearance of better-class Soviet fighter opposition in the autumn of 1944. Operational trainers for pilots engaged in ground-attack work were produced, under the designation Ju 87H, by converting various D sub-series to have dual controls and modified cock-pit hoods. When production of the Ju 87 series finally ended in September 1944, more than five thousand seven hundred of these aircraft had been built.

Dornier Do 17, Do 215 and Do 217

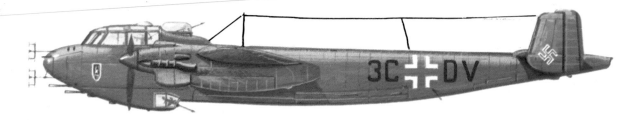

Dornier Do 217N-1 (3C + DV) of 11./NJG 4, France, 1943

Gruppe emblem of
III./KG 255

Gruppe emblem of
III./KG 2

Emblem of **Geschwader
Stab./KG 3**

Dornier Do 17Z-2 (U5 + DL) of 3./KG 2 'Holzhammer', Balkans theatre, spring 1941

Dornier Do 217K-1 (Z6 + BH) of I./KG 66, Chartres, summer 1943

Spectators watching the International Military Aircraft Competition at Zurich in July 1937 were duly impressed, as well they might have been – and were no doubt meant to be – when the Circuit of the Alps event was won by a twin-engined German bomber that outstripped in performance every single-engined fighter racing against it. What they did not know, then, was that they were watching the eighth prototype of a design that had first flown nearly three years previously and was already entering service with the still-new Luftwaffe. One other point unknown to the Zürich spectators was that the top speed of 276mph (444km/hr) shown by the V8 prototype was some 56mph (90km/hr) better than that of the Do 17E then entering Luftwaffe service, thanks to various aerodynamic refinements and the use of DB 600A engines instead of the 750hp BMW VIs of the Do 17E. Three prototypes of the Do 17, each with a single fin and rudder, were built originally as six-passenger high-speed mailplanes for DLH, the Do 17 V1 making its first flight in autumn 1934. DLH turned it down; but the RLM, in search of a new medium bomber, ordered additional prototypes, the first of these (the Do 17 V4) having twin fins and rudders and a shorter fuselage. The V4, V6 and V7 were powered, like the V1 to V3, with two 660hp Vee-type BMW VI, while the V5 had 775hp Hispano-Suiza 12 Ybrs engines. The specially-stripped V8, with 1,000hp boosted DB 600A engines, outclassed even the best single-seat fighters

when it appeared at the Zürich International Military Aircraft Competition in July 1937, but by this time the Do 17E-1 bomber and F-1 reconnaissance models, based on the V9, were already in production and service, the first recipients being units of KG 153 and KG 155. Both had 750hp BMW VI 7·3 engines, and the former a short-range internal bomb load of 750kg (1,653lb). While these early versions took part in the Spanish Civil War, the Yugoslav government, also impressed by the V8's performance at Zürich, ordered 20 export Do 17Ks with 980hp Gnome-Rhône 14 N radial engines, improved speed and range, and a 1,000kg (2,205lb) internal weapon load. Luftwaffe production meanwhile continued with the Do 17M bomber (900hp Bramo 323A-1 supercharged radials), based on the V8, and Do 17P reconnaisance-bomber (865hp BMW 132Ns), which entered production from late 1937 as successors to the E and F. The experimental Do 17L, R and S appeared in 1937–38, and by September 1938 combined production of the Do 17E, F, M and P for the Luftwaffe had reached 580. After a few Do 17Us, a pathfinder version with DB 600A engines, came the Do 17Z, the most numerous model, of which about 525 were built with Bramo 323 A-1 or 1,000hp Bramo 323P engines. Production of the Do 17 (about 1,200 of all models) ended in mid-1940. On 2 December 1939 the Luftwaffe had 493 Do 17s on strength; 352 of these were Do 17Zs, most of them probably Z-2 bombers. A small number of

(continued on page 113)

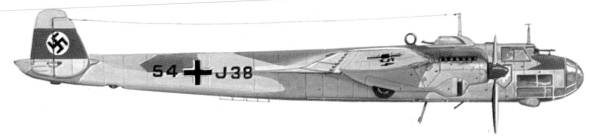

Dornier Do 17 E-1 of 8. 1 KG 255,
Memmingen, *ca* 1938.

Engines: Two 750hp BMW VI radials
Span: 59ft 0⅝in (18·00m)
Length: 53ft 3⅓in (16·25m)
Wing area: 592·0sq ft (55·00sq m)
Maximum take-off weight: 15,250lb
  (7,040kg)
Maximum speed: 220mph (354km/hr) at
  sea level
Service ceiling: 16,730ft (5,100m)
Operational radius: 311 miles (500km)

In July 1937 the Do 17 made a spectacular public debut at the International Military Aircraft Competition at Zurich, when it completely overshadowed in performance the French Dewoitine D 510, then regarded widely as the best single-seat fighter being built in Europe – although by this time Germany's own Messerschmitt Bf 109 fighter was also entering production.

The Do 217E entered production in 1941 following service trials with a small pre-series batch of Do 217A-0s in the preceding year. Numerous E sub-types appeared, powered by various models of the BMW 801 radial engine and differing in armament and other equipment. The Do 217E-5 carried additional radio gear for launching and guiding two underwing Hs 293 missiles. Many E-2s later became Do 217J night fighters.

Dornier Do 217E-2 of 5/KG.6, France, early 1943

Engines: Two 1,580hp BMW 801M
  radials
Span: 62ft 4in (19·00m)
Length: 56ft 9⅓in (17·30m)
Height: 16ft 4⅞in (5·00m)
Normal take-off weight: 33,069lb
  (15,000kg)
Maximum speed: 320mph (515km/hr) at
  17,060ft (5,200m)
Operational ceiling: 24,610ft (7,500m)
Maximum range: 1,429 miles (2,300km)
Armament: One 15mm MG 151 cannon in
  nose, one 13mm MG 131 machine-gun
  in dorsal turret and one in rear of
  under-nose cupola, one 7·9mm MG 15
gun in nose and one each side in rear of cabin; up to 5,512lb (2,500kg) of bombs internally and 3,307lb (1,500kg) externally

The Do 17 was an advanced bomber for its time, and the E and F initial production models duly underwent an operational blooding in the Spanish Civil War during 1937–39. They were superseded in service by the Do 17M and P series and finally by the Do 17Z. When production ended in 1940 about 1,200 Do 17s had been built, nearly half of these being Do 17Zs, the most numerous variant and the one most prominent in the Battle of Britain.

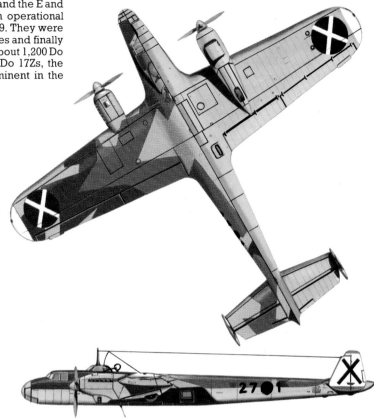

Dornier Do 17F-1 of *Aufklärungsstaffel*
1.A/88, Condor Legion, Spain October 1937

Engines: Two 750hp BMW VI 7·3
12-cylinder Vee type
Span: 59ft 0¾in (18·00m)
Length: 53ft 3¾in (16·25m)
Height: 14ft 2in (4·32m)
Take-off weight: 15,432lb (7,000kg)
Maximum speed: 222mph (357 km/hr) at sea level
Operational ceiling: 19,685ft (6,000m)
Maximum range: 1,274 miles (2,050km)
Armament: One 7·9mm MG 15 machine-gun at rear of crew cabin and one in lower front fuselage; up to 1,653lb (750kg) of bombs internally

In an attempt to overcome a severe shortage of specialised night fighters, the *Luftwaffe* in 1942 initiated the conversion of large numbers of Dornier 217 bombers to fulfil this function. Fundamentally, the airframe conversion entailed replacing the bulbous, glazed nose of the bomber with a more stream-lined 'solid' fairing containing additional guns.

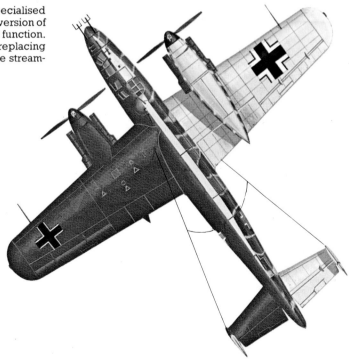

Dornier Do 217N-1 of an unidentified
Nachtjagdgeschwader, ca spring 1943

Armament: Four 20mm MG 151 cannon and four 7·9mm MG 17 machine-guns in fuselage nose, one 13mm MG 131 machine-gun in turret aft of cabin and one in rear of ventral cupola

A **Dornier Do 17Z-2 (U5 + AH) of Kampfgeschwader 2.** The Do 17Z was widely used during the campaigns in Poland, France and the Low Countries, and in the Battle of Britain

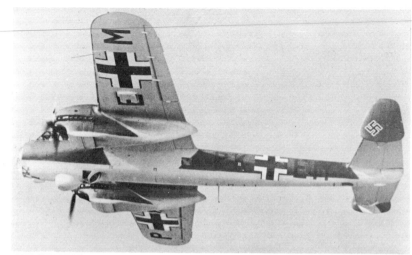

A **Do 215B-4 (PK + EM)** in factory markings. This reconnaissance version carried two aerial cameras, one of them in the 'chin' blister fairing

Dornier Do 217E-4/R19 (U5 + NT) in the markings of **KG 2 'Holzhammer'**. This model had BMW 801C engines and balloon cable-cutters on the wing leading-edges

An apparently hybrid **Do 217J** night fighter. Normally the J-1 had no Lichtenstein BC nose radar array, and the J-2 had no rear bomb bay, but this aircraft clearly has both

Z-3s were converted to Z-10 interim night fighters in 1940. Additional Do 17Ks had been built in 1939–40 by the Yugoslav state aircraft factory, and when Germany invaded that country in April 1941 there were 70 Do 17Ks in service with the Yugoslav Air Force. The few that survived the early fighting were allocated to the Croatian Air Force in early 1942. Two of the pre-production Do 17Z-0s, redesignated Do 215 V1 and V2, were turned into export demonstrators, powered respectively by Bramo and Gnome-Rhône 14 N engines. Only Sweden ordered the Do 215 (18 Do 215A-1s, with DB 601A engines), but these were commandeered before delivery by the Luftwaffe, which went on to order 101 Do 215Bs in several small series. Most of these were similar to one another except the B-5, a night fighter/intruder version with a six-gun 'solid' nose. By this time, however, mainstream development of the Do 17 was well advanced in the form of the Do 217. The first of many Do 217 prototypes flew in August 1938, outwardly resembling a slightly scaled-up Do 215B. All of the first six incorporated a novel four-leaf air brake, opening umbrella-style in operation and forming an extension of the rear fuselage when retracted. This feature proved troublesome to operate and was discarded on later models. Then came service trials with small batches of Do 217A-0s and C-0s preceding, in 1940, the first major series, the Do 217E. Numerous E sub-types appeared, powered by various models of the BMW 801 radial engine and differing primarily in armament and other equipment. The Do 217E-2, typically, carried up to 2,500kg (5,512lb) of bombs internally and a further 1,500kg (3,307lb) externally. It was armed with one 15mm MG 151 cannon and one 7·9mm MG 15 machine-gun in the nose; one MG 15 on each side at the rear of the cabin; and two 13mm MG 131 machine-guns—one in a dorsal turret and one in the rear of the under-nose gondola. The Do 217E-5 was a carrier for two underwing Hs 293A radio-controlled glider-bombs. In 1941–42, by which time virtually all Do 17/Do 215 units had re-equipped with Do 217s, the Luftwaffe began converting a number of Do 217 bombers for the night fighter role, the basic modification being to replace the bulbous, glazed nose with a more streamlined 'solid' one accommodating a battery of guns and, later, radar antennae. First subjects were 157 Do 217E-2s converted into Do 217J-1 intruders and J-2 night fighters, the latter with Lichtenstein BC radar. Both had four 20mm MG FF cannon and four 7·9mm MG 17 machine-guns in the nose, plus provision for one 13mm MG 131 ventral gun and another in the dorsal turret. The next bomber series, the Do 217K (1,700hp BMW 801D engines), featured a further-redesigned and even more bulbous nose than the E series. The K-2 and K-3 could carry anti-shipping weapons beneath extended-span (24·80m; 81ft 4·4in) wings. Vee-type engines—1,750hp DB 603As—appeared on the Do 217M bomber series, otherwise similar to the K-1; and on the Lichtenstein-equipped Do 217N-1 and N-2 night fighters which, in 1943, began replacing the J series. Fifty conversions from M to N were carried out. The final model was the Do 217P pressurised reconnaissance version, of which, however, only six development aircraft were built. Total Do 217 output, ending in June 1944, amounted to 1,905, of which all except 364 were bombers. The five Do 217Rs were in fact Do 317A-0 missile carriers, redesignated.

Aircraft type		Do 17Z-2	Do 217K-1	****Do 217N-1
Power plant		2 × 1,000 hp BMW-Bramo 323P	2 × 1,700 hp BMW 801D	2 × 1,750 hp DB 603A
Accommodation		4	4	4
Wing span	m : ft in	18·00 : 59 0·7	19·00 : 62 4·0	19·00 : 62 4·0
Length overall	m : ft in	15·79 : 51 9·7	16·98 : 55 8·5	18·90 : 62 0·1
Height overall	m : ft in	4·55 : 14 11·1	4·97 : 16 3·7	5·00 : 16 4·9
Wing area	m² : sq ft	55·00 : 592·01	57·00 : 613·54	57·00 : 613·54
Weight empty equipped	kg : lb	5,210 : 11,486	8,900 : 19,621	10,280 : 22,663
Weight loaded	kg : lb	8,590 : 18,937	16,580 : 36,553	13,200 : 29,101
Max wing loading	kg/m² : lb/sq ft	156·18 : 31·98	290·88 : 59·57	231·57 : 47·40
Max power loading	kg/hp : lb/hp	4·29 : 9·46	4·88 : 10·75	3·77 : 8·31
Max level speed	km/h : mph	360 : 224	515 : 320	515 : 320
at (height)	m : ft	4,000 : 13,125	4,000 : 13,125	6,000 : 19,685
Cruising speed	km/h : mph	300 : 186	400 : 248	425 : 264
at (height)	m : ft	4,000 : 13,125	4,000 : 13,125	5,400 : 17,715
Time to 1,000 m (3,280 ft)		3·3 min	3·5 min	3·0 min
Service ceiling	m : ft	7,000 : 22,965	8,200 : 26,905	8,900 : 29,200
Range	km : miles	*1,160 : 720	**2,300 : 1,429	***1,755 : 1,090

* with 500 kg (1,102 lb) bomb load and aux fuel   ** with max internal fuel   *** normal   **** weights and performance for N-2; N-1 similar

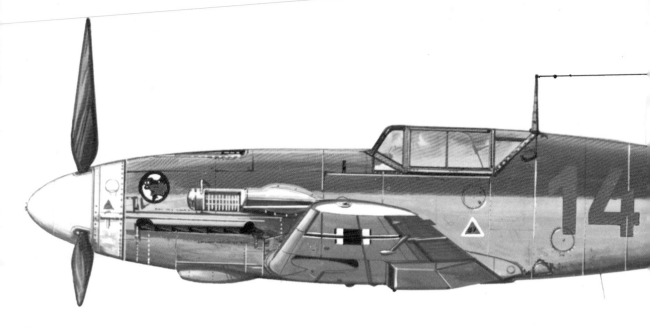

Messerschmitt Bf 109F-4/Trop. of 3./JG 27, Ain-El Gazala, Libya, mid-June 1942 (aircraft of the Staffelkapitän, Oberleutnant Hans-Joachim Marseille)

Geschwader emblem of **JG 51 'Mölders'**

Personal insignia of
Major Erich Hartmann

Messerschmitt Bf 109E-4/B of II./JG 54 'Grünherz', Eastern Front, 1942 (aircraft of the Geschwader Adjutant)

For 25 years the Bf 109 was in production somewhere in the world. It served the Luftwaffe for eight years, production during the years 1936–45 accounting for nearly two-thirds of Germany's entire output of single-seat fighters; and exported or licence-built versions equipped the air forces of nearly a dozen other nations. The total number built was well in excess of 33,000. Designed by the Bayerische Flugzeugwerke AG in 1933 around Germany's most powerful aero-engine of the time, the 610hp Junkers Jumo 210A, the Bf 109 V1 first prototype (D-IABI) actually made its first flight, on 28 May 1935, using a 695hp Rolls-Royce Kestrel V. A Jumo 210A powered the V2, which flew in January 1936, followed by the intended prototype for the initial production series, the V3. First in-service fighter versions were the Bf 109B-1 and B-2, based on the V4 and V7 prototypes and armed with two 7·9mm MG 17 machine-guns on top of the engine and a third MG 17 firing through the hollow propeller shaft. Deliveries of the B-1 (680hp Jumo 210Da) began in April 1937 to JG 132, which was dispatched to join the Luftwaffe's Condor Legion fighting in the Spanish Civil War. On 11 November 1937 the Bf 109 V13 (D-IPKY), with a specially boosted DB 601 engine, set a new world absolute speed record of 610·55km/h (379·38mph). Despite its successful combat record in Spain, the Bf 109B's armament left room for improvement, and the number of MG 17s was increased to four in the C-1 (two over the engine and two in the wings) and five in the C-3 (by restoring the centre gun). The Bf 109Cs, which had 700hp Jumo 210Ga engines, joined the Bs in Spain in 1938. In this year also, Arado, Erla, Fieseler, Focke-Wulf and WNF were brought into the Bf 109 production programme, and the BFW changed its name to Messerschmitt AG. Installation of the 986hp DB600Aa produced the Bf 109D series, with improved performance; small batches of Messerschmitt Bf 109Ds were also exported to Hungary and Switzerland. At the outbreak of World War 2 the Luftwaffe had a strength of 1,056 Bf 109s. Many of these were Bf 109Ds, but this series was already being replaced in increasing numbers by the Bf 109E. This had first appeared (as the V14) in mid-1938, and the E-1 was produced both as a fighter (with four MG 17s) and as a fighter-bomber (carrying one 250kg or four 50kg bombs). Later E-1s standardised on 20mm MG FF cannon in place of the two wing-mounted MG 17s. Against all types of opposing fighter throughout Poland, Czechoslovakia, France, Belgium, Holland and southern England, with the exception of the Spitfire (which it greatly outnumbered), the Bf 109E proved itself superior in both performance and manoeuvrability; only its range let it down. Production accelerated to the extent that Germany could afford to export substantial numbers of the Bf 109E-3 (which appeared at the end of 1939 and was the principal version to be used in the Battle of Britain) to Bulgaria, Hungary, Japan, Romania, Slovakia, Switzerland, the USSR and Yugoslavia. In addition, a small batch was built during 1941–43 by Dornier's Altenrhein factory in Switzerland. In July 1940 the Gerhard Fieseler-Werke began to convert 10 Bf 109E-1s to Bf 109T (for Träger: carrier) extended-span configuration. These were to have been development aircraft for the Bf 109T-1, intended for use aboard the proposed aircraft carrier Graf Zeppelin, but after the carrier programme was terminated the 60 T-1s ordered were completed instead as land-based T-2s. Various other E models, up to E-9, were produced for fighter and/or reconnaissance duties, with powerplant or equipment variations. Meanwhile, Messerschmitt had been developing what was to become the finest of all the many versions, the Bf 109F. Powered by either a 1,200hp DB 601N or a 1,350hp DB 601E engine, the Bf 109F represented a considerable advance over earlier series in terms of both performance and cleanliness of line, and at last gave the Luftwaffe a fighter that could outmanoeuvre the Spitfire V. The entire fuselage was cleaner aerodynamically, culminating in a more rounded rudder, an unbraced tailplane and a retractable tailwheel; the wings, of slightly increased span, were rounded off at the tips; and performance at all altitudes was better than that of earlier models. Production series ran from F-1 to F-6, with various sub-types. Several F-series aircraft were used as testbeds, the items evaluated including BMW 801 (radial) and Jumo 213 engines, a V-type tail unit, rocket weapons, and a nosewheel landing gear. A prototype never flown, but none the less of interest, was the Bf 109Z of 1943, in which two Bf 109Fs were 'twinned' by connecting them by a new, common wing centre-section and tailplane, the sole pilot being intended to occupy a cockpit in the port fuselage. By 1942 the Bf 109F had been supplanted in production and service by the most numerous version, the Bf 109G. Heavier and less manoeuvrable than the Fs, with DB 605 engines and additional equipment, the 'Gustavs' were individually less successful; they were, however, used widely in Europe, the Middle East, and on the Eastern Front. Production showed no sign of decreasing; indeed, from a total of 2,628 Bf 109s accepted during 1941, German output increased to 2,664 in 1942, to 6,379 in 1943, and to 13,942 in 1944, despite the ever-wider dispersal of production centres to avoid the depredations of Allied bombers; and the figures for 1943 and 1944 were increased still further by Hungarian and Romanian licence production. More than 70 per cent of all Luftwaffe Bf 109s were G-series aircraft, covering a huge variety of models from G-1 to G-16 (with numerous sub-types), for fighter, fighter-bomber or reconnaissance duties. The G-6 in particular, equipped with radar, was in widespread use as a night fighter from 1943. Recipients of export Bf 109Gs included Bulgaria, Finland, Hungary, Romania, Slovakia, Spain and Switzerland; and both Spain and Czechoslovakia continued licence production of various G models after the war. The final wartime models to be used operationally by the Jagdgeschwader were the Bf 109H and Bf 109K. Only a small number of the extended-span H-0 and H-1 were completed, as development priority for high-altitude fighter was by then being given to the Focke-Wulf Ta 152. A few Bf 109Ks, basically refined versions of the Bf 109G with the 'Galland hood' of the later Gs, entered service in late 1944, but did not see much combat; and the prototype Bf 109L (Jumo 213E) did not lead to a production series.

An exact total for production of all variants of the Messerschmitt Bf 109 is virtually impossible to determine, but it was approximately equal to the *combined* output of its great wartime opponents, the Hurricane and Spitfire, and thereby one of the most extensively produced aircraft of all time. Its final version, the Bf 109G, was alone built in numbers comparable to those of the Hurricane. Moreover the Bf 109, unlike its British contemporaries, remained basically a fighter or fighter-bomber all its operational life, apart from a few unprofitable excursions into other potential roles. First operational experience was gained in 1937 with Jagdgruppe 88 of the Condor Legion in Spain, and in the same year the Bf 109B entered service at home with the celebrated 'Richthofen' Geschwader. The Bf 109E series, which began to reach Luftwaffe fighter units at the beginning of 1939, formed the substantive service version right through the Battle of Britain. Superior in speed to the Hurricane at all altitudes, and faster in both climb and dive, the Bf 109E could, moreover, approximately match the Spitfire I in these areas, though it could be out-turned by both British fighters. But its very short tactical radius, leaving it fuel for only about 20 minutes combat once arriving over southern England, put it at a considerable disadvantage, and in the four months July–October 1940 the number of Bf 109s lost or damaged – not all due to combat – reached some 877. Best of all variants was the Bf 109F, which was the first version able to out-climb the Spitfire V. In the late summer of 1942, it was supplanted by the Bf 109G; but this version, despite its more powerful engine, was so much heavier that its performance was in fact poorer than the F. Post-war production of the Messerschmitt 109 took place in Czechoslovakia and Spain, and the type continued in service for some years after the end of hostilities in Europe.

Messerschmitt Bf 109B-2 of *Staffel 2*, J/88 Condor Legion, Spain 1937–38

Engine: One 700hp Junkers Jumo 210G 12-cylinder inverted-Vee type
Span: 30ft 3in (9·22m)
Length: 25ft 6in (7·77m)
Height: 7ft 5½in (2·27m)
Take-off weight: 4,850lb (2,200kg)
Maximum speed: 292mph (470km/hr) at 13,125ft (4,000m)
Operational ceiling: 26,575ft (8,100m)
Armament: Two 7·9mm MG 17 machine-guns in upper front fuselage and one firing through propeller hub. (*Weight and performance data are for Bf 109B-1 with 650hp Jumo 210Da*)

Messerschmitt Bf 109E-4 flown by Major Adolf
Galland while commanding III/JG.26, France,
June 1941

**Engine: One 1,150hp Daimler-Benz
 DB 601Aa inverted-Vee type**
Span: 32ft 4½in (9·87m)
Length: 28ft 4⅛in (8·64m)
Height: 11ft 1⅞in (3·40m)
Normal take-off weight: 5,523lb (2,505kg)
**Maximum speed: 357mph (575km/hr) at
 12,305ft (3,750m)**
Operational ceiling: 36,090ft (11,000m)
Normal range: 413 miles (665km)
**Armament: Two 7·9mm MG 17 machine-
 guns in upper front fuselage and one
 20mm MG FF cannon in each wing**

Messerschmitt Bf 109F-2 of 7./JG 54
'Grünherz', Leningrad area, winter 1941-42.
Best of all versions of this aircraft, the Bf 109F
first flew on 10 July 1940

**Engine: One 1,200hp Daimler-Benz
 DB 601N inverted-Vee type**
Span: 32ft 5¾in (9·90m)
Length: 29ft 0⅓in (8·85m)
Wing area: 174·4sq ft (16·20sq m)
Normal take-off weight: 6,173lb (2,800kg)
**Maximum speed: 373mph (600km/hr) at
 19,685ft**
Service ceiling: 36,090ft (11,000m)
**Range with under-fuselage drop
 tank: 528 miles (850km)**

Aircraft type		Bf 109E-3	Bf 109F-4	Bf 109G-6
Power plant		1 × 1,175 hp DB 601Aa	1 × 1,350 hp DB 601E-1	1 × 1,475 hp DB 605AM
Accommodation		1	1	1
Wing span	m : ft in	9·87 : 32 4·6	9·924 : 32 6·7	9·924 : 32 6·7
Length overall	m : ft in	8·64 : 28 4·2	8·848 : 29 0·3	8·848 : 29 0·3
Height overall	m : ft in	3·20 : 10 6·0	3·20 : 10 6·0	3·20 : 10 6·0
Wing area	m² : sq ft	16·40 : 176·53	16·20 : 174·38	16·20 : 174·38
Weight empty equipped	kg : lb	2,125 : 4,685	2,390 : 5,269	2,675 : 5,897
Weight loaded	kg : lb	2,665 : 5,875	2,900 : 6,393	3,150 : 6,944
Max wing loading	kg/m² : lb/sq ft	162·50 : 33·28	179·01 : 36·66	194·44 : 39·82
Max power loading	kg/hp : lb/hp	2·26 : 5·00	2·14 : 4·73	2·13 : 4·70
Max level speed	km/h : mph	560 : 348	625 : 388	621 : 386
at (height)	m : ft	4,440 : 14,565	6,500 : 21,325	6,900 : 22,640
Cruising speed	km/h : mph	375 : 233	571 : 355	***500 : 311
at (height)	m : ft	7,000 : 22,965	5,000 : 16,405	6,000 : 19,685
Time to height		5,000 m (16,405 ft) in 7·1 min	5,000 m (16,405 ft) in 5·2 min	5,000 m (16,405 ft) in approx 5·0 min
Service ceiling	m : ft	10,500 : 34,450	12,000 : 39,375	11,550 : 37,895
Range	km : miles	*660 : 410	**850 : 528	***1,000 : 621

* max, on internal fuel   ** with 300 litre drop-tank   *** approx

Messerschmitt Bf 109G-6/R6 Trop. of II./JG 53 'Pik-As', Italy, 1943–44

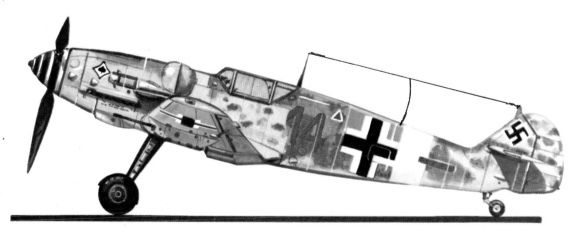

Messerschmitt Bf 109E-4/Trop. of I./JG 27, North Africa, summer 1941

An early-production **Messerschmitt Bf 109E-1** fighter of **2./JG 20**, bearing the Staffel emblem later used also by 8./JG 51 'Mölders'. At the outbreak of war I./JG 20, based at Fürstenwalde, formed part of Luftflotte 1 in north-eastern Germany

This **Bf 109G-6** has on its cowling the emblem of **JG 53 'Pik-As'** (Ace of Spades). The G-6, which entered production in late 1942, was powered by a DB 605 engine, with boosted performance at altitude, and had a 30mm MK 108 cannon mounted to fire through the propeller hub

Heinkel He 115

Heinkel He 115B-1, ex works with factory flight test codes, 1939–40

Engines: Two 970hp BMW 132K radials
Span: 73ft 1in (22·28m)
Length: 56ft 9in (17·30m)
Height: 21ft 7¾in (6·60m)
Maximum take-off weight: 22,928lb (10,400kg)
Maximum speed: 203mph (327km/hr) at 11,155ft (3,400m)
Operational ceiling: 17,060ft (5,200m)
Maximum range: 2,082 miles (3,350km)
Armament: Single 7·9mm MG 15 machine-guns in nose and dorsal positions; five 551lb (250kg) bombs, or two such bombs and one 1,764lb (800kg) torpedo or one 2,028lb (920kg) sea mine

It was to be expected that Ernst Heinkel, designer of several fine marine aircraft during World War 1, should produce one of the leading seaplanes of the 1939–45 conflict. The first He 115 prototype (D-AEHF) flew in 1937, being modified later for attempts on the prevailing world seaplane speed records, eight of which it captured on 20 March 1938. The definitive production aircraft was foreshadowed by the third and fourth prototypes, with an extensively glazed nose and long 'greenhouse' canopy, and, in the latter case, no wire bracing for the twin floats. Ten pre-production He 115A-0s and thirty-four He 115A-1s were completed in 1937 and 1938 respectively, the latter having an MG 15 gun in the nose as well as the observer's dorsal gun. The A-2 was the export equivalent of the *Luftwaffe*'s A-1, and was sold to Norway (six) and Sweden (twelve). The first large-scale domestic version, the He 115A-3, was soon followed by the He 115B series, comprising ten B-0s and eighteen B-1/B-2s. These had increased fuel capacity and could carry one of Hitler's much-vaunted 'secret weapons', the magnetic mine, in addition to their internal bomb load. With these they caused consider

able havoc to Allied shipping during the early years of the war. In 1940–41 there appeared the He 115C series, of which the C-0, C-1 and C-2 sub-types had an extra forward-firing 20mm MG 151 cannon in a fairing under the nose. On some aircraft, a 7·9mm MG 17 gun was installed in each wing root as well. The C series concluded with eighteen C-3 minelayers and thirty C-4 torpedo bombers, the latter having the dorsal MG 15 as its only defensive gun. One He 115A-1 was re-engined with 1,600hp BMW 801MA radials and equipped with five machine-guns and a cannon to become the He 115D; but although this was used operationally, no production of the D series was undertaken. Some Bs and Cs were, however, fitted with the undernose cannon during 1942–43, and others were given an MG 81Z twin gun in the rear cockpit, but the He 115 had been phased out of service by the end of 1944. Two of the Norwegian A-2s, which escaped to Britain after the invasion of Norway in 1940, were later employed in RAF colours to transport Allied agents between Malta and North Africa.

Fieseler Fi 156 Storch (Stork)

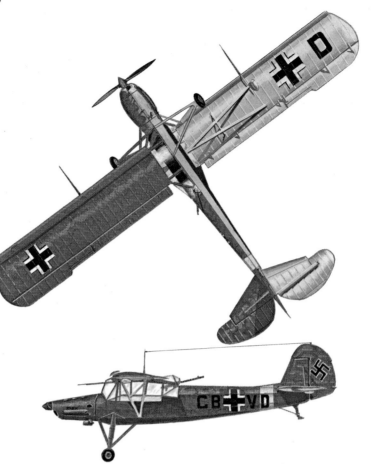

Fieseler Fi 156C-2 Storch, North Africa, *ca* spring 1941

Engine: One 240hp Argus As 10C-3 inverted-Vee type
Span: 46ft 9in (14.25m)
Length: 32ft 5½in (9.90m)
Height: 10ft 0in (3.05)
Normal take-off weight: 2,923lb (1,326kg)
Maximum speed: 109mph (175km/hr) at sea level
Operational ceiling: 17,060ft (5,200m)
Maximum range (standard fuel): 205miles (330km)
Armament: One 7.9mm MG 15 machine-gun in rear of cabin

Germany's counterpart to the Westland Lysander, the Fieseler Storch was also of pre-war design, three of the five prototypes being flown during 1936. A small pre-series batch of Fi 156A-0s was followed by the initial production model, the A-1, in 1937. No examples were completed of the Fi 156B, a projected civil version, and production continued with the Fi 156C series. The Fi 156C-0, which appeared late in 1938, introduced a defensive MG 15 machine-gun, mounted in a raised section at the rear of the 3-seat cabin, and was followed by C-1 staff transport and C-2 observation versions. All models thus far had been powered by Argus As 10C engines, but most of the multi-purpose C3s built were fitted with the As 10P version of this engine. Detail improvements introduced during the production life of the C-3 were incorporated in its successor, the C-5, which was able to carry such optional items as three 110lb (50kg) bombs, a 298lb (135kg) mine, a pod-mounted reconnaissance camera or an auxiliary drop-tank with which its range was increased to 628 miles (1,010km). Final models were the Fi 156D-0 (As 10C) and Fi 156D-1 (As 10P), with increased cabin space and enlarged doors to permit the loading of a stretcher. From 1942 until the

end of the war the C-5 and D-1 were the principal models in production. The Fi 156E-0 was a successful but experimental-only version with caterpillar-track landing gear for operation on rough or soft terrain. The Storch's remarkable STOL qualities enabled it to take off and land in extremely short distances, due to the full-span Handley Page leading-edge wing slats, and the slotted flaps and ailerons extending over the entire trailing edge. The wings could be folded back alongside the fuselage. Wartime production of the Storch, which amounted to two thousand five hundred and forty-nine aircraft, was transferred during 1944 to the Mraz factory in Czechoslovakia (which built sixty-four) and to the Morane-Saulnier works at Puteaux. The Storch served with the *Luftwaffe*, the *Regia Aeronautica*, and in small numbers with the air forces of Bulgaria, Croatia, Finland, Hungary, Romania, Slovakia and Switzerland. Both companies continued to build the type after the war, the Mraz version being known as the K-65 Cap (Stork) and the French version as the Criquet (Locust). The Fi 256 was a wartime Puteaux-built prototype for an enlarged 5-seat development.

Heinkel He 112

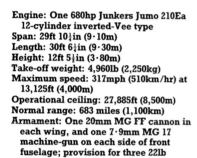

Heinkel He 112B-0 of III/JG 132 of the
Luftwaffe, Fürstenwalde, late summer 1938

Engine: One 680hp Junkers Jumo 210Ea
  12-cylinder inverted-Vee type
Span: 29ft 10½in (9·10m)
Length: 30ft 6¼in (9·30m)
Height: 12ft 5½in (3·80m)
Take-off weight: 4,960lb (2,250kg)
Maximum speed: 317mph (510km/hr) at
  13,125ft (4,000m)
Operational ceiling: 27,885ft (8,500m)
Normal range: 683 miles (1,100km)
Armament: One 20mm MG FF cannon in
  each wing, and one 7·9mm MG 17
  machine-gun on each side of front
  fuselage; provision for three 22lb
  (10kg) bombs beneath each wing

The He 112 was evolved in the mid-1930s as a contender to vie with the Messerschmitt Bf 109 and others for *Luftwaffe* orders, and from the aesthetic viewpoint at least was a more attractive aeroplane than its now-famous contemporary. Like the Bf 109, the He 112V1 first prototype (D-IADO) was also powered by a Rolls-Royce Kestrel V engine, although the Junkers Jumo 210 was the powerplant for which it had been designed. It flew for the first time in the summer of 1935, being followed in November by a Jumo-engined second prototype with a 3ft 3¼in (1·00m) shorter wing span and a third, armed machine similar to the second. The He 112V4, V5, V6 and V8 were completed as prototypes for an He 112A production model, the last of these four having a 1,000hp DB 600A engine. In the event, however, the He 112A version was not built; the first to go into production was the He 112B, based upon the V7 and V9 prototype aircraft. A batch of thirty He 112B-0s was built, and these were delivered to the *Luftwaffe* for service trials in 1938. Later that year seventeen of them, flown by German

crews, carried out a brief period of operations with *Grupo 5-G-5* of the Spanish Nationalist forces in the Civil War. All but two of these survived that war to serve on in the new Spanish Air Force in Morocco. Meanwhile twelve of the other He 112B-0s had been sold to the Japanese Naval Air Force in the spring of 1938, but plans to use these operationally against China were frustrated and they were utilised only as instructional airframes. No further He 112s were built for the *Luftwaffe*, despite the favourable opinion of the fighter held by German pilots. The only other batch to be built was a total of twenty-four (thirteen B-0s and eleven B-1s) delivered to the Romanian Air Force in the autumn of 1939, and these were the only He 112 fighters to serve operationally – albeit briefly – in World War 2. Three of the B-1s were later re-sold to Hungary. Two other prototypes were completed: the DB 601A-powered V10 and the Jumo 210G-engined V11, but no production of either version ensued.

DFS 230A-1 (LC + 1-186) of an
unidentified unit, *ca* 1942

Aircraft type		DFS 230A-1
Accommodation		1 + 9/2 + 8
Wing span	m : ft in	21·98 : 72 1·3
Length overall	m : ft in	11·24 : 36 10·5
Height overall	m : ft in	2·74 : 8 11·9
Wing area	m² : sq ft	41·26 : 444·12
Weight empty	kg : lb	860 : 1,896
Weight loaded	kg : lb	2,100 : 4,630
Max wing loading	kg/m² : lb/sq ft	50·90 : 10·43
Max gliding speed	km/h : mph	280 : 180
Max aero-tow speed	km/h : mph	210 : 130
Normal aero-tow speed	km/h : mph	180 : 112
Best glide ratio (loaded)		18

In service with LLG 1, 42 DFS 230 assault gliders took part, on 10 May 1940, in the storming of Eben-Emael and three nearby bridges in Belgium, the first time that glider-borne troops had been used in a military operation. Designed by Hans Jacobs of the Deutschen Forschungsinstitut für Segelflug, it first flew in late 1937 and an experimental airborne unit was formed in autumn 1938 with a small pre-production quantity of DFS 230A-0s. Deliveries of the major production DFS 230A-1 and dual-control A-2 began in October 1939, followed about a year later by the improved B-1 and B-2 models. Total DFS 230A/B production amounted to 1,593, from three main German manufacturers (Gotha, Erla and Hartwig) except for 410 built in Czechoslovakia. The B series had a strengthened airframe, an under-fuselage brake 'chute, and a 7.9mm MG 15

machine-gun aft of the cockpit. Much routine use was made of the DFS 230 as a freighter by various Lastenseglerstaffeln, but from 1941 they figured in airborne operations on the Corinth canal, the invasion of Crete, and the relief of Kholm on the Eastern Front (1942), Budapest (1945) and Breslau (1945). In September 1943 the spectacular rescue of Mussolini from prison on the Gran Sasso Massif was made possible by a special force of about a dozen DFS 230C-1s, converted from B-1s by adding three Rheinmetall-Borsig braking rockets under the nose. In another attempt to improve the glider's already excellent ability at pin-point landings, a DFS 230B fuselage was fitted with wheels and a three-blade rotor to become the Focke-Achgelis Fa 225 experimental rotor-glider.

Arado Ar 196A-3 (7R + BK) of 2./SAGr 125, Aegean theatre, winter 1941/42

Staffel emblem of **2./SAGr 125**

Aircraft type		Ar 196A-3
Power plant		1 × 960 hp BMW 132K
Accommodation		2
Wing span	m : ft in	12·44 : 40 9·8
Length overall	m : ft in	11·00 : 36 1·1
Height overall	m : ft in	4·45 : 14 7·2
Wing area	m² : sq ft	28·35 : 305·16
Weight empty	kg : lb	2,577 : 5,681
Weight loaded	kg : lb	3,310 : 7,297
Wing loading	kg/m² : lb/sq ft	116·75 : 23·91
Power loading	kg/hp : lb/hp	3·45 : 7·60
Max level speed	km/h : mph	312 : 194
at (height)	m : ft	4,000 : 13,125
Cruising speed	km/h : mph	253 : 157
at (height)	m : ft	— : —
S/L rate of climb	m/min : ft/min	300 : 984
Service ceiling	m : ft	7,000 : 22,965
Range	km : miles	*800 : 497

* at 253 km/h (157 mph)

Arado Ar 196A-2 (BB + YC) twin-float seaplane on its beaching trolley

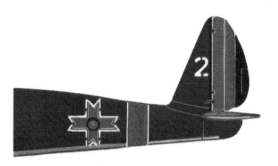

Bulgarian Air Force markings (No. 161 Squadron)
on an **Ar 196A-3**, *ca* 1943

Romanian Air Force markings (No. 102 Squadron)
on an **Ar 196A-3**, spring 1944

Arado Ar 196A-3 of 2/*Bordfl. Gruppe* 196,
southern Italy, 1942

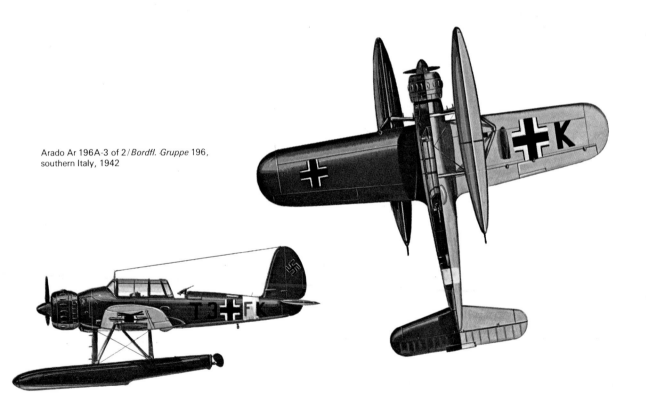

This maritime reconnaissance, patrol and attack seaplane, designed in 1936 to replace the Heinkel He 60, first flew in mid-1937, the Ar 196 V1 (D-IEHK) and V2 both being of twin-float configuration. Three additional prototypes and a small number of pre-production Ar 196B-0s were built later with a central main float and twin outboard stabilising floats, but the main Ar 196A production series followed the twin-float arrangement. Ten pre-production Ar 196A-0s were followed by 20 A-1s and a total of 506 A-3, A-4 and A-5 models, this total including 23 A-3s by SNCASO at St Nazaire in France and 69 A-5s by Fokker in the Netherlands. The Ar 196A entered service in late 1938 and during the war served under

Bordfliegergruppe 196 on board the major German warships *Admiral Graf Spee, Admiral Scheer, Bismarck, Gneisenau, Lützow, Prinz Eugen, Scharnhorst* and *Tirpitz*; and with seven SAGr (Seeaufklärungsgruppen), KG 100 and 200, and Küstenfliegergruppe 706, from coastal bases in virtually every European, Mediterranean and Balkan theatre of operations. All except the Ar 196A-5 (which had an MG 81 Z twin gun) mounted a single movable 7·9mm MG 15 gun in the rear cockpit; the A-2 to A-5 had also a cowling-mounted MG 17 and two wing-mounted 20mm MG FF cannon; all models had provision for carrying a 50kg bomb beneath each wing.

Messerschmitt Bf 110

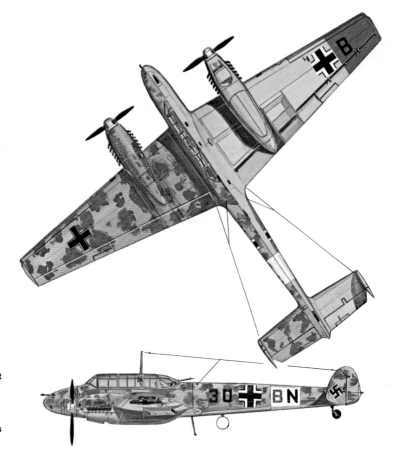

Messerschmitt Bf 110C-1 of 5/ZG.26, North
Africa, 1942

Engines: Two 1,050hp Daimler-Benz
 DB 601A-1 inverted-Vee type
Span: 53ft 4¾in (16·28m)
Length: 39ft 7½in (12·07m)
Height: 13ft 6⅜in (4·13m)
Normal take-off weight: 13,294lb
 (6,030kg)
Maximum speed: 336mph (540km/hr) at
 19,685ft (6,000m)
Operational ceiling: 32,810ft (10,000m)
Maximum range: 876 miles (1,410km)
Armament: Two 20mm MG FF cannon
 and four 7·9mm MG 17 machine-guns
 in fuselage nose, and one 7·9mm
 MG 15 gun in rear cockpit

The Bf 110 was the second production warplane designed by Prof Willy Messerschmitt after joining the Bayerische Flugzeugwerke AG, and was evolved in response to an RLM specification of early 1934 for a long-range escort fighter and *Zerstörer* (destroyer) aircraft. Three prototypes were completed with DB 600 engines, and the first of these was flown on 12 May 1936. The second, delivered early in the next year to the *Luftwaffe* for service trials, was received with mixed feelings. It was fast for a relatively heavy twin-engined machine, but was also heavy on the controls and less manoeuvrable than was desired. Four pre-series Bf 110A-0s were ordered, and these, due to the comparative scarcity of DB 600 engines, were fitted instead with 680hp Jumo 210Da units. These proved clearly inadequate, and were succeeded in the spring of 1938 by ten Bf 110B-0 aircraft with 670hp Jumo 210 Ga to carry out trials for the initial Bf 110B-1 production series. Plans to evaluate the B-1 operationally in the Spanish Civil War were forestalled when that conflict was resolved before it was ready for service. Thus, the first model to go into active service was the Bf 110C, in which increased power was provided by the use of DB 601A engines. Other refinements appearing in the C model included squared-off wingtips to improve the manoeuvrability, and a modified crew enclosure. The Bf 110C entered service in 1939, over three hundred of this model being on the *Luftwaffe*'s strength by the end of that year. Some were produced for the fighter-bomber and reconnaissance roles, and the Bf 110 was employed primarily in

ground-attack manoeuvres during the invasion of Poland. Hence it was not until it was fully exposed as a fighter, in the Battle of Britain, that its shortcomings in that capacity became apparent. Losses then became so heavy that the Luftwaffe was obliged to send Bf 109s with the bomber formations to protect their Bf 110 escorts. Production of the C model continued, latterly with 1,200hp DB 601N engines, but many of the earlier machines were withdrawn to such second-line duties as glider towing. Attempts to boost the aircraft's range resulted in the Bf 110D, produced both as a fighter (D-0 and D-1) and as a fighter-bomber (D-2 and D-3), but by mid-1941 most of the C and D versions were operational only in the Middle East or on the Eastern Front. The more versatile Bf 110E (DB 601N) and Bf 110F (DB 601F) appeared later that year, variants including the rocket-firing F-2 and the F-4 night fighter. By late 1942, when it became apparent that the Me 210 was not going to be a satisfactory replacement for its predecessor, Bf 110 production was stepped up again and the Bf 110G was introduced. This followed the pattern of earlier series, including the G-4 night fighter with 1,475hp DB 605B engines, two or four 20mm cannon and four 7·9mm machine-guns. The four-seat Bf 110G-4/R3 was the first variant to incorporate Lichtenstein SN-2 airborne interception radar. The Bf 110H series, differing chiefly in carrying even heavier armament, was produced in parallel with the G series, and was the last production model. Total Bf 110 production, in all versions, was approximately six thousand and fifty, and ended early in 1945.

Bf 110D long range Zerstörer with 'Dackelbauch' (dachshund-belly) ventral fuel tank, a feature soon discarded when its jettison mechanism proved to be unreliable

The **'Englandblitz'** insignia carried by most Nachtjagdgeschwader aircraft

Emblem of **1./NJG 3**

Messerschmitt Bf 110G-4d/R3 (D5 + DS) of 8./NJG 3, 1944

127

Arado Ar 96

Arado Ar 96 V3 (third prototype), *ca 1938-39.*
Data apply to Ar 96 A-1 production version

Engine: One 240hp Argus As 10C-3
   8-cylinder inverted-Vee type
Span: 36ft 1in (11·00m)
Length: 28ft 9¾in (8·78m)
Height: 8ft 8in (2·64m)
Take-off weight: 3,307lb (1,500kg)
Maximum speed: 171mph (275km/hr) at
   9,845ft (3,000m)
Operational ceiling: 16,075ft (4,900m)
Range: 590 miles (950km)
Armament: None

The Arado Ar 96 began to enter *Luftwaffe* service in the spring of 1939 and it had become a standard German trainer type by 1940. The original Ar 96V1 prototype (D-IRUU) was designed and flown in 1938, followed by the V2 which incorporated modifications to the tandem-seat cockpit enclosure. These two machines formed the basis for the initial production version, the Ar 96A-1, which was powered by a 240hp Argus As 10C-3 engine. Even with this modestly-rated powerplant the Ar 96 exhibited excellent flying qualities and performance, and the installation of a 350hp As 410 engine in the Ar 96V3 gave clear indication of what might be accomplished with a more powerful installation. Thus the Ar 96V6 was earmarked as prototype for the next production model, the Ar 96B, in which was installed the 465hp Argus As 410A-1 engine. The bigger engine resulted in an increase of 1ft 1¾in (0·35m) in the overall length, and brought a marked increase in performance over the Ar 96A, including an in-crease of 34mph (55km/hr) in the maximum level speed. Three main sub-types of the Ar 96B were produced from 1939. The standard pilot trainer model was the B-1, while the B-2 could be equipped for gunnery training with one or more 7·92mm MG 17 machine-guns; the B-5 was similar to the B-2 except for the addition of radio equipment. A futher endeavour to increase power and performance resulted in the Ar 96C, fitted with a 480hp As 410C engine, but this did not, in the event, enter production. Overall production of the Ar 96, by Arado and AGO in Germany and later by Avia and Letor in Czechoslovakia, totalled more than 11,500 and included small batches for Hungary and Romania. In addition to their training role, many were employed for reconnaissance, liaison and communications duties. A much-developed version, the Ar 396, was produced in some numbers after the war in France (by SIPA) and Czechoslovakia.

Focke-Achgelis Fa 223 Drache (Dragon)

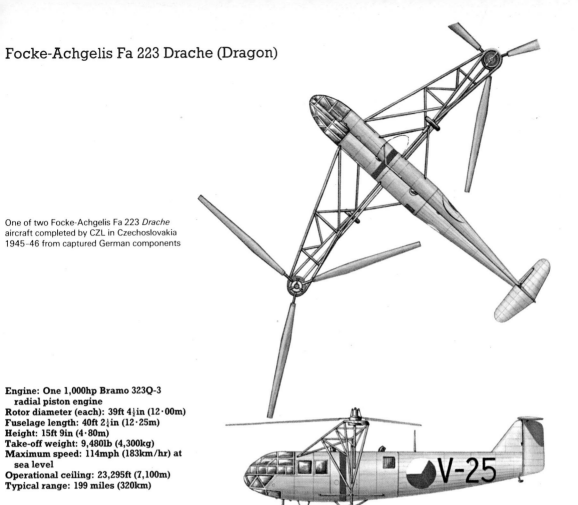

One of two Focke-Achgelis Fa 223 *Drache* aircraft completed by CZL in Czechoslovakia 1945–46 from captured German components

Engine: One 1,000hp Bramo 323Q-3 radial piston engine
Rotor diameter (each): 39ft 4½in (12·00m)
Fuselage length: 40ft 2¼in (12·25m)
Height: 15ft 9in (4·80m)
Take-off weight: 9,480lb (4,300kg)
Maximum speed: 114mph (183km/hr) at sea level
Operational ceiling: 23,295ft (7,100m)
Typical range: 199 miles (320km)

A helicopter with extremely advanced capabilities for its time, the Fa 223 was fundamentally an extension of the concept which produced the smaller Fw 61 (page 98) and employed a generally similar arrangement of twin counter-rotating rotors mounted on outriggers from the main airframe and driven by a fuselage-mounted radial engine. In the case of the Fa 223, however, the engine was installed amidships in the fabric-covered steel-tube fuselage to the rear of the 4-seat passenger compartment. The forward part of this cabin was a multiple-panelled enclosure made up of flat Plexiglas panels, and the aircraft was fitted with a tricycle undercarriage. Usual powerplant was a 1,000hp Bramo 323Q-3 radial engine. The Fa 223 originated in the late 1930s as an experimental design, of which several variants were planned. One of these was the Fa 266 Hornisse (Hornet), powered by an 840hp Bramo engine, which had an estimated top speed of 118mph (190km/hr) and a climb rate of 1,575ft/min (8m/sec). Although none of the three Fa 266 prototypes was completed, another prototype (D-OCEB) was completed in autumn 1939; this was the Fa 223 V1, which by then had been adapted for a military role. Manufacturer's trials with the Fa 223V1 revealed slight instability at the lower end of the speed range, but the heli-copter's general handling and controllability were excellent and on 28 October 1940 D-OCEB was flown to a record height of 7,100m (23,294ft). Official acceptance trials early in 1942 were followed by an order for one hundred Fa 223E pro-duction helicopters; by July a second prototype (D-OCEW)

had flown but the ten other Fa 223s completed that year were destroyed by Allied air attack. Further raids in July 1944 destroyed six of the eight additional aircraft then completed and flown, together with all others under assembly. The only other example to be built was one completed at a new Berlin factory set up to build Fa 223s at the rate of four hundred per month for the German armed forces, and by VE-day only three airworthy Fa 223s survived. One of these, flown in September 1945 to the Airborne Forces Experimental Estab-lishment in southern England, became the first helicopter to fly the English Channel, exactly seventeen years after the first rotorcraft crossing by the Cierva C.8L Autogiro. Unfortun-ately, on only its third test flight in Britain, it was written off when it crashed from 60ft (18m) after a vertical take-off. Three known examples were completed after the end of World War 2, all from captured or salvaged components. One of these was built, with the assistance of Professor Henrich Focke, by the SNCA du Sud-Est in France with the designation S.E. 3000 and flown on 23 October 1948. The other pair, designated VR-1, were built at the Ceskoslovenské Závody Letecké (formerly Avia) factory in Czechoslovakia. Uncompleted German war-time projects included proposals to produce a 4-rotor heli-copter by joining two Fa 223s together in tandem with a new fuselage centre-section; and the much larger Fa 284 crane helicopter to be powered by two 1,600 or 2,000hp BMW engines and capable in the latter form of lifting a 7,000kg (15,432lb) payload.

Junkers Ju 88

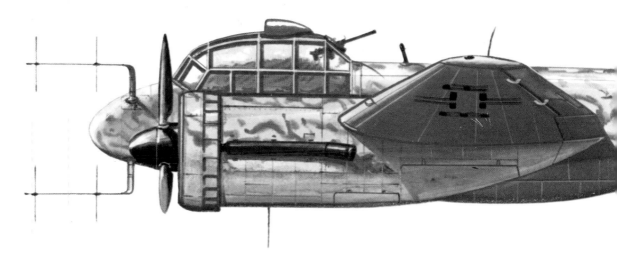

Junkers Ju 88G-6c (4R + BR) of 7./NJG2 (aircraft of the Staffelkapitän, Oberleutnant W. Briegleb), Luftflotte Reich, winter 1944/45

Aircraft type			Ju 88A-4	Ju 88C-6c	Ju 88G-7b
Power plant			2 × 1,340 hp Jumo 211J-1	2 × 1,340 hp Jumo 211J-1	2 × 1,725 hp Jumo 213E
Accommodation			4	3	4
Wing span	m	: ft in	20·00 : 65 7·4	20·00 : 65 7·4	20·00 : 65 7·4
Length overall	m	: ft in	14·40 : 47 2·9	14·36 : 47 1·4	16·36 : 53 8·1
Height overall	m	: ft in	4·85 : 15 10·9	5·07 : 16 7·6	4·85 : 15 10·9
Wing area	m²	: sq ft	54·50 : 586·63	54·50 : 586·63	54·50 : 586·63
Weight empty equipped	kg	: lb	9,860 : 21,738	9,060 : 19,974	9,300 : 20,503
Weight loaded (max)	kg	: lb	14,000 : 30,865	12,350 : 27,227	14,675 : 32,353
Max wing loading	kg/m²	: lb/sq ft	256·88 : 52·61	226·61 : 46·41	269·27 : 55·15
Max power loading	kg/hp	: lb/hp	5·18 : 11·43	4·57 : 10·08	4·25 : 9·38
Max level speed	km/h	: mph	470 : 292	495 : 307	626 : 389
at (height)	m	: ft	5,300 : 17,390	5,300 : 17,390	9,100 : 29,855
Cruising speed	km/h	: mph	400 : 248	423 : 263	560 : 348
at (height)	m	: ft	5,000 : 16,405	6,000 : 19,685	9,000 : 29,530
Time to height			5,400 m (17,715 ft) in 23·0 min	6,000 m (19,685 ft) in 12·7 min	9,200 m (30,185 ft) in 26·4 min
Service ceiling	m	: ft	8,200 : 26,905	9,900 : 32,480	10,000 : 32,810
Range (standard fuel)	km	: miles	1,790 : 1,112	1,040 : 646	2,250 : 1,398

The most versatile German combat aircraft of World War 2, and among the most widely used, the Ju 88 was evolved to a 1935 RLM requirement for a three-seat Schnellbomber (high-speed bomber). The Ju 88 V1 first prototype (D-AQEN) flew for the first time on 21 December 1936, powered by two 1,000hp DB 600Aa engines. The V2 was similar, but the Jumo 211 was substituted in the Ju 88 V3, and this engine powered the majority of Ju 88s subsequently built; the characteristic multi-panelled glazed nose first appeared on the four-seat V4. Following 10 pre-series Ju 88A-0s completed in mid-1939, deliveries of the Ju 88A-1, based on the V6, began in the following August. The A series continued, with very few gaps, through to the A-17, and included variants for such diverse roles as dive-bombing, anti-shipping strike, long-range reconnaissance and conversion training. Probably the most common model was the Ju 88A-4, which served in Europe and North Africa. This was the first version to incorporate modifications from experience gained in the Battle of Britain: it had extended-span wings, Jumo 211J engines, a 1,500kg (3,307lb) bomb load and increased defensive armament. Twenty-three Ju 88A-4s were supplied to Finland in 1943, 52 A-4s and D-1s to the Regia Aeronautica, and other A-4s to the Romanian Air Force. In parallel with the Ju 88A bomber series, Junkers pursued development of the basic airframe as a 'heavy' fighter, or Zerstörer, for which its speed and sturdy construction made it particularly suitable. This emerged as the Ju 88C (the pre-war Ju 88B having followed a separate course to become the Ju 188), and the first such model was the Ju 88C-2, a few conversions of the Ju 88A-1 with a 'solid' nose mounting three 7·9mm MG 17 machine-guns and a 20mm MG FF cannon, plus two aft-firing MG 15 guns. The C-2 entered service with II./NJG 1 in July 1940, being followed by small batches of the C-4 (with the A-4's extended-span wings) and the C-5 (BMW 801 D engines). Armament was improved in the C-6, the first major fighter version, powered by Jumo 211J engines and having (in the C-6b) Lichtenstein BC or C-1 radar.

Final C sub-type was the C-7 which, like the C-6, operated both as a Zerstörer and as a night fighter. The Ju 88D series, of which nearly 1,500 were built, were developed versions of the Ju 88A-4 for the strategic reconnaissance role; they, too, were used by the Hungarian and Romanian air forces. Night fighter developments continued with the Ju 88G, which utilised the angular vertical tail of the Ju 188 bomber and carried the improved Lichtenstein SN-2 radar. The G series appeared from spring 1944, principal sub-types being the G-1 and G-4 (BMW 801 D engines), G-6a and G-6b (BMW 801 G), G-6c (Jumo 213A), and G-7 (Jumo 213E). Small batches were built of the Ju 88H-1 (long-range reconnaissance) and H-2 (Zerstörer). A specialised version, produced primarily for service on the Eastern Front, was the Ju 88P. This was a ground attack/anti-tank aircraft with a 'solid' nose and either a 75mm PaK 40 cannon (in the P-1), two 37mm BK 3·7 cannon (in the P-2 and P-3), or a 50mm BK 5 cannon (in the P-4) mounted in a ventral pack. Next bomber series was the Ju 88S, produced in three small sub-series as the S-1 (BMW 801 G), S-2 (BMW 801 TJ) and S-3 (Jumo 213A). The S series, which entered service in autumn 1943, differed from earlier bomber models in having a smaller, fully-rounded glazed nose. They were only lightly armed, but offered considerably better performance than the Ju 88A and D series. Bomb load varied from 910kg (2,006lb) internally to 2,000kg (4,409lb) externally. The Ju 88T-1 and T-3 were photo-reconnaissance counterparts of the S-1 and S-3, introduced in early 1944. Towards the end of the war, many Ju 88s ended their days as explosive-laden lower portions of Misteln composite attack weapons, carrying a Bf 109 or Fw 190 fighter on their backs to guide them to their targets. Production, which ended in 1945, included more than 8,800 bombers, about 3,950 fighters and about 1,900 reconnaissance variants, overall output (excluding prototypes) reaching 14,676—built, in addition to Junkers, by Arado, Dornier, Heinkel, Henschel and Volkswagen factories.

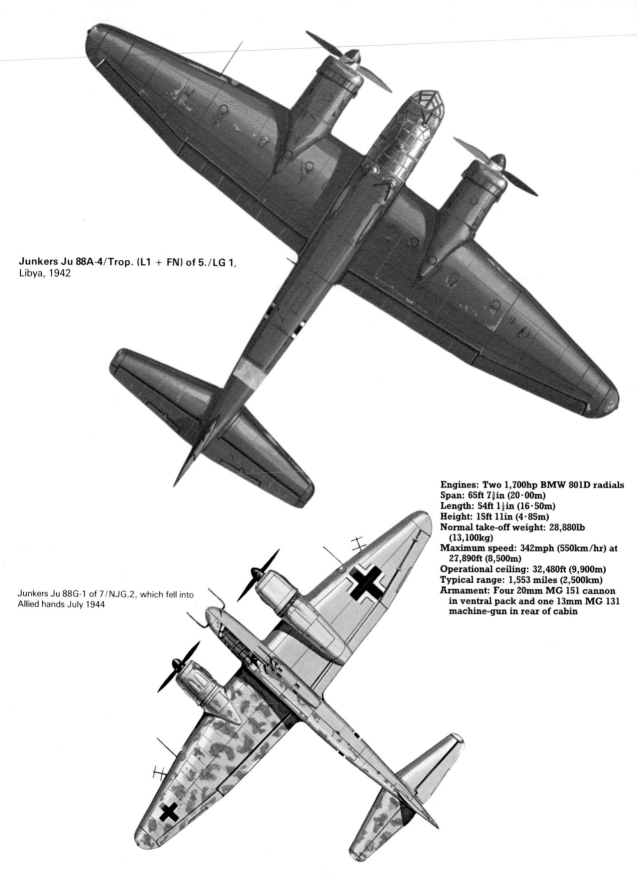

Junkers Ju 88A-4/Trop. (L1 + FN) of 5./LG 1,
Libya, 1942

Junkers Ju 88G-1 of 7/NJG.2, which fell into
Allied hands July 1944

Engines: Two 1,700hp BMW 801D radials
Span: 65ft 7½in (20·00m)
Length: 54ft 1½in (16·50m)
Height: 15ft 11in (4·85m)
Normal take-off weight: 28,880lb
   (13,100kg)
Maximum speed: 342mph (550km/hr) at
   27,890ft (8,500m)
Operational ceiling: 32,480ft (9,900m)
Typical range: 1,553 miles (2,500km)
Armament: Four 20mm MG 151 cannon
   in ventral pack and one 13mm MG 131
   machine-gun in rear of cabin

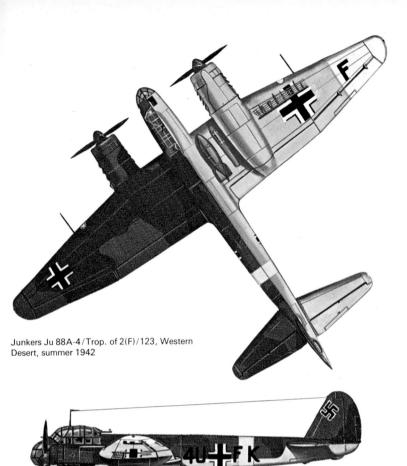

Junkers Ju 88A-4/Trop. of 2(F)/123, Western
Desert, summer 1942

Gruppe emblem of **II./LG 1**

Gruppe emblem of **II./KG 3**

Junkers Ju 88A-4 (5K + VN) of 5./KG 3
'**Blitz**', northern USSR, summer 1941

Blohm und Voss Ha 139

Blohm und Voss Ha 139 V2 *Nordwind* in Deutsche Luft Hansa livery, *ca* 1938; used by the *Luftwaffe* during the invasion of Norway in 1940

Engines: Four 600hp Junkers Jumo 205C
twelve-cylinder diesels
Span: 88ft 7in (27.0m)
Length: 63ft 11½in (19·50m)
Wing area: 1,259·38sq ft (117.0sq m)
Catapult take-off weight: 38,581lb
(17,500kg)
Maximum speed: 196mph (315km/hr) at
sea level
Operational ceiling: 11,480ft (3,500m)
Maximum range: 3,295 miles (5,300km)

In so far as it is possible for a large, four-engined aeroplane to look attractive, when it has plank-like gull wings, a strut-braced tailplane with twin fins and rudders, and is mounted on two large floats, the Ha 139 probably represented the best compromise possible in the late 1930s between operational considerations and aerodynamic cleanliness. Deutsche Luft Hansa made known in 1935 a requirement for a new commercial floatplane, capable of flying across the North and South Atlantic after being launched by catapult from German depot ships, but capable also of taking off from and landing on rough water if necessary. Two years earlier the Blohm und Voss shipbuilding company had set up an associate company, Hamburger Flugzeugbau GmbH, for aircraft manufacture, and under the design leadership of Dr Ing Richard Vogt this company prepared a design, the Ha 139, to meet the DLH requirement. The first of these, the Ha 139V1 (D-AMIE, named *Nordmeer* = North Sea), was completed in 1936 and delivered to the airline in March of the following year, together with the Ha 139V2 (D-AJEY *Nordwind* = North Wind). Between mid-August and the end of November 1937 these two aircraft, operating from the MSS *Schwabenland* off the Azores and *Friesenland* off Long Island, made seven experimental return crossings of the North Atlantic between Horta and New York. They carried a four-man crew and a 1,058lb (480kg) payload. The North Atlantic trials revealed a few shortcomings in the design, notably in the cooling of the engines and in directional stability. Modifications to rectify these faults were made during the winter of 1937-38, from which the aircraft emerged with the original circular fins and

rudders replaced by new surfaces of different shape and greater area. A third prototype (D-ASTA *Nordstern* = North Star) was delivered to DLH in 1938, this being somewhat larger overall and having the restyled tail surfaces and such other improvements as lower-mounted engines and much smaller attachment fairings between the floats and the wings. Luft Hansa gave the designation Ha 139A to the first two aircraft, referring to the Ha 139V3 as the Ha 139B. All three floatplanes were in operation before the end of 1938, at first on further experimental flights over the Horta-New York route and later on regular South Atlantic services between Bathurst, Natal (Brazil) and Recife. The one hundredth crossing (forty over the North Atlantic and sixty over the South Atlantic) was made in June 1939. A projected maritime reconnaissance bomber development was not proceeded with, but upon the outbreak of World War 2 the three DLH floatplanes and their crews were impressed for military service and the Ha 139V3 underwent extensive conversion for the reconnaissance role. The principal alterations involved the provision of a glazed observation station in a lengthened nose, the substitution of larger, roughly-triangular fin and rudder surfaces, and the fitting of an unwieldy external structure for de-gaussing magnetic mines. In this form, in which it was first flown on 19 January 1940, it was redesignated Ha 139V3/U1. Armament comprised four 7.9mm MG 15 guns in nose, dorsal and two beam positions. All three aircraft were pressed into emergency use as transports during the invasion of Norway later in 1940.

Blohm und Voss BV 138

Blohm und Voss BV 138C-1 of an unidentified *Aufklärungsgruppe* (Reconnaissance Group), possibly in the Baltic Sea area, *ca* 1942–43

Engines: Three 880hp Junkers Jumo 205D vertically-opposed diesel type
Span: 88ft 4¼in (26·93m)
Length: 65ft 1⅛in (19·85m)
Height: 19ft 4¼in (5·90m)
Normal take-off weight: 31,967lb (14,500kg)
Maximum speed: 177mph (285km/hr) at sea level
Operational ceiling: 16,400ft (5,000m)
Maximum range: 2,760 miles (4,355km)
Armament: Two 20mm MG 151 cannon (one each in bow and rear turrets), one 13mm MG 131 machine-gun aft of central engine, and provision for one

7·9mm MG 15 gun in starboard side of hull; three or six 110lb (50kg) bombs or four 331lb (150kg) depth charges beneath starboard centre-section

A product of Hamburger Flugzeugbau, the aircraft division of the Blohm und Voss shipbuilding company, the prototype of this three-engined flying boat was designated Ha 138V1 when it made its first flight on 15 July 1937. A second prototype, with a modified hull and tail surfaces, was flown on 6 November 1937, both being powered by 600hp Junkers Jumo 205C engines. In 1938 the 'Ha' designations were discarded, the third machine to be completed being designated BV 138A-01. This was the first of six pre-production aircraft, embodying a much-enlarged hull, redesigned booms and tail, and a horizontal wing centre section. Production began late in 1939 of twenty-five similar Bv 138A-1s, intended for well-equipped, long-range maritime patrol duties, but this initial version was not a conspicuous success, and the first pair were actually employed as 10-passenger transports in Norway. It made its combat debut in October 1940, at about which time the A-1

was beginning to be replaced by the BV 138B-1, twenty-one of which were built with a turret-mounted nose cannon, a similar gun in the rear of the hull and 880hp Jumo 205D engines. The major version in service was the BV 138C-1, two hundred and twenty-seven of which were produced between 1941 and 1943. The C-1, with more efficient propellers and a 13mm upper gun, offered slightly better performance and defence than its predecessor. Despite an indifferent start to its career, the BV 138 eventually proved to be both robust and versatile, and was employed with increasing effect both on convoy patrol in Arctic waters and, in association with the U-boat patrols, on anti-shipping missions over the North Atlantic and the Mediterranean. A few were also converted for sweeping or 'de-gaussing' minefields (these were designated BV 138MS), and many more were adapted for launching from catapults.

Focke-Wulf Fw 200 Condor

Focke-Wulf Fw 200C-4 (F8 + CD) of Stab.II./KG 40, autumn 1942

Focke-Wulf Fw 200 V2 Condor *Westfalen* of
Deutsche Lufthansa, 1938

**Engines: Four 720hp BMW 132G-1 nine-
cylinder radials**
**Span (V2): 107ft 9in (32·84m); span
(production version): 108ft 3¼in
(33·00m)**
Length: 78ft 3in (23·85m)
**Wing area (V2): 1,270·1sq ft
(118·00sq m); wing area (production
version): 1,291·7sq ft (120·00sq m)**
Take-off weight: 32,188lb (14,600kg)
**Cruising speed: 202mph (325km/hr) at
9,845ft (3,000m)**
Service ceiling: 21,980ft (6,700m)
Normal range: 777 miles (1,250km)

Engines: Four 1,200hp BMW-Bramo
323R-2 Fafnir radials
Span: 107ft 9½in (32.85m)
Length: 76ft 11½in (23·45m)
Height: 20ft 8in (6·30m)
Maximum take-off weight: 50,045lb
(22,700kg)
Maximum speed: 224mph (360km/hr) at
15,750ft (4,800m)
Operational ceiling: 19,030ft (5,800m)
Range (standard fuel): 2,212 miles
(3,560km)
Armament: One 20mm MG 151/20
cannon in the front of the ventral
gondola, one 15mm MG 151 machine-
gun in forward dorsal turret, and three
7·9mm MG 15 guns (one in the rear of
the ventral gondola and one in each
beam position); up to 4,630lb (2,100kg)
of bombs internally and externally

Several of the German warplanes of World War 2 originated before the outbreak of hostilities in designs intended to meet joint military and civil requirements. One which originated purely as a commercial transport design was the Focke-Wulf Condor, developed to meet a Lufthansa requirement for a 26-passenger long-range airliner. Design work, led by Prof Dipl Ing Kurt Tank, began in the spring of 1936 and in the following autumn Focke-Wulf began the construction of three prototypes, and made plans for a pre-series production batch of nine more. The Fw 200 V1 first prototype, which flew on 27 July 1937, was powered by four 875hp Pratt & Whitney Hornet S1EG radial engines. Shortly after this flight it received the identity D-AERE *Saarland*. The V2 (D-AETA *Westfalen*) was essentially similar, but was powered by 720hp BMW 132G-1 engines. The similarly-powered V3, one of two Condors acquired by the Luftwaffe as VIP transports for the use of Adolf Hitler and his staff and advisers, became D-2600 and was named *Immelmann III*; later in its career its markings were varied as WL+2600 and later still as 26+00. The BMW 132 was retained for seven of the nine Fw 200A-0 pre-production batch, five of which were allocated to Deutsche Lufthansa. Two BMW-powered Fw 200A-0s were delivered to the Danish airline DDL. The remaining two which were Hornet-powered, were delivered to Sindicato Condor SA of Brazil in August 1939. The Condor first demonstrated its long-range capabilities outside Germany when the V4 made a flight from Berlin to Cairo on 27 June 1938, and soon after this DLH and DDL put the Condor into airline service. Further publicity came on 10 August 1938, when the Fw 200 V1 left Berlin for a non-stop flight to New York, for which it was redesignated Fw 200 S1, re-registered D-ACON and renamed *Brandenburg*. On 28 November 1938 it began an equally spectacular flight, this time reaching Tokyo in 42 hours 18 minutes flying time from Berlin. Unfortunately the aircraft was lost shortly afterwards, but its visit brought an order for five Fw 200Bs from Dai Nippon KKK, and a request from the Japanese Navy for a sixth equipped as a potential reconnaissance-bomber. In the event, the fulfilment of this order – and of another from Aero O/Y of Finland for two Fw 200Bs – was

prevented by the outbreak of war in Europe, but four B-series Condors were completed and allocated to Deutsche Lufthansa. One other Condor – D-ASVX *Thüringen*, the first Fw 200C-0 – was allocated to Lufthansa, but before delivery it and the rest of the DLH fleet were acquired by the Luftwaffe in the spring of 1940 and employed as troop transports during the German invasion of Norway. The two Danish Condors continued to operate a Copenhagen-Amsterdam-UK service for some months after the outbreak of war, until one was impounded in Britain early in April 1940. It subsequently flew for a time in BOAC markings. Although none of the aircraft ordered by Japan were delivered, the Condor was adapted, as the Fw 200C, for ocean patrol and bombing duties with the *Luftwaffe*. Early production Fw 200Cs were powered by 830hp BMW 132H engines and carried a crew of 5, but with successive variations in armament the crew later increased to 7 men, and from the Fw 200C-3 onward Bramo 323R engines became the standard powerplant. The Fw 200C-1 first entered service in the maritime role towards the end of 1940, with *Kampfgeschwader* 40, followed by the C-2 and C-3 models during 1941. The principal sub-type was the C-4, with more advanced radar and radio equipment, which entered production early in 1942. Subsequent variants included the C-6 and C-8, adapted to carry two Hs 293 guided missiles. The latter was the final military variant, a total of two hundred and seventy-six Condors (including prototypes) having been built when production ended early in 1944. Considering the small quantity built, the Condor established a considerable reputation as a commerce raider during the early war years, operating independently or in conjunction with U-boat patrols against the Allied convoys. It was not ideally suited to the rigours of maritime warfare, however, and many were lost through structural failure when indulging in strenuous manoeuvres. When its initial successes began to diminish after the appearance of the CAM ships and such Allied types as the Beaufighter and Liberator, it was progressively transferred to the transport role for which it had first been designed.

Focke-Wulf **Fw 190A-4/Trop.** (unit unknown), North Africa, 1943

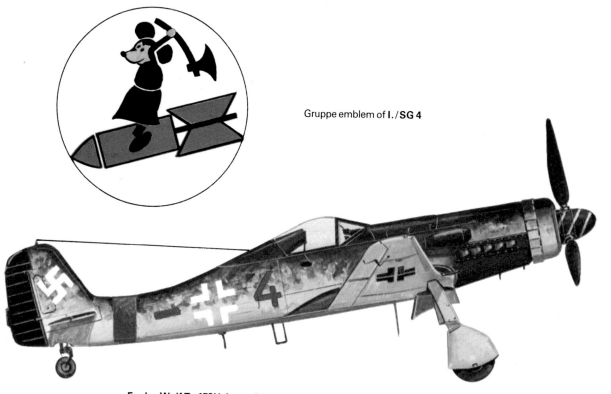

Gruppe emblem of **I./SG 4**

Focke-Wulf **Ta 152H-1**, possibly an aircraft of **Stab./JG 301**, 1945

Gruppe emblem of **I./JG 54 'Grünherz'**

To Dipl-Ing Kurt Tank, one of the most progressive aircraft designers of the past three decades, belongs the distinction of producing what is generally acknowledged as Germany's most successful single-seat fighter of World War 2, the Focke-Wulf Fw 190. By the time the RLM specification for the Fw 190 was issued, in 1937, the Messerschmitt Bf 109 was well established in production, but the thirty-nine-year old Tank's design was superior to it in many respects. It was a well-proportioned and aerodynamically clean-looking aircraft, the most noticeable characteristics being a very wide-track main landing gear and a large but neatly cowled BMW 139 engine. The Fw 190 V1 (D-OPZE), designed by Dipl-Ing Kurt Tank and Oberingenieur R Blaser to a 1938 RLM requirement, first flew on 1 June 1939, this aircraft and the V2 each being powered by a 1,550hp BMW 139 two-row radial engine. Subsequent aircraft, with the larger and more powerful BMW 801C, included 40 pre-series Fw 190A-0s ordered in 1940, most of them with a 1·00m (3ft 3·4in) greater wing span which later became standard. Full-scale production started with 100 four-gun Fw 190A-1s, which entered service with II./JG26 in summer 1941, and continued with the better-armed A-2 and A-3, the latter having six guns (two MG 151/20 and four MG 17) and a BMW 801D-2 engine. Early operational use was made of the Fw 190 in the Jagdbomber role, in low-level hit-and-run raids over southern England during 1942. The A-4 series (2,100hp boosted BMW 801D-2) included the A-4/U8 fighter-bomber (carrying a drop-tank and 500kg; 1,102lb of bombs, with armament reduced) and the A-4/R6 bomber interceptor with underwing rocket projectiles. By the end of 1942 more than 2,000 Fw 190s had been delivered and were in widespread service in Europe, the Mediterranean and on the Eastern Front. The A-5 was produced chiefly for close support; the A-6 and A-7 featured further improvements in firepower; the A-8s were mostly bomber interceptors or Zerstörern, although some were employed as all-weather fighters and others as two-seat trainers. As a fighter, at altitudes up to about 20,000ft (6,100m), the Fw 190 could match or improve upon the performance of the Spitfire V, then the best of its Allied adversaries. Above such heights, however, performance of the Fw 190 began to fall off rapidly, and improvement became an absolute necessity in the face of high-level daytime raids by USAAF bomber formations in the middle war years. The Fw 190B and C series were discarded, after a few prototypes with boosted BMW 801D or DB 603A engines, in favour of the long-nosed Fw 190D or 'Dora'. The D series, of which some 650–700 were built, evolved from prototypes with the 1,776hp Jumo 213A-1 engine, fitted with an annular cooling duct that maintained the 'radial' appearance. Early Fw 190D-0s and D-1s were characterised, apart from their longer cowlings, by lengthened rear fuselages and (on the D-1) increased fin area. The major production version (numbered to follow on from the A-8) was the Fw 190D-9 interceptor, which entered service with III./JG 54 in 1944 and was armed with two MG 151/20 wing cannon and two MG 131s over the engine. Regarded by many as the Luftwaffe's finest piston-engined fighter of the war, the Fw 190D-9 was to have been followed by the D-11, 12, 13, 14 and 15; but no substantial production of these models was undertaken. The Fw 190F and G (the E reconnaissance fighter and high altitude H series not being built) were short-nosed models, based on the Fw 190A. The Fw 190F series' principal model, the F-8, had provision for underwing rocket projectiles. Both the F and G were BMW 801-powered, the latter being mostly fighter-bombers in which gun armament was reduced to permit (on the G-1) a single 1,800kg (3,968lb) bomb, or (on other G models) up to 1,000kg (2,205lb) of smaller bombs, to be carried. Total Fw 190 production, which ended in 1945, was approximately 19,500. It was the first fighter to give the Luftwaffe a combat advantage over the early Spitfires. Its overall versatility, too complex to list here, was characterised by several dozen kits to adapt production aircraft to different roles, and the allocation of some 80 Versuchs numbers to individual development aircraft.

(continued on page 142)

Focke-Wulf Fw 190A-4/R6 equipped with underwing launching tubes for two W Gr 21 rocket missiles, a weapon used with some success in the bomber interception role

Fw 190F-8 with MG 131 machine-guns in a bulged cowling, under-fuselage rack for a 250kg bomb, and underwing racks for four 50kg bombs

Fw 190 V53 (DU + UC), converted from an A-7 as a pre-production (D-0) development aircraft for the long-nosed Fw 190D series with Jumo 213A-1 engine

Focke-Wulf Fw 190 V30/U1 (GH + KT), converted from an Fw 190C as the second development aircraft for the high altitude Ta 152H fighter

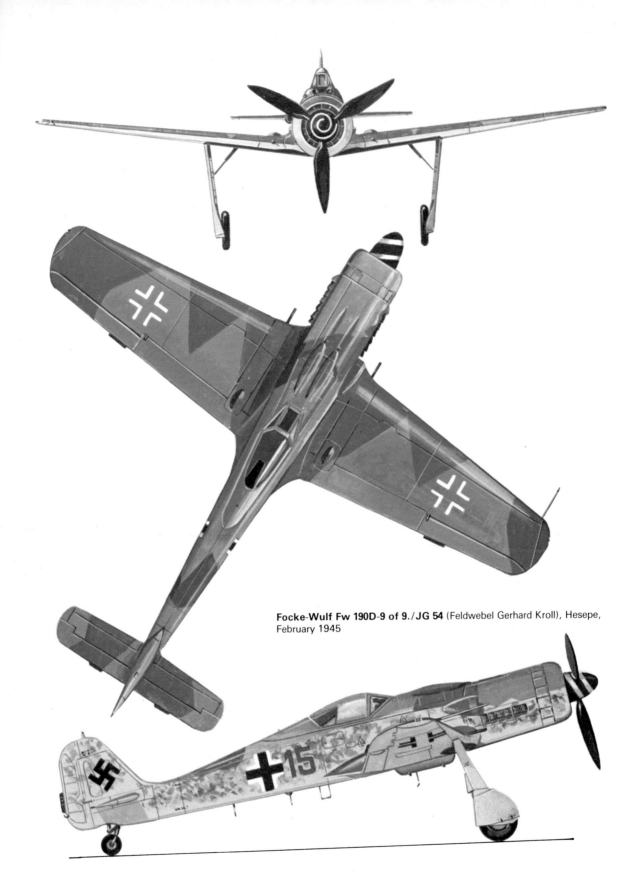

Focke-Wulf Fw 190D-9 of 9./JG 54 (Feldwebel Gerhard Kroll), Hesepe, February 1945

Aircraft type		Fw 190A-8	Fw 190D-9	Ta 152H-1
Power plant		1 × 1,700 hp BMW 801D-2	1 × 1,776 hp Jumo 213A-1	1 × 1,750 hp Jumo 213E-1
Accommodation		1	1	1
Wing span	m : ft in	10·506 : 34 5·6	10·506 : 34 5·6	14·44 : 47 4·5
Length overall	m : ft in	8·95 : 29 4·4	10·192 : 33 5·3	10·71 : 35 1·6
Height overall	m : ft in	3·96 : 12 11·9	3·36 : 11 0·3	3·36 : 11 0·3
Wing area	m² : sq ft	18·30 : 196·98	18·30 : 196·98	23·30 : 250·80
Weight empty equipped	kg : lb	3,470 : 7,650	3,490 : 7,694	3,920 : 8,642
Weight loaded	kg : lb	4,380 : 9,656	4,840 : 10,670	4,750 : 10,472
Max wing loading	kg/m² : lb/sq ft	239·34 : 49·02	264·48 : 54·17	203·86 : 41·75
Max power loading	kg/hp : lb/hp	2·57 : 5·68	2·72 : 6·01	2·71 : 5·98
Max level speed	km/h : mph	657 : 408	686 : 426	760 : 472
at (height)	m : ft	6,300 : 20,670	6,600 : 21,655	12,500 : 41,010
S/L rate of climb	m/min : ft/min	716 : 2,349	950 : 3,117	1,050 : 3,445
Service ceiling	m : ft	10,300 : 33,790	11,300 : 37,075	14,800 : 48,555
Range (internal fuel)	km : miles	800 : 497	837 : 520	1,215 : 755

Several of the latter helped in evolving the Ta 152, virtually a total redesign, derived from the Fw 190D and first flown in autumn 1944. First production (and only operational) series was the Ta 152H, with long-span wings for high altitude flying, which saw limited service with JG 301 in 1945. Proposed variants included the Ta 152A, B, E and S; but the only other version to begin serious development before the war ended was the medium altitude Ta 152C (2,100hp DB 603L), first flown in November 1944 and capable of 463mph (745km/hr) at 34,100ft (10,400m).

Focke-Wulf Fw 190 D-9 in typical Luftwaffe home defence colour scheme, spring 1945. Only a handful of Fw 190s now survive from some 20,000 built. *Inset:* Cockpit interior of an Fw 190A.

Focke-Wulf Fw 189 Uhu (Owl)

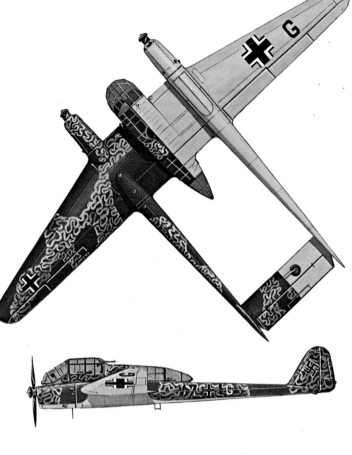

Focke-Wulf Fw 189A-2 of 1(H)/32 serving with *Luftflotte* 5, Eastern Front (White Sea area) October 1942

Engines: Two 465hp Argus As 410A-1
  inverted-Vee type
Span: 60ft 4¾in (18·40m)
Length: 39ft 5½in (12·03m)
Height: 10ft 2in (3·10m)
Normal take-off weight: 8,708lb (3,950kg)
Maximum speed: 218mph (350km/hr) at
  7,875ft (2,400m)
Operational ceiling: 23,950ft (7,300m)
Normal range: 416 miles (670km)
Armament: Four 7·9mm MG 81 machine-
  guns (two in dorsal position and two in
  rear of nacelle), and one 7·9mm MG 17
  gun in each wing root; four 110lb (50kg)
  bombs beneath the wings

The Fw 189 was designed originally to a 1937 specification for a tactical reconnaissance aircraft. The Fw 189V1 prototype (D-OPVN), first flown in July 1938, was an unorthodox aeroplane, with two 430hp Argus As 410 engines mounted in slender booms that also carried the tail assembly. The crew members were accommodated in an extensively glazed central nacelle. A second and third prototype were completed to generally similar configuration, the Fw 189V2 carrying guns and external bomb racks. The first series version to go into production was the Fw 189B dual-control trainer, three B-0s and ten B-1s being completed in 1939–40. Production of the first reconnaissance series began in the spring of 1940, ten Fw 189A-0 pre-series aircraft being followed by the A-1, the better-armed A-2 and a smaller quantity of A-3 trainers. First deliveries to the *Luftwaffe* were made in the autumn of 1940, but it was not until the end of the following year that the Fw 189 began to appear in front-line units in any numbers. Thereafter the *Uhu*, as it was known to its crews, became employed in increasing numbers, especially on the Eastern Front. It was popular with those who flew it, and its delicate appearance belied what was in fact an adaptable, manoeuvrable and sturdily built aeroplane. Production of the Fw 189A series was undertaken by the parent company, which built one hundred and ninety-seven, excluding prototypes; at the Aero factory in Czechoslovakia, which built three hundred and thirty-seven; and at Bordeaux-Mérignac in France, where two hundred and ninety-three were completed. Small numbers were supplied to the air forces of Hungary and Slovakia. Meanwhile, in 1939 the Fw 189V1 had been reflown after being modified to have a very small but heavily armoured central nacelle seating two crew members. This and the generally similar Fw 189V6 were prototypes for a proposed attack version, the Fw 189C, but the latter did not go into production. The float-fitted Fw 189D, the Fw 189E with Gnome-Rhône engines, and the more powerful Fw 189G were all projects that did not come to fruition, but a small number of Fw 189F-1s, with 580hp As 411 engines, did become operational.

Focke-Wulf Fw 189A-2 (5D + FH) of 1.(H)/31, Eastern Front, summer 1942

Staffel emblem of **1.(H)/31**

National insignia of the **Slovak Air Force**

Staffel emblem of **5.(H)/12**

Gotha Go 242 and Go 244

Aircraft type			Go 242A-1
Accommodation			2 + 21
Wing span	m	: ft in	24·50 : 80 4·6
Length overall	m	: ft in	15·80 : 51 10·0
Height overall	m	: ft in	4·40 : 14 5·2
Wing area	m²	: sq ft	64·40 : 693·20
Weight empty equipped	kg	: lb	3,236 : 7,134
Weight loaded (max)	kg	: lb	7,300 : 16,093
Max wing loading	kg/m²	: lb/sq ft	113·35 : 23·22
Max gliding speed	km/h	: mph	290 : 180
Max aero-tow speed	km/h	: mph	240 : 149
Ceiling with Ju 52/3m	m	: ft	2,200 : 7,220
Ceiling with He 111 or Bf 110	m	: ft	3,800 : 12,465

Gotha Go 242A-1 (F7 + 8-12) on an unidentified Feldflugplatz on the Eastern Front, 1943

Gotha Go 244B-1 (4V + ES) of 8./TG 3, Hagenow, summer 1942

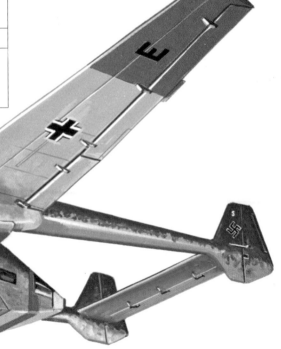

A direct result of early wartime success with the DFS 230, the larger Go 242 transport/assault glider was ordered 'off the drawing board' of Dipl-Ing Kalkert in autumn 1940, two prototypes being flown in the following spring. The Go 242A-1 freighter had deeper tailbooms than the pre-production A-0, and was delivered from August 1941; the assault-troop A-2 was similar except for a brake parachute. Go 242As first appeared in Greece, Sicily and North Africa in early 1942, usually towed by Heinkel He 111s and sometimes having rocket-assisted take-off. The original six Gotha Staffeln formed the basis for the later Schleppgruppen, serving also as supply and evacuation transports on the Eastern Front. A non-jettisonable wheeled landing gear characterised the B series, which comprised the B-1 and B-2; their B-3 and B-4 personnel counterparts with rear exit doors; and the B-5 trainer. A few A-1s were converted to C-1s, a water-landing version delivered to 6./KG200 in autumn 1944 for an attack (never mounted) on the Home Fleet at Scapa Flow. Of 1,528 Go 242s built, 133 B-1 to B-5s were converted (and another 41 built new) as powered Go 244B-1 to B-5s, most with captured French Gnome-Rhône engines and others with 660hp BMW 132Zs or captured Soviet 750hp Shvetsov M-25As. Underpowered and vulnerable, they were withdrawn in 1942 after only a few months' limited service, mostly in the Mediterranean and southern Russia, and allocated to the training of airborne troops.

Blohm und Voss BV 222 Wiking (Viking)

The **BV 222 V1** first prototype during a test flight in the autumn of 1940

Aircraft type			BV 222A-0 (V4)			
Power plant			6 × 1,200 hp BMW-Bramo 323R-2			
Accommodation			6 + 16			
Wing span	m	: ft in	46·00	: 150	11·0	
Length overall	m	: ft in	36·50	: 119	9·0	
Height overall	m	: ft in	10·90	: 35	9·1	
Wing area	m²	: sq ft	255·00	: 2,744·79		
Weight empty equipped	kg	: lb	28,550	: 62,942		
Weight loaded (max)	kg	: lb	45,600	: 100,531		
Max wing loading	kg/m²	: lb/sq ft	178·82	: 36·63		
Max power loading	kg/hp	: lb/hp	6·33	: 13·96		
Max level speed	km/h	: mph	296	: 184		
at (height)	m	: ft	S/L			
Cruising speed (econ)	km/h	: mph	250	: 155		
at (height)	m	: ft	S/L			
Time to 6,000 m (19,685 ft)			49·0 min			
Service ceiling	m	: ft	6,500	: 21,325		
Range (max)	km	: miles	*7,450	: 4,630		

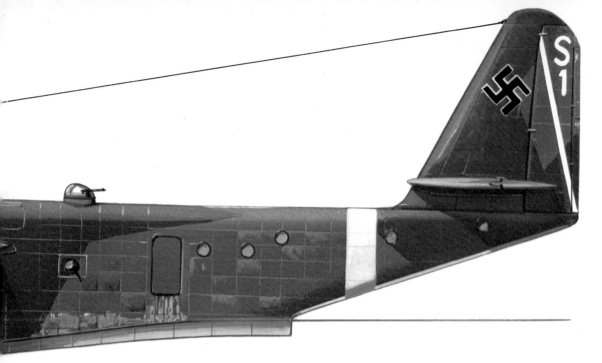

Blohm und Voss BV 222 V1 (X4 + AH) as in service with **Lufttransportstaffel (See) 222**, Tobruk, spring/summer 1942

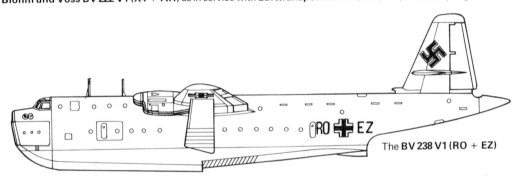

The **BV 238 V1 (RO + EZ)**

The aptly-named Wiking, whose design was evolved under the leadership of Dr Ing Richard Vogt, was originally conceived as a trans-Atlantic passenger-carrying flying-boat for Deutsche Luft Hansa, which placed an order for three in the autumn of 1937. Planned gross weight was 99,208lb (45,000kg) and maximum range in excess of 4,350 miles (7,000km). The intended accommodation was for 24 day or 16 night-time passengers, but the aircraft never went into commercial service, for war had broken out before the BV 222V1 first prototype (D-ANTE) made its first flight on 7 September 1940, some twenty months after construction had begun. Instead the prototype was used, beginning in July 1941, as an unarmed freight transport on behalf of the *Luftwaffe*, but by the following winter it had become obvious that a defensive armament was necessary. This took the form of a 13 mm MG 131 machine-gun in each of two dorsal turrets and five 7·9mm MG 81 guns, four amidships firing to left and right and a fifth in the nose, and in this form the aircraft became operational with LTS (*Lufttransportstaffel*) See 222 in the following spring. In August 1942 it was joined by the second prototype (BV 222V2), which had first flown a year previously and had incorporated armament from the outset. It had originally had two additional MG 131 guns in fairings under the inboard wing sections, but these were removed and a deeper keel fitted before the V2

entered service. The V3 (first flight 28 November 1941) was essennialy similar except that the armament, consisting originally of only a single nose-mounted MG 81, was later increased to three 20mm MG 151 cannon, one MG 131 and two MG 81 in three fuselage and two wing turrets, with no gun at all in the nose. Subsequently the V2, V4 and V5 prototypes were brought up to a similar standard, prior to being employed by the *Fliegerführer Atlantik* in a maritime reconnaissance role from the spring of 1943. By this time the V1, V6 and V8 had been lost, the V1 in a landing accident and the other two shot down; and in June 1943 the V3 and V5 also were destroyed, while at moorings, by Allied air attack. All of these seven aircraft were powered by Bramo Fafnir 323R radial engines, and were designated BV 222A by the *Luftwaffe*. The V7 machine, prototype for the BV 222C, had meanwhile been flown on 1 April 1943 with a powerplant of six 1,000hp Junkers Jumo 207C twelve-cylinder diesel engines. (The BV 222B was an unbuilt project for a Jumo 208-powered commercial transport.) Armament in the V7 again varied, the three 20mm guns being retained with one MG 131 in the nose and four more amidships. The ninth Wiking was the first true production example of the BV 222C, and was placed in service together with three similar aircraft and the V7 aircraft in the summer of 1943. Only one other Wiking, the

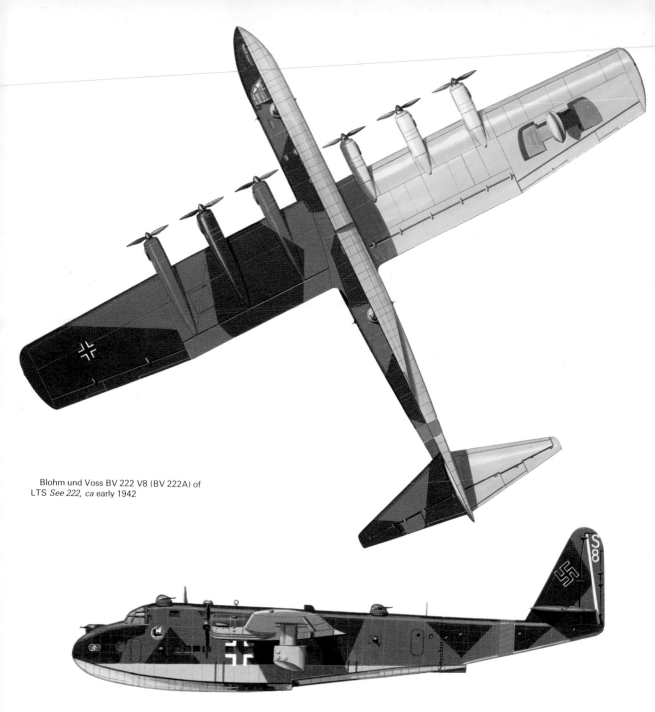

Blohm und Voss BV 222 V8 (BV 222A) of
LTS *See 222, ca* early 1942

thirteenth aircraft, was subsequently completed. Originally to
have been the first BV 222D, with Jumo 205D diesel engines, it
was in the event fitted with Jumo 205Cs. The BV 222D series,
and a proposal to replace the six-engined layout with four of
the more powerful BMW 801 radial engines, were both abandoned, and when work on the BV 222 was halted in 1944 (to
give priority to more urgently-needed combat aircraft) four
additional C-series flying-boats were left uncompleted. The
Wiking was the largest flying-boat in production and service
during World War 2; only three BV 222Cs, of the thirteen
Wikings built, survived the war; one was then brought to the
UK for study and two sent to the USA. Huge as the BV 222 was
for its time, an even larger flying-boat was built by Blohm and

Voss during the war years. This was the BV 328, intended as a
replacement for the much smaller BV 138 and was originally
proposed early in 1941 with four Jumo 323 diesel engines.
Later that year the design was adapted for six DB 603 or
BMW 801 engines, and four prototypes were ordered. Only
the BV 238V1, with 1,750hp DB 603V engines, was flown, and
that not until 1944; by the end of the war in Europe the V2 and
V3 were still incomplete, as was the first prototype of a land-
based development, the BV 250. The BV 238V1 had a wing
span of 197ft 5in (60·17m), length of 142ft 3in (43·36m), normal
take-off weight of 154,324lb (70,000kg), maximum speed of
264mph (425km/hr) and a range of 3,790 miles (6,100km).

Flettner Fl 282 Kolibri (Humming-Bird)

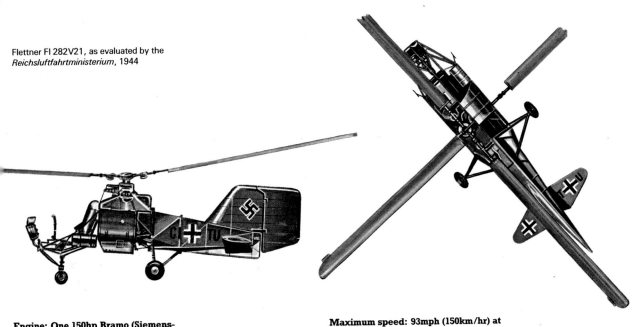

Flettner Fl 282V21, as evaluated by the
Reichsluftfahrtministerium, 1944

Engine: One 150hp Bramo (Siemens-
 Halske) Sh.14A seven-cylinder radial
Rotor diameter (each): 39ft 2⅜in (11·96m)
Fuselage length: 21ft 6⅓in (6·56m)
Height: 7ft 2⅜in (2·20m)
Maximum take-off weight: 2,205lb
 (1,000kg)

Maximum speed: 93mph (150km/hr) at
 sea level
Operational ceiling: 10,825ft (3,300m)
Normal range: 106 miles (170km)

The pioneer work of Anton Flettner is often overshadowed by the more publicised activities of his contemporaries Focke and Sikorsky; yet Flettner's first fully practical helicopter, the Fl 265, was far superior to the Fw 61 and made a successful free flight several months before the VS-300 began tethered flights. Flettner's first rotorcraft, flown in 1932, had a 2-blade rotor 98ft (29·87m) in diameter, with a 30hp Anzani engine mounted part of the way along each blade driving a propeller – a form of propulsion similar to that used by the Italian Vittorio Isacco on his so-called 'helicogyres' developed in the USSR in the 1930s. The Flettner machine made a successful tethered take-off, but later overturned during a gale and was written off. His next significant design was the Fl 184 single-seat autogyro; powered by a 150hp Sh.14 radial engine, it flew in 1935 and was due to be evaluated by the German Navy when it, too, was unfortunately destroyed. The next design was the Fl 185, whose prototype (D-EFLT) flew in 1936 and had a 3-blade main rotor. The centrally-mounted Sh.14A engine drove, in addition to the rotor, two small anti-torque propellers on outriggers each side of the cabin and a large cooling fan in the nose. By this time, however, Flettner had developed the idea of counter-rotating, intermeshing twin rotors. Many of his advisers thought that the airflow disturbed by the intermeshing blades would make this system less efficient than one using a single rotor; but Flettner believed that any problems thus encountered would be more than offset by the reduced drag resulting from having no external rotor-carrying structure. He proved his point by installing such a system in the Fl 265, whose prototype (D-EFLV) flew in May 1939. At this time encouragement for the development of small helicopters came mostly from the German Navy, on whose behalf six Fl 265s had been ordered in 1938 with a view to developing a machine suitable for shipboard re

connaissance and anti-submarine patrol. Service trials of the Fl 265 were more than satisfactory, and plans were made for series production; but by this time work was well advanced on a later model, the Fl 282, which could carry 2 men and was more versatile. The RLM therefore agreed to wait for the Fl 282, to hasten whose development it ordered thirty prototypes and fifteen pre-production aircraft in spring 1940. Maiden flight was made in 1941. The first three prototypes were completed as single-seaters and had fully enclosed cabins made up of a series of optically flat Plexiglas panels, faired-in rotor pylons and well-contoured fuselages. The Fl 282V3 was fitted with endplate auxiliary fins and a long underfin beneath the rear fuselage. Later machines had more utilitarian bodies and some had semi-enclosed cockpits; others, like the example illustrated, had a completely open pilot's seat. Like the Fl 265, the Fl 282 underwent exhaustive service trials, and several were used operationally from 1942. Usually they flew from platforms above the gun turrets of convoy escort vessels in the Baltic, Aegean and Mediterranean, often in extreme weather conditions, and revealed control and performance qualities well above expectations. By VE-day, only three of the twenty-four prototypes completed by Flettner at Johannisthal still survived, the others having been destroyed to prevent capture. Two of these, the V15 and V23, were taken to the United States, and the other to the Soviet Union. The RLM had placed an order in 1944 for one thousand Fl 282s from BMW, but Allied bombing attacks prevented production from being started. At least two other Flettner helicopters were under development when the war ended. These were the Fl 285, another fleet spotter with an Argus As.10C engine, capable of making a 2-hour flight and carrying two small bombs; and the Fl 339, a large transport helicopter project powered by a BMW 132A engine.

Messerschmitt Me 321 and Me 323 Gigant (Giant)

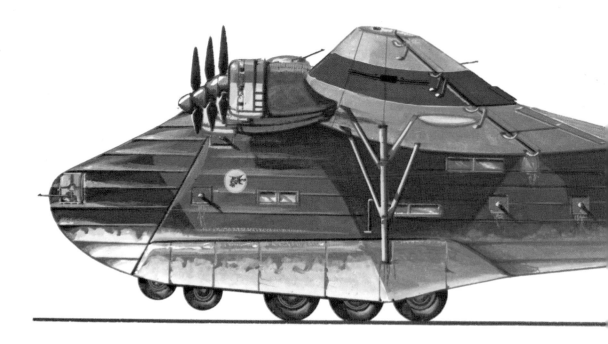

Aircraft type			Me 323E-2
Power plant			6 × 1,140 hp Gnome-Rhône 14N 48/49
Accommodation			11 + 130
Wing span	m	: ft in	55·00 : 180 5·4
Length overall	m	: ft in	28·50 : 93 6·0
Height overall	m	: ft in	9·60 : 31 6·0
Wing area	m²	: sq ft	300·00 : 3,229·17
Weight empty equipped	kg	: lb	29,600 : 65,256
Weight loaded	kg	: lb	45,000 : 99,208
Max wing loading	kg/m²	: lb/sq ft	150·00 : 30·72
Max power loading	kg/hp	: lb/hp	6·57 : 14·50
Max level speed	km/h	: mph	285 : 177
at (height)	m	: ft	S/L
Cruising speed	km/h	: mph	250 : 155
at (height)	m	: ft	S/L
S/L rate of climb	m/min	: ft/min	120 : 394
Service ceiling	m	: ft	4,500 : 14,765
Range	km	: miles	*1,300 : 808

*at 4,000 m (13,125 ft)

Messerschmitt Me 323E-2 (C8 + CB) of I./TG 5, Odessa, March 1944

The huge Me 321 Gigant transport glider, hurriedly designed in the autumn of 1940, flew for the first time on 25 February 1941 and was in service in large numbers less than four months later. It could accommodate up to 200 troops, or some 22 tonnes of cargo or military equipment, and served principally on the Eastern Front; two versions (100 of each) were built as the Me 321A-1 and B-1. The initial aero-tow method of launch using a trio of Bf 110s, usually with rocket assistance, proved unsatisfactory; later, the use of a single Ju 290A-1 or 'twin' He 111Z proved more practical. In 1941, Ing Degel of Messerschmitt undertook the development of a self-powered version, the Me 323, avoiding encroachment upon domestic engine production by utilising captured French Gnome-Rhône 14 N radial engines. Two prototypes were converted from Me 321s, the four-engined Me 323 V1 (prototype for the Me 323C) making its first flight in spring 1942. However, it was quickly apparent that four engines were insufficient, and all effort was concentrated on the Me 323D prototype, the six-engined V2. The Me 323D followed the Me 321 into production, a pre-series batch of 10 D-0s being delivered from August 1942, followed a month later by the D-1 initial production model, with accommodation for 120 troops, 60 stretcher cases or equivalent cargo. (The D-2, differing only in having two-blade wooden, instead of three-blade metal propellers, was less satisfactory.) The D-1's four 7·9mm MG 15 machine-guns were replaced by five 13mm MG 131s in the chief production model, the Me 323D-6; however, additional weapons were often carried, and the experimental Me323E-2/WT mounted no fewer than 11 cannon and four machine-guns. The E-1 and E-2 series, based on the V13 prototype, had strengthened airframes, carried more fuel, and in the E-2 introduced, between the centre and outer engines on each wing, a 20mm MG 151 cannon in a power-operated turret. The V14 and V16 were powered respectively by Jumo 211F and 211R engines, the latter being a prototype for the proposed Me 323F series, but no Jumo-engined version was after all produced. Overall Me 323 production, by Messerschmitt and Zeppelin factories, amounted to 198, excluding prototypes. The Me 323 was an invaluable supply transport on the Eastern Front, but in North Africa and elsewhere its slow speed and difficult handling made it vulnerable, despite being well-armed and battleworthy. After heavy losses in the evacuation of Tunisia, little more was heard of it.

Messerschmitt Me 210 and Me 410 Hornisse (Hornet)

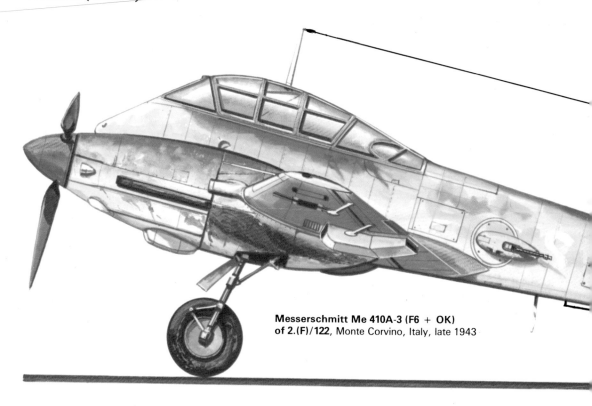

Messerschmitt Me 410A-3 (F6 + OK)
of 2.(F)/122, Monte Corvino, Italy, late 1943

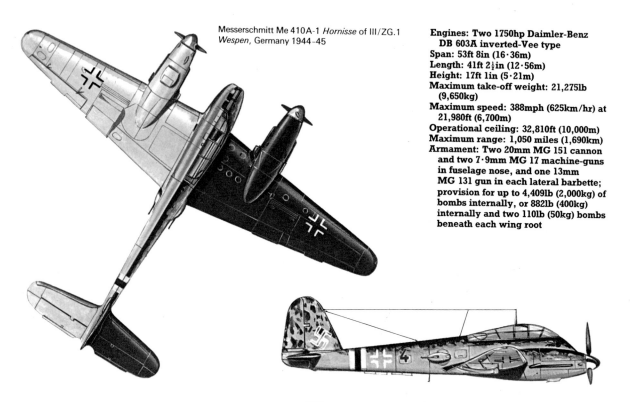

Messerschmitt Me 410A-1 *Hornisse* of III/ZG.1
Wespen, Germany 1944–45

Engines: Two 1750hp Daimler-Benz
DB 603A inverted-Vee type
Span: 53ft 8in (16·36m)
Length: 41ft 2½in (12·56m)
Height: 17ft 1in (5·21m)
Maximum take-off weight: 21,275lb
(9,650kg)
Maximum speed: 388mph (625km/hr) at
21,980ft (6,700m)
Operational ceiling: 32,810ft (10,000m)
Maximum range: 1,050 miles (1,690km)
Armament: Two 20mm MG 151 cannon
and two 7·9mm MG 17 machine-guns
in fuselage nose, and one 13mm
MG 131 gun in each lateral barbette;
provision for up to 4,409lb (2,000kg) of
bombs internally, or 882lb (400kg)
internally and two 110lb (50kg) bombs
beneath each wing root

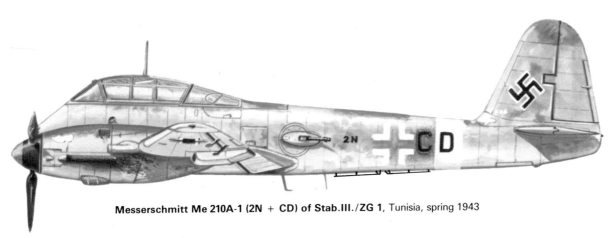

Messerschmitt Me 210A-1 (2N + CD) of Stab.III./ZG 1, Tunisia, spring 1943

The Me 210 was designed as a potential successor to the Bf 110, and RLM approval of the project in 1937 was followed on 5 September 1939 by the first flight of the twin-finned Me 210V1 prototype. This aircraft showed marked instability in flight, and attempts to remedy this resulted in a large-area single fin and rudder being introduced on the second machine. This still did not eliminate all the Me 210's control problems, but the RLM had committed itself to a substantial order for one thousand aircraft of this type before the first prototype had flown. The three production models – the Me 210A-1, A-2 and C-1, were all similarly powered, with 1,395hp DB 601F engines; the A-2 was fitted with external bomb racks, while the C-1 had the two MG 17 guns deleted and carried two aerial reconnaissance cameras. In April 1942, however, the RLM halted production of the Me 210. It was later resumed for a brief period, but the final total completed in Germany was only three hundred and fifty-two, plus two hundred and sixty-seven built under licence in Hungary with DB 605B engines. In the search for a replacement type, the RLM passed over the pressurised Me 310 project in favour of a simpler derivative, the Me 410, which was also powered by DB 603A engines. Known as the *Hornisse*, the Me 410 entered production late in 1942. By 1944 a total of one thousand one hundred and sixty had been manufactured. Several A and B sub-types were produced, with armament or equipment variations, for service as 'heavy' fighters, bomber destroyers and photographic reconnaissance aircraft. The Me 410A-3 and B-3 had bulged bomb bay fairings containing three aerial cameras; the B-5 and B-6 carried torpedoes for anti-shipping duties.

Henschel Hs 129

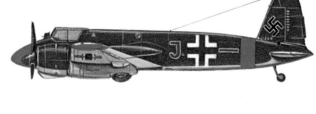

Henschel Hs 129B-2/R2 of an unidentified
Schlachtgeschwader, Eastern Front, late
summer 1943

**Engines: Two 700hp Gnome-Rhône 14M
04/05 radials**
Span: 46ft 7in (14·20m)
Length: 31ft 11⅛in (9·75m)
Height: 10ft 8in (3·25m)
Normal take-off weight: 9,259lb (4,200kg)
**Maximum speed: 253mph (407km/hr) at
12,565ft (3,830m)**
Operational ceiling: 29,525ft (9,000m)
Normal range: 429 miles (690km)
**Armament: Two 20mm MG 151 canon
and two 7·9mm MG 17 machine-guns
in fuselage nose, and one 30mm MK
101 canon in ventral fairing**

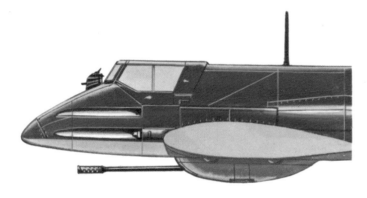

Inboard profile showing the ventral
installation of a 30mm MK 103 cannon on
the **Hs 129B-2/R2**

Henschel Hs 129B-2/R2 of 4./Sch G1, Eastern Front, summer 1943

The 1937 RLM specification that resulted in the Hs 129 was prompted by the need, revealed during the Spanish Civil War, for a specialised close support and ground-attack aeroplane. Dipl-Ing Nicolaus of Henschel designed the Hs 129 around the use of twin Argus As 410 engines, three prototypes being completed. The first of these was flown in the spring of 1939, and in 1940 a small pre-series batch of Hs 129A-0s were sent to a *Luftwaffe* trials unit for evaluation. Pilots' reports were highly unfavourable, chiefly due to the aircraft's inadequate power, and were sufficiently damning to prevent the Argus-engined Hs 129A from entering production. The existing Hs 129A-0s were not, evidently, too unsatisfactory to pass on to the Romanian Air Force, which used them for some months on the Russian Front. Meanwhile, Herr Nicolaus's team produced an alternative design, known originally by the project number P.76, but this was rejected by the RLM, which directed instead that the Hs 129A be adapted to take captured French Gnome-Rhône 14M radial engines. Thus re-engined, and with cockpit and other internal modifications, the type became known in 1941 as the Hs 129B. The Hs 129B-1, following a batch of ten pre-series Hs 129B-0s, entered production in March 1942, and became operational with *Luftwaffe* units in the Crimea that spring. Later, the Hs 129B appeared in numbers in North Africa, being employed primarily as an anti-tank aircraft in both theatres. Several B-1 sub-types were produced, with various combinations of armament. Standard equipment, as installed in the B-1/R1, comprised two 20mm MG 151 cannon and two 7·9mm MG 17 machine-guns, with provision for a small external bomb load. Without bombs, and with a fixed ventral 30mm MK 101 cannon, it was designated B-1/R2; the B-1/R3 had the big cannon replaced by a ventral tray of four more MG 17s; the B-1/R4 and B-1/R5 each carried the standard quota of guns, but with a more varied bomb load and photo-reconnaissance camera respectively. The B-1/R2 was notably successful in the anti-tank role, and prompted the evolution of the all-gun B-2 series. The B-2/R1 was similar to the B-1/R1 except that 13mm MG 131s replaced the nose MG 17s; to this the B-2/R2 added a 30mm MK 103 cannon; while the B-2/R3 discarded the two MG 131s in favour of two more MG 151s (making four in all) and a 37mm cannon. Final version was the B-2/R4, with a huge 75mm ventral cannon whose muzzle projected nearly 8ft (2·44m) ahead of the aircraft's nose. A total of eight hundred and forty-eight Hs 129Bs were built before production ceased in September 1944.

Heinkel He 177 Greif (Griffin) and He 277

Heinkel He 177A-5/R6 *Greif* of *Staffel* 6,
II/KG.40, Bordeaux-Mérignac, *ca* November
1943

Engines: Two 2,950hp Daimler-Benz
 DB 610A-1/B-1 (coupled DB 605)
 radials
Span: 103ft 1¾in (31·44m)
Length: 72ft 2⅛in (22·00m)
Height: 21ft 0in (6·40m)
Normal take-off weight: 59,966lb
 (27,200kg)
Maximum speed: 273mph (440km/hr) at
 20,010ft (6,100m)
Operational ceiling: 26,245ft (8,000m)
**Maximum range with two Hs 293
 missiles:** 3,417 miles (5,500km)

Armament: One 20mm MG 151 cannon in
front of under-nose cupola and one in
tail; two 13mm MG 131 machine-guns
in forward dorsal barbette and one in
rear dorsal turret; and one 7·9mm
MG 81 gun in nose and two in rear of
under-nose cupola; up to 2,205lb
(1,000kg) of bombs internally and two
mines, torpedos or missiles externally

The fact that the He 177 was the only German long-range strategic bomber to go into series production during World War 2 was doubtless due chiefly to the official indecision and political interference with its development that gave little chance of its initial design faults being satisfactorily overcome before it was pressed into service. Had it been permitted a natural and uninterrupted development, its story might have been very different, for it was basically a conventional design in all but one respect. This was the radical decision to employ pairs of coupled engines, each pair in a single nacelle, driving a single propeller. It was designed to a 1938 specification for a dual-purpose heavy bomber and anti-shipping aircraft, and was, unbelievably, required to be stressed for dive bombing. The first prototype, flown on 19 November 1939, just managed to keep within the overall weight limits of the specification, but service variants of the He 177 became progressively heavier. More ominous, however, was the curtailment of the first flight due to engine overheating, which was to plague the He 177 throughout its career. Eight prototypes were completed, followed by thirty-five pre-production He 177A-0s built by Arado and Heinkel and one hundred and thirty Arado-built He 177A-1s. The early aircraft in this batch

were used for further trials, and after a brief and unhappy operational debut the remainder were also withdrawn from service. From late 1942 they were replaced by one hundred and seventy Heinkel-built A-3s and eight hundred and twenty-six A-5s, which had longer fuselages and repositioned engine nacelles. Main combat area of these models was the Eastern Front, where the bomber's use also for ground-attack produced some interesting variations in armament. Other He 177As were employed as transports, and certain variants were equipped to carry Hs 293 or FX 1400 missiles externally. A few A-5s were converted into A-6s and A-7s, but attention was then diverted to developing the *Greif* with four separately mounted engines. When the German forces evacuated Paris the prototype He 274A (formerly the He 177A-4) was still awaiting its first flight at the Farman factory at Surèsnes. One He 177A-3 airframe became the four-engined He 277, to which Heinkel gave the false designation He 177B to overcome official disapproval of the re-engined design. This flew late in 1943 with four 1,730hp DB 603A engines, followed by two more prototypes and a small production batch, but these did not enter squadron service.

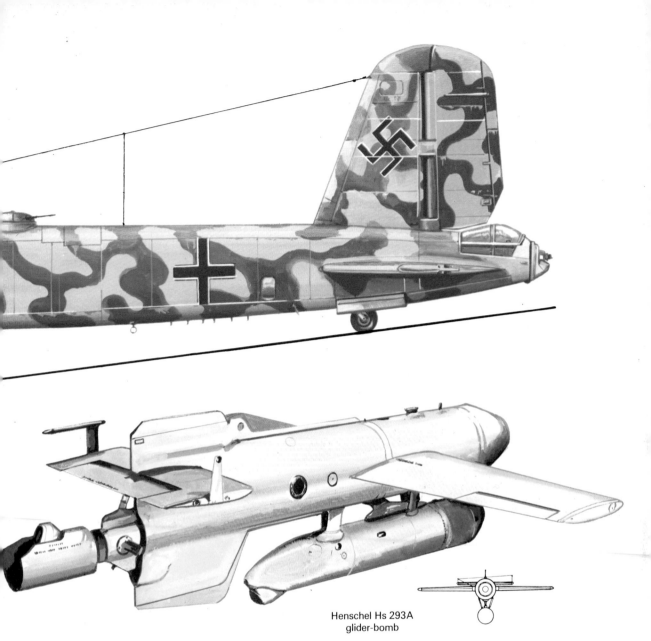

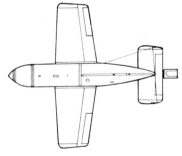

Henschel Hs 293A
glider-bomb

Aircraft type		Hs 293A-1
Power plant		1 × 600 kg (1,323 lb) st HWK 109-507B
Wing span	m : ft in	3·10 : 10 2·0
Length overall	m : ft in	3·82 : 12 6·4
Body diameter	m : ft in	0·47 : 1 6·5
Wing area	m² : sq ft	1·92 : 20·67
Weight of warhead	kg : lb	295 : 650
Launch weight	kg : lb	1,045 : 2,304
Max wing loading	kg/m² : lb/sq ft	544·27 : 111·49
Max power loading	kg/kg st : lb/lb st	1·74 : 1·74
Max speed	km/h : mph	435–900 : 270–559
Launch altitude	m : ft	400–2,000 : 1,310–6,560
Range	km : miles	3·5–18 : 2·2–11·2

157

Arado Ar 232

Arado Ar 232 V2 (VD + YB) in typical mid-war camouflage scheme. This aircraft was used by the Luftwaffe in the winter of 1942/43 to support the 6th Army at Stalingrad, and later by the Arado-Staffel of the Ergänzungs-Transport Gruppe

Side elevation of **Ar 232B-0**

Aircraft type			Ar 232 V1	Ar 232B-0
Power plant			2 × 1,600 hp BMW 801MA	4 × 1,200 hp BMW-Bramo 323R-2
Accommodation			4 + cargo	4 + cargo
Wing span	m	: ft in	21·80 : 71 6·3	33·50 : 109 10·9
Length overall	m	: ft in	23·52 : 77 2·0	23·52 : 77 2·0
Height overall	m	: ft in	5·70 : 18 8·4	5·70 : 18 8·4
Wing area	m²	: sq ft	— : —	142·60 : 1,534·93
Weight empty	kg	: lb	16,600 : 36,597	12,780 : 28,175
Weight loaded	kg	: lb	21,130 : 46,584	20,000 : 44,092
Max wing loading	kg/m²	: lb/sq ft	— : —	140·25 : 13·03
Max power loading	kg/hp	: lb/hp	6·60 : 14·56	5·00 : 11·02
Max level speed	km/h	: mph	338 : 210	308 : 191
at (height)	m	: ft	5,500 : 18,045	4,000 : 13,125
Cruising speed	km/h	: mph	— : —	288 : 179
at (height)	m	: ft	— : —	2,000 : 6,560
Time to 2,000 m (6,560 ft)			—	7 min
Service ceiling	m	: ft	— : —	6,900 : 22,640
Range	km	: miles	— : —	1,335 : 830

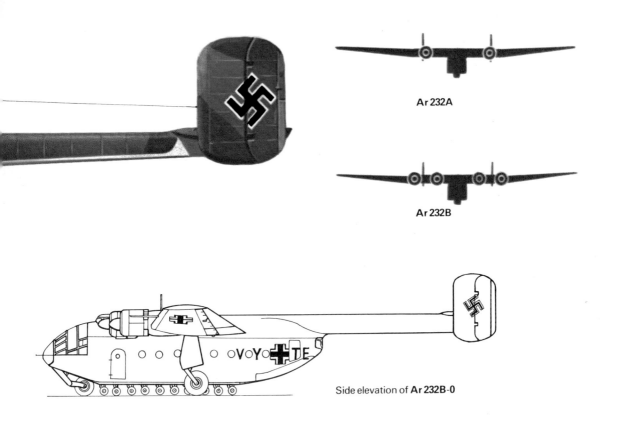

Ar 232A

Ar 232B

Side elevation of **Ar 232B-0**

One of several attempts to evolve a successor to the Junkers Ju 52/3m, the Arado Ar 232 was designed to a 1939 RLM specification and flew for the first time in the early summer of 1941. The V1 and V2 prototypes were each powered, as specified, by two 1,600hp BMW 801MA engines, but the Ar 232A production model based on them was abandoned when priority for the supply of these engines was needed by the Fw 190 fighter programme. Development therefore continued with the Ar 232B series, whose V3 (B-01) prototype was flown in May 1942. This differed mainly in having a 1·70m (5ft 6·9in) increase in wing span, to accommodate four BMW—Bramo 323R-2 engines. Of distinctive layout, the Ar 232B featured a pod-and-boom fuselage, with a hydraulically operated rear-loading door; a retractable tricycle landing gear; and a row of ten pairs of small idler wheels (11 pairs on the V1/V2) under the fuselage centreline, on to which the aircraft could sink to lower the cabin floor to truck-bed height for the loading of

vehicles, troops or equipment. A dorsal turret aft of the flight deck mounted a 20mm MG 151/20 cannon, and there were single movable 13mm machine-guns in the nose and above the rear-loading door. This armament could be supplemented, if required, by up to eight 7·9mm MG 34 infantry machine-guns firing through the side windows. Eight pre-production Ar 232B-0s (V4-V11) are known to have been built, though 10 more B-series aircraft were ordered. Arado retained one as a testbed (and later as supply transport for the Ar 234 programme); most of the others (including the V1 and V2) were assigned to Luftwaffe transport or special-duty units on the Eastern Front from the winter of 1942–43. Two (the V8/B-05 and V11/B-08) served with Wekusta 5 in Norway, the latter having a non-retractable ski undercarriage and the former a powerplant of four 700hp Gnome-Rhône 14M radial engines.

Doblhoff WNF-342

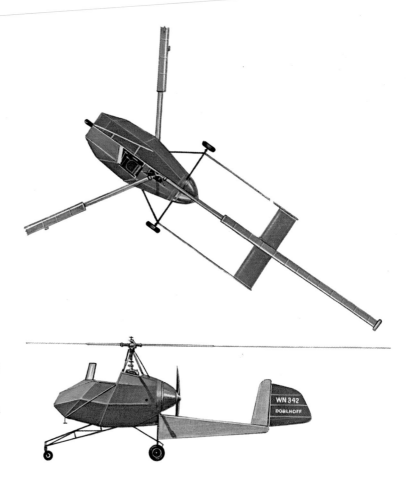

Doblhoff WNF-342V4, 1945

Engine: One 140hp Bramo (Siemens-
  Halske) Sh.14A seven-cylinder radial
Rotor diameter: 32ft 8⅛in (9·96m)
Fuselage length: approx 16ft 7½in (5·07m)
Height: approx 7ft 10½in (2·40m)
Maximum take-off weight: 1,411lb
  (640kg)
Maximum speed: 25mph (40km/hr) at sea
  level

First helicopter in the world to take off and land using blade-tip jets to drive the rotor, the WNF-342 was the work of three engineers – Friedrich von Doblhoff, A Stepan and Theodor Laufer – at the Wiener Neustadter Flugzeugwerke in Vienna. Doblhoff first built, in 1942, a ground test rig to prove the principle of his proposed rotor drive system, this rig consisting basically of a trio of hollow rotor blades mounted on a scaffold with the fuel/air mixture fed through each blade to a small jet unit at the tip. The demonstration proved so successful that the rotor actually 'took off' from its moorings, lifting about a yard into the air an anvil that had been attached to it to hold it down. Encouraged by this success, Doblhoff and his team then applied the principle in the small single-seat WNF-342V1 which he hoped would meet a German Navy requirement for an observation helicopter to be carried by submarines or small naval vessels. This first prototype, powered by a 60hp Walter Mikron II engine, was flown in spring 1943. The airframe, constructed from welded steel tube and fabric covered, had a gross weight of 360kg (794lb), twin tail fins and a tricycle undercarriage. Flight testing revealed the need for rather more side area, but performance was otherwise satisfactory, and when the WNF factory was damaged during an Allied air attack in mid-August 1943 the aircraft was moved to a safer site west of Vienna, at Obergraffendorf. Here a second machine, the WNF-342V2, was built, being a somewhat heavier aircraft at 460kg (1,014lb) gross weight, despite its open-framework fuselage. The main difference lay in the sail-like tail unit, this comprising a large single rectangular fin and

an elongated rudder pivoting about a horizontal axis. Experience with the first two machines showed that the high fuel consumption of the tip-jets would make the WNF-342's operating costs prohibitive, and so a major design change was introduced in the V3 and V4 prototypes. The tip-drive system was retained for take-off, hovering and landing only, a selective clutch enabling the engine (now a 140hp Siemens-Halske Sh.14A radial) to drive either the air compressor for jet propulsion or a conventional pusher propeller for forward flight while the rotor blades 'free-wheeled' in autorotative pitch. To clear this propeller the rotor pylon was raised above the cabin and the tail unit was redesigned as a twin-boom assembly, that of the V3 carrying two end-plate oval fins and rudders while that of the V4 had a single fin and rudder mounted on the tailplane centre. Gross weight of the V3, a single-seater with 9·88m (32ft 5in) diameter rotors, was 548kg (1,208lb). The V4 had side-by-side open cockpits for a crew of two. The V3 was destroyed early in its test programme by ground resonance vibration, but the V4 had completed 25 hours of testing before, in April 1945, it was hastily taken westwards to prevent its capture by the advancing Soviet forces. It eventually fell into American hands, Doblhoff later accompanying it back to the United States to assist with further tests before joining McDonnell to work on development of the XV-1. Stepan, who had done most of the test flying on the WNF-342, joined Fairey in the United Kingdom after the war, while Laufer went to work for the SNCA du Sud-Ouest in France.

Junkers Ju 188

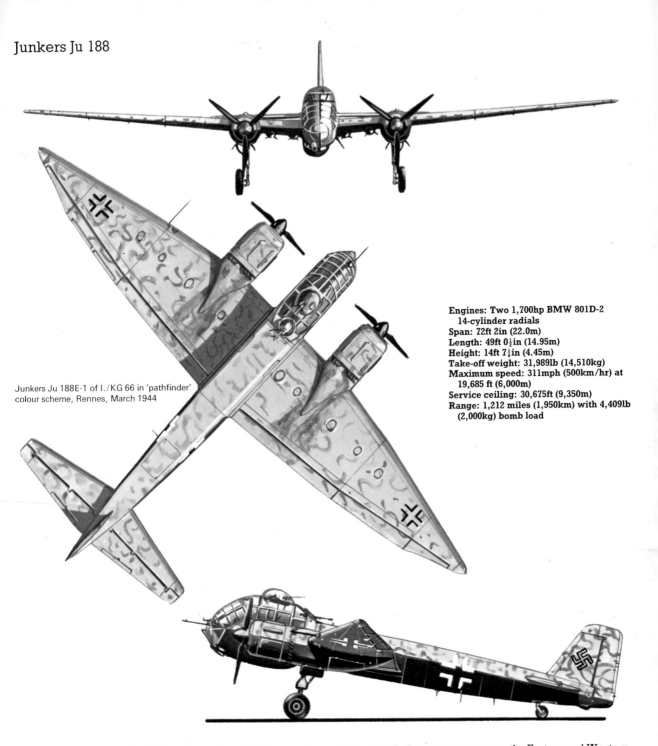

Junkers Ju 188E-1 of I./KG 66 in 'pathfinder' colour scheme, Rennes, March 1944

Engines: Two 1,700hp BMW 801D-2 14-cylinder radials
Span: 72ft 2in (22.0m)
Length: 49ft 0½in (14.95m)
Height: 14ft 7½in (4.45m)
Take-off weight: 31,989lb (14,510kg)
Maximum speed: 311mph (500km/hr) at 19,685 ft (6,000m)
Service ceiling: 30,675ft (9,350m)
Range: 1,212 miles (1,950km) with 4,409lb (2,000kg) bomb load

This descendant of the Ju 88 first flew in late 1942, the prototypes being modified Ju 88s with pointed wingtips, square-cut vertical tails and BMW 801MA engines. Jumo 213A-1s powered the Ju 188A-0, A-2 and A-3, the A-3 having Hohentwiel radar and carrying two 800kg torpedos underwing. The A models were preceded by the Ju 188E series (BMW 801s), comprising the E-0, E-1 and torpedo-bomber E-2; the E-1 entered service in mid-1943. The other major series, representing more than half of the 1,100 or so Ju 188s built, were the Ju 188F-1 and F-2 with BMW 801s. All of these were basically reconnaissance variants, and were employed widely with Aufklärungsgruppen on the Eastern and Western Fronts and in Italy. The projected C and G (bomber) and H and M (reconnaissance) series did not enter production, and the Ju 188J, K and L were developed separately as the Ju 388J, K and L. The Ju 188R, modified from the E, was an experimental night figher; the Ju 188S-1 and T-1 were respectively unarmed intruder and reconnaissance versions with Jumo 213E-1 engines, redesigned forward fuselages, and cabins pressurised for high-altitude flight. The Ju 188S-1/U armoured close-support version mounted a 50mm BK 5 cannon in an under-fuselage fairing.

Heinkel He 219A-7/R4 (G9 + TH) of 1./NJG 1, Sylt-Westerland, spring 1945

After an initial lack of interest when proposals for this multi-purpose fighter were first submitted to it in August 1940, the RLM authorised Heinkel, late in 1941, to begin detailed design work on the project. The first He 219 prototype was flown on 15 November 1942, powered by two 1,750hp DB 603A engines, and underwent armament trials during the following month. An initial order was placed for one hundred production aircraft, and this figure was increased to three hundred by the time tooling-up began in April 1943. About twenty pre-series He 219A-0s had been completed by the summer, and were followed by forty examples of the He 219A-2 (the A-1 having been abandoned). The A-2 was a 2-seat model; proposals for the 3-seat A-3 bomber and the high-altitude reconnaissance A-4 sub-types were not adopted. Production thus continued with the A-5, A-6 and A-7; most of these were powered by variants of the DB 603 engine, but Jumo 213Es were installed in the A-7/R5 and Jumo 222s in

the A-7/R6. The A-5 was a 3-seater and carried additional internal fuel. Total production of the He 219A-series aircraft was two hundred and sixty-eight, and these, together with some twenty prototype or pre-production machines and a few 2-seat He 219B-2s (developed from the A-6) were the only models to serve operationally with the *Luftwaffe*. The He 219 was widely regarded as the best-equipped night fighter of World War 2, and could compete on equal terms with the British Mosquito. It was fortunate for the Allies that that RLM cancellations and counter-cancellations prevented more from being produced. Prototype airframes were completed of the He 219C-1 night fighter and C-2 fighter-bomber, but when VE-day arrived these still awaited delivery of their Jumo 222 engines. The C series were to have carried a 4-man crew, the additional member manning a tail turret with four MG 131 machine-guns.

Engines: Two 1,800hp Daimler-Benz
   DB 603E inverted-Vee type
Span: 60ft 8⅜in (18·50m)
Length: 51ft 0⅛in (15·55m)
Height: 13ft 5⅜in (4·10m)
Maximum take-off weight: 33,730lb
   (15,300kg)
Maximum speed: 416mph (670km/hr) at
   22,965ft (7,000m)
Operational ceiling: 32,150ft (9,800m)
Maximum range: 1,243 miles (2,000km)
Armament: Four 20mm MG 151 cannon
   in ventral pack and one in each wing
   root

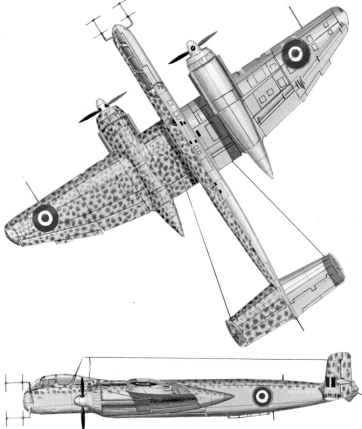

Heinkel He 219A-5/R2 *Uhu*, captured aircraft
with RAF markings superimposed, *ca* late
autumn 1945

Messerschmitt Me 262

Messerschmitt Me 262A-2a of 1./KG 51, Achmer, spring 1945

Me 262A-2a of 1./KG 51

Two-seat **Me 262B-1a**

Geschwader emblem of
KG 51 'Edelweiss'

Design of the Me 262 jet fighter, which had the Messerschmitt Projekt number 1065, began about a year before the outbreak of World War 2. But, due to delays in the development and delivery of satisfactory engines, the depredations caused by Allied air attacks, a troublesome development programme, and Hitler's refusal to be advised regarding its most appropriate role, it was six years before the aircraft entered Luftwaffe squadron service. A mockup of the aircraft was completed during the latter half of 1939, examination of which prompted the RLM to order three flying prototypes in the spring of 1940. These were all completed by early 1941, long before the arrival of their engines; so, to test the basic attributes of the airframe, the Me 262 V1 (PC + UA) made its first flight on 18 April 1941 with dummy jet-engine nacelles under the wings and a single 700hp Jumo 210G piston engine mounted in the nose. On 25 March 1942 it made a barely-successful attempt to fly with two underwing BMW 003 jet engines, but still with the nose-mounted Jumo 210G. The first all-jet flight was made on 18 July 1942, when the Me 262 V3 (PC + UC) took off under the power of two 840kg (1,852lb) st Jumo 004A turbojets. Many more prototypes were completed and used for trials with various armament and equipment installations, and from the V5 onward (first flight 26 June 1943) a tricycle landing gear was substituted for the original tailwheel type. Plans for priority mass-production were seriously affected by Allied air attacks upon Messerschmitt's Regensburg factory, and there were numerous development

problems involving engine fires and failures, landing gear collapses, guns jamming, and in-flight break-ups. Engine deliveries began in earnest in June 1944, permitting deliveries of production Me 262As to begin, and 513 had been accepted by the Luftwaffe by the end of the year—less than 40 per cent of the planned number. The Me 262's flying qualities were excellent, and a pre-series batch of 23 A-0s was accepted in the spring of 1944. These were allocated to the Erpro-bungsstelle at Rechlin and the conversion unit EKdo 262, the latter unit becoming, on 25 July 1944, the first to fire the Me 262's guns in anger. The two principal basic production versions to become operational were the Me 262A-1a Schwalbe (swallow) interceptor and the Me 262A-2a Sturm-vogel (stormbird) fighter-bomber. The former was built in numerous sub-types with four 30mm MK 108 cannon in the nose, or alternative armament installations; the latter, produced as a result of Hitler's insistence upon developing the aircraft as a bomber, had external racks for one 1,000kg or two 500kg bombs. Other variants included the A-1a/V 083, with a single 50mm BK 5 cannon in the nose; the A-1b, with twelve 55mm R4M unguided rocket projectiles under each wing; the one-off A-2a/U2 with a glazed nose-cap over a prone bomb-aiming position; the ground attack Me 262A-3a; and the photo-reconnaissance Me 262A-1a/U3 and Me 262A-5a. A tandem two-seat trainer version was designated Me 262B-1a, and one prototype was completed of a proposed two-seat night fighter, the Me 262B-2a. This incorporated a longer fuselage, containing more fuel, and a Schräge Musik installation of two MK 108 cannon aft of the cockpit, firing upward. The B-2a did not enter production, but several B-1as were converted for night fighting (without the extended fuselage) and redesignated Me 262B-1a/U1. These were employed quite successfully by the Kommando Welter, or 10./NJG 11 as it was later known. The few Me 262C models completed before VE-day were fitted with various rocket motors in the fuselage to boost the fighter's climb rate. Although little more than 500 Me 262s had been produced by December 1944, by the end of the war the total had risen to about 1,430. Probably less than a quarter of these saw front-line service, and losses among them were quite heavy, even though relatively few losses were realised in combat. Despite this, their destruction of Allied bombers and fighters was greater than one for one, and JV 44, the top-scoring Me 262 interceptor unit, achieved some 50 'kills' in little more than a month's operations in 1945. In air-to-air combat the Me 262 never engaged its British counterpart, the twin-jet Gloster Meteor (which was slower and less well armed); conversely, many Me 262s were destroyed by Allied Mustang, Spitfire, Tempest and Thunderbolt piston-engined fighters.

FZG 76 (V-1) flying bomb in typical 1944 colour scheme

Aircraft type			Fi 103		
Power plant			1×300 kg (661 lb) st As 109–014		
Wing span (untapered)	m	: ft in	5·30	: 17	4·7
Length overall	m	: ft in	7·90	: 25	11·0
Body diameter	m	: ft in	0·838	: 2	9·0
Wing area	m²	: sq ft	4·80	: 51·67	
Weight empty	kg	: lb	815	: 1,796	
Warhead	kg	: lb	850	: 1,874	
Weight loaded	kg	: lb	2,180	: 4,806	
Max level speed	km/h	: mph	645	: 401	
at (height)	m	: ft	2,000	: 6,560	
Launching speed	km/h	: mph	378	: 235	
Service ceiling	m	: ft	3,000	: 9,845	
Range (typical)	km	: miles	240	: 149	

Fieseler Fi 103 Reichenberg III

Known alternatively as the FZG 76 (Flakzielgerät: anti-aircraft aiming device 76) or Vergeltungswaffe Eins (Reprisal Weapon 1), or more simply as the V1, the Fi 103 flying bomb had an airframe designed by Dipl-Ing Robert Lüsser of Fieseler, and a Siemens guidance system. It could be launched from a 50m (152ft) inclined ramp by a Walter steam-driven catapult, or air-dropped from a carrier aircraft (usually an He 111). The weapons were launched against Britain (from 13 June 1944) and targets in continental Europe, and more than 30,000 were manufactured by Henschel, Mittelwerke and Volkswagen factories. An Askania gyroscope fed signals to the elevators and rudder to control attitude and direction, and

the terminal dive was initiated when a pre-set distance had been flown. Operational air launches were mostly made from He 111Hs of KG 3 (later KG 53); but, whatever the launch method, about a quarter of the weapons failed in use and only about a quarter of the remainder got through Allied defences. Even more of a desperation weapon was the 'Reichenberg' piloted series, of which there were four versions: the single-seat and two-seat unpowered Fi 103R-I and R-II, the single-seat powered R-III trainer, and the proposed operational R-IV. About 175 were so converted, but none was used in combat.

Messerschmitt Me 163 Komet (Comet)

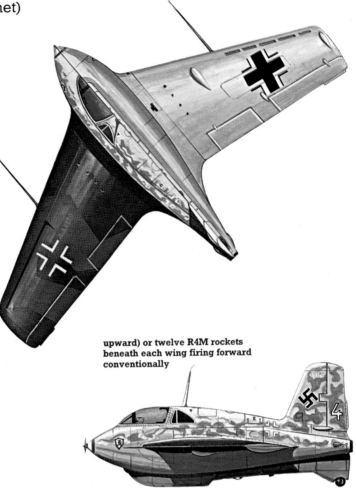

Messerschmitt Me 163B-1 *Komet* of
1/JG.400, Zwischenahn, summer 1944

Engine: One 3,748lb (1,700kg) st Walter
HWK 109-509A-1 liquid rocket motor
Span: 30ft 7¼in (9·33m)
Length: 19ft 2¼in (5·85m)
Height: 9ft ½in (2·76m)
Normal take-off weight: 9,502lb (4,310kg)
Maximum speed: 596mph (960km/hr) at
9,845ft (3,000m)
Operational ceiling: 39,700ft (12,100m)
**Maximum endurance (including
climb):** 7½ minutes, after which the
aircraft returned to earth in a glide
Armament: One 30mm MK 108 cannon in
each wing root, and four 5cm R4M
rockets in each wing (firing vertically
upward) or twelve R4M rockets
beneath each wing firing forward
conventionally

Probably the most ingenious and radical German combat aeroplane to serve during World War 2, the Me 163 achieved no small degree of success during the nine months or so that it was in active service, although it reached operational units too late and in numbers too small to affect the ultimate outcome. It was based on the experimental DFS 194, designed in 1938 by Prof Alexander Lippisch and transferred, together with his staff, to the Messerschmitt AG for further development. But for the subsequent clash of personalities between Lippisch and Prof Willy Messerschmitt, and the delay in delivery of its rocket engines in later years, it would almost certainly have been in service much earlier. The first two Me 163 prototypes were flown in the spring of 1941 as unpowered gliders, the Me 163V1 being transferred to Peenemünde later that year to receive its 1,653lb (750kg) st HWK R.II rocket motor. The first rocket-powered flight was made in August 1941, and in trials the fighter soon exhibited speeds of more than 620mph (1,000km/hr). Ten unpowered Me 163As were completed late in 1941 as conversion trainers, and development of the fighter was accelerated. The airframe of the third prototype (for the seventy Me 163B-0 and B-1 production machines ordered) was completed in May 1942,

but over a year elapsed before its new engine, the HWK 509A, became available. By then more than half of the original production batch were also complete except for their power-plants. Additional Me 163 production was undertaken by Hans Klemm Flugzeugbau, the overall total being slightly more than three hundred and fifty. The first *Luftwaffe* unit to receive the Me 163B acquired its fighters in June/July 1944, making its operational debut in mid-August against US Eighth Air Force B-17s over Germany. The Komet's spectacular speed, and the element of surprise, resulted in many early successes against Allied bomber formations. However, the definitive version was nearly a ton heavier than its original design weight, necessitating the use of auxiliary booster rockets for take-off, while landings were hazardous in the extreme. All too often the Me 163, landing directly on its fuselage keel-skid and with some of the highly inflammable fuel still left in the tank, would come to a literally comet-like end, with fatal results for its pilot. When the war ended the pressurised and improved Me 163C (HWK 509C motor) had reached the pre-production stage, and a prototype had also been flown of a derivative known first as the Me163D and later as the Me 263, but this too was too late to go into production.

Arado Ar 234 Blitz (Lightning)

Aircraft type			Ar 234B-2	
Power plant			2 × 900 kg (1,984 lb) st Jumo 004B	
Accommodation			1	
Wing span	m	: ft in	14·11 : 46	3·5
Length overall	m	: ft in	12·64 : 41	5·6
Height overall	m	: ft in	4·30 : 14	1·3
Wing area	m²	: sq ft	26·40 : 284·17	
Weight empty	kg	: lb	5,200 : 11,464	
Weight loaded	kg	: lb	***9,850 : 21,715	
Max wing loading	kg/m²	: lb/sq ft	373·11 : 76·42	
Max power loading	kg/hp or kg/kg st	lb/hp or : lb/lb st	5·47 : 5·47	
Max level speed	km/h	: mph	****742 : 461	
at (height)	m	: ft	6,000 : 19,685	
Cruising speed	km/h	: mph	— : —	
at (height)	m	: ft	— : —	
Time to 6,000 m (19,685 ft)			—	
Service ceiling	m	: ft	10,000 : 32,810	
Range	km	: miles	*1,100 : 684	

Arado Ar 234 V1 on its take-off trolley

Arado Ar 234B-2 (F1 + AS) of 8./KG76, Laerz, January 1945

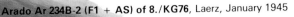

This clean and attractive twin-jet aircraft's design started in late 1940, around a pair of 840kg (1,852lb) st Jumo 004A turbojets, but through delays in engine development the Ar 234 V1—first of 40 Versuchs machines eventually ordered—did not fly until 15 June 1943. The V3 had a pressurised cabin, ejection seats and Walter assisted take-off rockets, and the V5 was powered by 900kg (1,984lb) st BMW 003As for comparison. The intended Ar 234A production series was abandoned after trials with a jettisonable take-off trolley; skids beneath the engine and fuselage were provided for landing. The first production version was therefore the Ar 234B, based on the V9. First flown on 10 March 1944, this had retractable tricycle landing gear. After small numbers of the Ar 234B-0 and B-1 for unarmed reconnaissance, which entered service in July 1944, the Ar 234B-2 was the first production bomber—the first in the world with turbojet power. It entered service in late 1944 with KG 76, and could carry a bomb load of 1,500kg (3,307lb); some aircraft were armed with two rearward-firing 20mm MG 151 cannon in the lower aft fuselage. By this time the Blitz enjoyed a high production priority, and 210 Ar 234B-1/B-2s were built, but due to accidents in training (mostly because the techniques of handling jet aircraft were unfamiliar) comparatively few became operational. Their employment during 1944–45 was primarily for reconnaissance over the UK and northern Italy, or for bombing over the Western Front, notably during the Ardennes offensive and the Rhine crossing in the spring of 1945. The next production model, the Ar 234C, was a multi-purpose series with four 800kg (1,764lb) st BMW 003A-1 engines. The C-1 was intended for reconnaissance, the C-2 for bombing, and the C-3 for bombing, ground attack (with anti-personnel bombs) or night fighting (with two additional MG 151s in a forward-firing ventral pack), but only 14 C-1/C-3s were completed. Further C variants, for reconnaissance, night fighting or bombing, were under development in the spring of 1945, and 10 prototypes had been started for the Ar 234D, to be powered by two Heinkel Hirth HeS 011A turbojets. Other projects included the Ar 234E (a Zerstörer variant of the D), Ar 234F, Ar 234P night fighter and rocket-powered Ar 234R.

Dornier Do 335 Pfeil (Arrow)

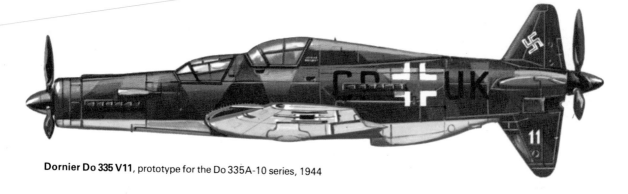

Dornier Do 335 V11, prototype for the Do 335A-10 series, 1944

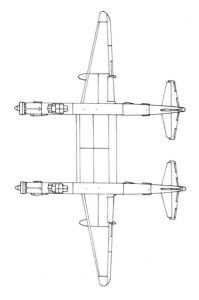

Junkers Ju 8-635 (originally **Do 635**) project for a 'twin' version of the Do 335

Aircraft type		Do 335A-0
Power plant		2 × 1,750 hp DB 603A-2
Accommodation		1
Wing span	m : ft in	13·80 : 45 3·3
Length overall	m : ft in	13·85 : 45 5·3
Height overall	m : ft in	5·00 : 16 4·8
Wing area	m² : sq ft	38·50 : 414·41
Weight empty	kg : lb	6,530 : 14,396
Weight loaded	kg : lb	9,510 : 20,966
Max wing loading	kg/m² : lb/sq ft	247·01 : 50·59
Max power loading	kg/hp : lb/hp	2·72 : 5·99
Max level speed	km/h : mph	732 : 455
at (height)	m : ft	7,100 : 23,295
Cruising speed	km/h : mph	633 : 393
at (height)	m : ft	5,700 : 18,700
Time to 8,000 m (26,245 ft)		14·5 min
Service ceiling	m : ft	9,500 : 31,170
Range	km : miles	2,150 : 1,336

Dornier Do 335A-07, one of several A-0s used by **Erprobungskommando 335** in late 1944

Reviving a principle patented in 1937, Dornier designed the radical centreline-thrust Do 335 to a 1942 requirement for a day/night fighter, fighter-bomber and reconnaissance aircraft. The Do 335 V1 (CP + UA) first flew at Oberpfaffenhofen on 26 October 1943, with one 1,800hp DB 603E engine in the nose and another, driving a pusher propeller, in the rear fuselage. By the war's end, 36 Do 335s had been completed: 13 Versuchs (prototype) aircraft, 10 pre-production A-0s, 11 A-1s, and two A-12 tandem two-seat trainers; over 80 other A-series aircraft remained uncompleted. First armed prototype was the V5; the V9 was prototype for the A series, which had two 15mm MG 151/15 guns in the upper forward fuselage and a 30mm MK 103 cannon firing through the front spinner. The A-1 could carry one 500kg or two 250kg bombs internally. No Do 335s saw combat service, though operational evaluation of the Do 335A-0 was carried out from autumn 1944 by Erprobungskommando 335. Prototypes for other versions included the Do 335A-4 (one A-0 converted for unarmed photo-reconnaissance); the V10 (A-6) tandem two-seat night fighter; the V11 (A-10) and V12 (A-12) tandem-seat trainers; and the V13 (B-1) and V14 (B-2) Zerstörern. Uncompleted prototypes included the V4 (Do 435) night fighter, with side-by-side seats and 2,500hp Jumo 222 engines; and the V15 to V20, prototypes for the B-1, B-2 and B-3 Zerstörern and the B-6 and B-7 night fighters. The B-4 and B-8 were proposed high altitude versions, with extended span, the corresponding trainer version being the B-5. The Do 635 (later redesignated Ju 8-635) was a long range reconnaissance project.

Heinkel He 162

Heinkel He 162A-2 of I./JG 1, Leck/Holstein, April 1945

Engine: One 1,764lb (800kg) st BMW 003E-1 or E-2 turbojet
Span: 23ft 7½in (7.20m)
Length: 29ft 8¼in (9.05m)
Height: 8ft 6½in (2.60m)
Maximum take-off weight: 6,184lb (2,805kg)
Maximum speed: 562mph (905km/hr) at 19,685ft (6,000m)
Service ceiling: 39,370ft (12,000m)
Typical range: 370–385 miles (595–620km)

One of the most rapidly conceived warplanes ever produced, the He 162 home defence fighter existed as a wooden mock-up within 15 days of the issue, on 8 September 1944, of the RLM requirement. Seven days later a huge production contract was placed; detail design drawings were completed by the end of October; and on 6 December 1944 – less than 13 weeks from initiation of the programme – the He 162 V1 (or A-01) made its first flight. Dubbed, for propaganda purposes, the Volksjäger or People's Fighter, the He 162 was of attractive if unorthodox appearance and was built largely of wood and other non-strategic materials. Its looks, however, belied a dangerous instability and some vicious handling characteristics, and troubles were also encountered (as in the Focke-Wulf Ta 154) with the wood-bonding adhesive used. Under the high priority given to fighter programmes in 1944–45, manufacture of the He 162, under the code name Salamander, was assigned to numerous factories. It was planned to produce 2,000 a month by May 1945 and 4,000 a month ultimately, and about 800 were in various stages of assembly when the war in Europe ended. A further 280 or so He 162A-0s, A-1s and A-2s had actually been completed. These differed primarily in their armament, the A-1 having two 30mm MK 108 cannon in the lower forward fuselage and the A-2 a pair of 20mm MG 151s. The first Luftwaffe unit to fly the He 162A was Erprobungskommando 162, which began to receive these aircraft in January 1945; but the first operational units, I. and II./JG 1, were still working up at the beginning of May. Consequently, very few He 162s were actually encountered in combat. Proposed later versions included He 162A sub-types up to A-14, the He 162B (one or two pulse-jet engines), the He 162C (swept-forward wings), the He 162D (swept-back wings), and models with combined jet and rocket propulsion.

Dornier Do 27

Dornier Do 27A-4 of the Luftwaffe, *ca* 1963

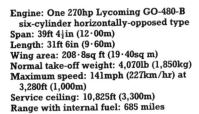

Engine: One 270hp Lycoming GO-480-B
six-cylinder horizontally-opposed type
Span: 39ft 4¼in (12·00m)
Length: 31ft 6in (9·60m)
Wing area: 208·8sq ft (19·40sq m)
Normal take-off weight: 4,070lb (1,850kg)
Maximum speed: 141mph (227km/hr) at
3,280ft (1,000m)
Service ceiling: 10,825ft (3,300m)
Range with internal fuel: 685 miles
(1,100km)

This useful little post-war German aeroplane was a true 'general purpose' type. Seating from six to eight people, it could be used for observation, liaison, casualty evacuation and utility transport roles; and a substantial number were built for the civil market. It was, however, as a training aircraft that its chief military use lay, and of the six hundred and eighty Do 27s built, four hundred and twenty-eight were for the Federal German armed forces as training and liaison aircraft. The Schweizerische Flugwaffe had ten for utility roles, the Nigerian Air Force ten (later increased) for training; other forces to have employed the Do 27 include those of Belgium, Nigeria, Portugal, South Africa, Sweden, Turkey and Zaïre. Fifty were built under licence in Spain, for the Ejército del Aire, as the CASA C.127, and in fact it was in Spain that the aeroplane had its origins, in the Do 25 which was powered by a 150hp ENMA Tigre G-IVB and flown for the first time on 25 June 1954. The prototype Do 27 was also begun in Spain, but the parts were then taken to Germany for assembly prior to the first flight on 27 June 1955. Altogether, three Do 27 prototypes were completed; series production in Germany began in the following year and ended in 1966, at which time six hundred and twenty had been built. The production facility was, however, kept open, and a further sixty aircraft were subsequently completed. Most military examples were Do 27As or Do 27Bs, basically similar but with dual controls in the B model for pilot training.

Transall C-160

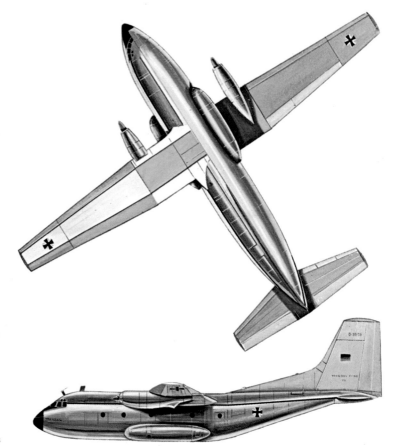

Transall C-160: first prototype aircraft

Data apply to initial production version
Engines: Two 6,100hp Rolls-Royce Tyne
Mk 22 turboprops
Span: 131ft 3in (40.00m)
Length: 106ft 3½in (32.40m)
Height: 38ft 3in (11.66m)
Maximum take-off weight: 112,440lb
(51,000kg)
Maximum cruising speed: 319mph
(513km/hr) at 18,050ft (5,500m)
Operational ceiling: 27,900ft (8,500m)
Range with 17,640lb payload: 2,832 miles
(4,558km)

The C-160 is an early example of international collaboration between European powers to develop an aeroplane that satisfies the air force requirements of all the countries concerned. In this case they were France and Germany, who began to compare notes on a joint transport requirement in the late 1950s, when both were considering the matter of a replacement for the Nord Noratlas. The name Transall is derived from *Transporter Allianz*, and design and production was shared between the two countries. The wings, engines and undercarriage were the responsibility of French companies, while Germany took care of fuselage and tail assembly; the Tyne engines were built jointly by a four-nation consortium. The first of three flying prototypes was flown on 25 February 1963, and the first of six pre-production Transalls in May 1965. Initial production orders comprised one hundred and ten C-160Ds for the *Luftwaffe*, fifty C-160Fs for the *Armée de l'Air* and nine C-160Zs for the South African Air Force. German and French units to equip with Transalls were, respectively, *Lufttransportgeschwader* (LTG) 61 and 63, and the 61e *Escadre de Transport*; the SAAF aircraft went into service with Nos 25, 28 and 44 Squadrons. Twenty ex-German C-160Ds were later transferred to the Turkish Air Force, and four C-160Fs were modified to C-160P in 1972–73 for civilian mail transport in France. The C-160 has a first-class short-field STOL performance, and an excellent carrying capacity.

Typical tactical payload is eight tonnes (which can be doubled over short ranges); alternatively, ninety-three troops, eighty-one paratroops or sixty-two casualty litters can be transported. The effective cargo volume of the Transall's fuselage is nearly five thousand cubic feet. Although primarily for tactical or strategic transport missions, the C-160 could have other applications such as survey, weather reconnaissance or air/sea rescue. Manufacture of the first series of 169 was completed in 1972, but five years later the C-160 was put back into production, mainly to provide the French *Armée de l'Air* with a further twenty-nine aircraft, and these are in service with the 64e Escadre de Transport at Evreux. Ten of these second-series Transalls are fitted with hose-and-drogue gear, enabling them to double as in-flight refuelling tankers both for the French Air Force and for carrier-based aircraft of the French Navy. A further five are configured for rapid adaptation as tankers if required, and from 1987 four others will serve as communications relay aircraft in support of France's nuclear deterrent forces, in addition to carrying tanker/receiver gear. The second production run also included six Transalls for the Indonesian government, which is using them in a programme to transfer families from over-inhabited Java and resettle them in some of the less densely populated islands.

MBB BO 105

BO 105, first prototype in manufacturer's demonstration finish, 1966

Data apply to 1985 BO 105CB production version
Engines: Two 420shp Allison 250-C20B shaft-turbines
Main rotor diameter: 32ft 3½in (9·84m)
Fuselage length: 28ft 1in (8·56m)
Height: 9ft 10in (3·00m)
Normal take-off weight: 5,291lb (2,400kg)
Maximum speed: 167mph (270km/hr) at sea level
Operational ceiling: 17,000ft (5,180m)
Normal range: 357 miles (575km)

Design of the BO 105 lightweight general purpose helicopter was begun by Bölkow (now a constituent of Messerschmitt-Bölkow-Blohm) in July 1962, utilising basic experience gained by the company in the preceding few years in building the Bö 102 and Bö 103. The former was a non-flying, ultra-light helicopter trainer, and the Bö 103, flown for the first time on 9 September 1961, was essentially the same aircraft minus its fixed base. An enlarged version of the Bö 103 was proposed as the Bö 104, but this project was supplanted by the more promising BO 105. The first BO 105 prototype, powered by a pair of Allison 250-C18 shaft turbine engines and using a conventional hinged-rotor installation, encountered ground resonance problems which eventually caused its destruction. The second machine, which flew for the first time on 16 February 1967, was similarly powered but introduced the 4-blade rigid rotor which is standard on production aircraft. The third prototype (first flight 20 December 1967) was powered by two MAN-Turbo 6022 turboshafts. Two pre-production aircraft followed, one of which had 400shp Allison 250-C20 engines, and a choice of the -C18 or -C20 was offered to customers for the production helicopter. In addition to the pilot the BO 105 will accommodate 4 or 5 passengers with their baggage. The non-articulated rotor, whose foldable blades are reinforced with glassfibre, was developed over several years by Bölkow in association with Sud-Aviation and was initially flight tested by the French company on its own Alouette II Astazou light helicopter. By 1985 production of BO 105 variants had passed the one thousand mark, with current models powered by the 420shp Allison 250-C20B. Principal military variants, both for the German Army, are the BO 105M for liaison and light scout duties (one hundred built), and the anti-tank BO 105P or PAH-1 (*Panzer Abwehr Hubschrauber:* tank defence helicopter), of which two hundred and twelve were delivered between 1980–84. The latter version is armed with six HOT missiles on cabin-side outriggers, with a stabilised sight on the port side of the cabin roof. The armed forces of Indonesia, Mexico, Spain and Sweden are among other military and naval operators of the BO 105, and there are licence assembly lines in Indonesia and the Phillipines.

Panavia Tornado

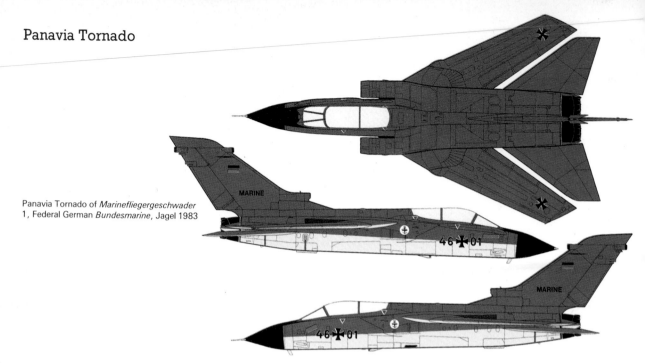

Panavia Tornado of *Marinefliegergeschwader* 1, Federal German *Bundesmarine*, Jagel 1983

Engines: Two approx 15,800lb (7,167kg) st Turbo-Union RB199-34R Mk 101 afterburning turbofans
Span: 45ft 7½in (13.91m) spread, 28ft 2½in (8.60m) swept
Length: 54ft 10¼in (16.72m)
Height: 19ft 6⅛in (5.95m)
Maximum take-off weight with external stores: approx 60,000lb (27,215kg)
Maximum speed (without stores): more than 1,320mph (2,135km/hr) at high altitude
Service ceiling: over 50,000ft (15,240m)

Typical combat radius: 863 miles (1,390km)
Armament: Two 27mm IWKA-Mauser cannon in lower front fuselage (one in ADV); three underfuselage (four on ADV) and four underwing stations for approx 19,840lb (9,000kg) of stores such as an MW-1 munitions dispenser, air-launched missiles (e.g. Sidewinder, Sky Flash, Alarm, Harm, Sea Eagle and Kormoran), bombs, rocket launchers, reconnaissance and ECM pods, and drop-tanks

Currently the principal interdictor/strike (IDS) aircraft of three major NATO powers, the swing-wing Tornado was known until 1976 as the MRCA (multi-role combat aircraft). It is produced by a British/German/Italian consortium called Panavia, formed for the purpose seven years earlier, whose industrial members are British Aerospace, MBB (Germany) and Aeritalia. A parallel consortium of Rolls-Royce, MTU and Fiat, known as Turbo-Union, produces the engines. Design was finalised in 1972, and the development programme involved nine prototypes (first flight 14 August 1974) and six pre-series Tornados. Four of the latter will eventually be upgraded to form part of the eight hundred and nine production aircraft being built for the three member nations. More than five hundred of these had been delivered by the end of 1985, by which time export orders had been placed by Saudi Arabia (forty-eight IDS Tornados and twenty-four of the air defence variant or ADV) and Oman (eight ADVs). Among the original customers, Britain's Royal Air Force will have two hundred and twenty IDS Tornados (designated GR Mk 1) and one hundred and sixty-five ADVs designated F Mks 2 and 3. The Italian Air Force will have a hundred IDSs, while Germany will receive two hundred and twelve for the *Luftwaffe* and one hundred and twelve for the Federal German Navy (*Bundesmarine*). Germany and Britain each have a 42½ per cent share of the production work, and Italy the other 15 per cent. In the *Luftwaffe*, the Tornado is already operational with four squadrons of *Jagdbombergeschwader* 31 and 32, and eventually will completely replace the American F-104G

Starfighter for battlefield interdiction, counter-air and close support duties. *Marinefliegergeschwader* 1, with two squadrons operational by 1986, is tasked with carrying out strike missions against sea and coastal targets, and with a reconnaissance role. The *Luftwaffe* also plans to have up to forty more Tornados specially equipped for ECR (electronic combat and reconnaissance) in the late 1980s. Italy's Tornados are also primarily a Starfighter replacement, taking over the air superiority, ground attack and reconnaissance roles previously performed by F and RF versions of the American fighter. Most of the RAF's GR Mk 1 Tornados are based in Germany (planned strength is seven strike and two reconnaissance squadrons), and are equipped to carry tactical nuclear stores and Hunting JP 233 runway denial weapons. Others, armed with Sea Eagle missiles, are replacing RAF Buccaneers in the maritime strike role. Maritime combat air patrols will also be one important task for the RAF's F Mks 2 and 3 air defence version. Distinguishable by a 4ft 5⅝in (1.36m) longer nose, they will replace seven Phantom and two Lightning squadrons, and will be mainly UK-based, covering an air defence region from the Atlantic approaches to the Baltic and from Iceland to the English Channel. Primary armament is a built-in 27mm cannon, with four Sky Flash snap-up/snap-down missiles under the fuselage and two or four underwing Sidewinders. Like all Tornados, the ADVs are equipped both for in-flight refuelling and for the carriage of external drop-tanks.